Buried Dreams Plan  eality
that is grief. This _____ those
experiencing loss, and for the people closest to them. The combined
perspectives from Katie and Kevin make this book a unique and
invaluable resource. I only wish it had been available fourteen years
ago as I walked through this valley. Watching this book come to
fruition has been a work of God that I have been blessed to witness.

–WENDIE GARDEN

I am an attorney and have specialized in injury and death claims almost
exclusively since 1985. I have represented hundreds of individuals who
have suffered loss as a result of all kinds of circumstances. On October
9, 2014, Katie Neufeld suffered just such a tragic loss. The collision she
was involved in would be termed catastrophic. Anyone looking at the
photographs of her automobile would not believe anyone could have
survived it. Katie did, although her passenger and fiancé, Jerod, did not.
I had the privilege and honor of representing Katie in this heartbreaking
case. Although Katie's life was spared physically, it could easily have
been taken emotionally or spiritually. Thankfully, it was not. I am an
eyewitness to how God got Katie and her family through this tragedy.
This book, which chronicles the journey of Katie and her dad, Kevin,
and their family through this season of sorrow and sadness, will help
anyone who encounters difficult situations. I recommend it to all.

–ALBERT E. JONES, ATTORNEY

Jerod Hicks was one of the brightest lights I have ever met on this
earth. His incredible energy and zest for life were made possible
because of the grace and salvation he had found in Jesus. Our Mellow
Mushroom lunch conversations and phone calls often focused on
grace. Jerod knew he had received it, but wanted to understand it
enough to give it away to others as much as humanly possible to the
measure he had received. When Katie and Jerod met, an amazing
thing happened and his life burned brighter still. These two would
truly be better together and would give strength to one another. Katie
goes further and grows stronger to this day as displayed in her courage
to share her story and provide all of us with the strength to hope.

–PAUL RICHARDSON, LEAD PASTOR OF MINISTRY AT WEST RIDGE CHURCH

Buried Dreams Planted Hope is a must read for readers seeking encouragement while traveling down the lonely road of grief. Neufeld shares the journey of life, love, and loss in a captivating page-turner that provides courage in the darkness and a hope for the hopeless. A useful resource for understanding the grief process and walking alongside the hurting. This book is truly an inspirational narrative of personal growth intertwined with Jesus Christ's everlasting, never-failing omnipresence.

–Denise Rountree, MS, NCC, LPC, Clinical Mental Health Therapist

This story strips away all the external shells and masks we hide behind and exposes what's on the inside of a young woman and her father. They represent other family members and friends who journeyed along and how God has been faithful and is healing hearts. To know the girl, then see the woman and hear her heart is rare, but to read these words where she bears her soul and how God fathers her through this journey is absolutely amazing. Having served alongside Kevin in ministry and having a daughter myself, the weight of his words help me to be a more devoted father to my family and to my Lord Jesus. As you read this book and walk with them in this journey, you will find the strength and the hope found in Jesus that will allow you to plant your hope and "dance your dances" in the days ahead. This book is a must read for anyone that has suffered loss, experienced grief or needs to lay their hands on hope.

–Ryan (and Lisa) Tyler, associate pastor of discipleship and church growth at Highland Baptist Church in Florence, Alabama

I was excited to read Katie's book. I had just met Katie and had no idea of her life outside the hospital, but I knew she had a story to tell. Reading her book was going to give me insight on who she was. Not only was this the story of a terrible accident that would change her life, but it also opened my eyes to the hurt that was in my own heart. She gave me words to the feelings I had bottled up inside and I couldn't wait for her to email me every next chapter! The last chapter was so unexpected and I loved her father's insight.

–Kim Yeager

BURIED DREAMS

PLANTED HOPE

author: Katie Neufeld

co-author: Kevin Neufeld

Finding Hope in Life's Darkest Moments

All Scripture quotations, unless otherwise indicated, are taken from the Holy Bible, New International Version®, NIV®. Copyright © 1973, 1978, 1984, 2011 by Biblica, Inc.™ Used by permission of Zondervan. All rights reserved worldwide. *www.zondervan.com* The "NIV" and "New International Version" are trademarks registered in the United States Patent and Trademark Office by Biblica, Inc.™

Scripture quotations marked (ESV) are from The ESV® Bible (The Holy Bible, English Standard Version®), copyright © 2001 by Crossway, a publishing ministry of Good News Publishers. Used by permission. All rights reserved.

Scripture quotations marked (NLT) are taken from the Holy Bible, New Living Translation, copyright © 1996, 2004, 2015 by Tyndale House Foundation. Used by permission of Tyndale House Publishers, Inc., Carol Stream, Illinois 60188. All rights reserved.

Scripture quotations marked (MSG) are taken from *THE MESSAGE*, copyright © 1993, 2002, 2018 by Eugene H. Peterson. Used by permission of NavPress. All rights reserved. Represented by Tyndale House Publishers, Inc.

Printed in the United States of America
First Printing, 2019

ISBN: 978-1-09-689155-0

Cover design: Amy Hultquist
Editor: Dawn Kinzer
Interior Design: Wordzworth Ltd.
Photography: Virginia Greene Photography, Signs and Wonders Photography and Amanda Wilson Photography

Visit the author's website at
www.plantedhope.com

This book is dedicated to Jerod,
my fiancé and best friend.

TABLE OF CONTENTS

ACKNOWLEDGEMENTS

They say it takes an army.

They were right.

It has been incredible to behold God putting together our army, our tribe, right before our eyes. Some were already family. Some were friends. Some were strangers turned into dearest friends. It's been breathtaking to watch God inspire and organize this book every step of the way. Even in the waiting, God was working.

To Paige: Thanks for helping me be intentional about creating the time and space to write. Your writing tips have proven invaluable and I cherish our friendship.

To Dan and Amy Hultquist: We are grateful for the valuable guidance and input from a published author. Thank you for showing us the ropes, Dan. Our deepest gratitude to you, Amy, for creating such a beautiful cover. We absolutely love that it captures so much of the heart of this book and think it is perfect!

To Debbie Hicks: Thanks for helping to set my writing foundation so many years ago. I didn't enjoy correcting the countless red marks on my papers then, but am thankful for them now. Thank you for helping me then and thank you now with this endeavor.

To Dawn: We and our readers thank you, our editor, for dramatically improving our writing and helping to bring the reader into the story with us. Thank you for a job well done!

To Virginia: Thanks for answering endless book questions as we were in new waters way over our heads. I value our friendship and adore the photos you've so graciously taken for the book.

To Denise: Thanks, my counselor, for helping me to move through grief and process the trauma and loss. Thank you for your shared tears, godly wisdom, and advice.

To Louie and Shelley Giglio: Though we have not officially met, endless thanks for being faithful to God's call on your lives and helping to raise up a generation of faith. Your timely words and talks helped me to see that I would not die in this valley, but live and tell the world what God has done. God has used you both to bring so much hope and healing to my heart.

To my Work Family: Thanks for supporting and loving me to this day. You all truly are a family to me. For as long as I live, I will never forget how special you all made me feel at work on my first Valentine's Day after losing Jerod and beyond. I love you!

To Wendie and Kristen: Two of my dearest and best friends, born out of the ashes of the darkest season of my life, I treasure your friendships to no end and am deeply grateful for your shared tears and wise words, even when it hurt to hear them. I am profoundly grateful for the time I had with you, Kristen. God shared you with me when I needed you most. The ache for your friendship will only grow on this side of heaven, but I look forward to the day when we are all reunited and without sorrow.

To our Proofreaders: Thanks for all the helpful input and encouragement.

To our Army of Prayer Warriors: Thanks to all of those who prayed us through this journey. Thank you for relentlessly storming the gates of heaven on our behalf.

To Dusty Rose: Just a little shout-out to my fluffiest, faithful and loving companion through the darkness, my Dusty Rose Doodle. You give the best snuggles.

To Jerod's Family: (Carol, Megan, and Frank) Thank you for taking me in and loving me as one of your own. Your love and support has been invaluable to me as we have faced these darkest days together. I consider you my family, love you dearly, and will continue to do so into eternity when we finally group tackle Jerod with all that we have.

To my Family: Thank you will never be enough to my family who has sacrificed endless amounts of time, energy, and sleep throughout these most difficult years to support me and help carry me through.

Our shared tears and joys have only drawn us closer and I am eternally grateful for you. I love you!

Thank you to the many of you who encouraged me on countless occasions to write this book. Thank you for believing in me! Your words helped to bring this book into reality.

To the Reader: My prayer and desire is that as you read these words, you would see that this is not *my* story, but God's story being written and experienced through me. Every time I sat down to write the pages of this book, I prayed God would put His words on my heart and these pages. May this story help you see what God may be writing through the broken and beautiful parts of your own life. I pray these words have helped faith and hope to rise up where you are in your story even now. Don't give up!

PREFACE

She came into our world on September 14, 1989, in Austell, Georgia—our second child, but first and only daughter. Katie was the apple of our eye and immediately had this father's heart. She was lovely, especially when her mother curled her hair into ringlets, which she despised and I adored. A bit shy in public, she showed her chatty personality to those of us close to her in doses, which we sometimes had to limit. It became clear early on that she was going to be more fragile than we had hoped or expected. When she was only eighteen months old, I found myself doing CPR on her in the living room at the end of a long trip home from Michigan. She was rushed by ambulance to the hospital where tests and observation began in an attempt to diagnose the problem. The glucose tolerance test was the worst, and she learned that pain came along with people in white coats.

Prior to my current job as a loan officer, I'd served in the ministry. After the church service, Katie used to come upstairs from Sunday school to where I'd be talking with members of my congregation. As she passed by each week, she would say, "Hi, Daddy," give me a hug, and go find her mother. One Sunday, I was told by a children's church leader that she had not been feeling well just before my wife ran up to me with Katie in her arms, relaying that something was wrong and we had to get to the hospital. On the way there, she stopped breathing, and my wife and I both prayed aloud as we sped the one exit up the highway to the hospital.

When bodily functions failed, we were horrified, but by the time we reached the hospital she was conscious, breathing, and recovering. After a series of tests and a few more incidents, Katie was diagnosed with a seizure disorder. The good news—there was medicine that would help. The bad news—the medicine masked her developing personality. She went a number of years without incident, so they decided to try weaning her off the medicine to see if she had outgrown the seizures. Only one incident occurred, and that turned out to be heat-related. She came out of her shell, and the Katie who had been hidden was released from captivity.

She had a wonderful childhood and exhibited the uncanny ability to sense special moments while she was in them. She also had some memories of her seizures and along with it some anxiety. In school, she was a good student but liked to blend into the background.

Then, she discovered volleyball. She had a fantastic coach her first couple of years who scared her to death but really brought out the talent. Her skills flourished, and during one game she had eighteen straight service wins with several aces. She could serve, set, dig, and spike and grew into one of the best players on the team. Her volleyball skills were exceeded by her academic skills, and she ended up graduating third in her class. She was always a bit timid socially, though very talkative at home where she was comfortable.

We thought she would live at home and go to college locally, maintaining the safe environment she so enjoyed. But, she surprised us by announcing that she wanted to go away to college. A couple visits and her choice was settled. Her journey to become a nurse would begin at North Georgia College & State University.

Katie had always seemed a bit fragile, but she was about to prove just how tough she could be. She worked part-time throughout college, kept her grades up, and was involved in a number of college activities. Only one in seven applicants accomplished admission into the school of nursing, but she did it on the first try. She endured clinicals and passed, failing only one check-off. My recollection is clear as she prepared for her second and final try on the failed check-off—pass and you move on, fail and you're out of the program. I was stressed, and I wasn't even there! In a crowning achievement, she was approached by her professor on her final project for her BSN degree who informed her that she would like to help Katie get her paper published. A few months after pinning and graduation, her article was published in *AORN*, a nursing journal.

She proceeded to get her dream job at a pediatric hospital in Atlanta where she had done her nursing school pediatric clinical rotation. Now, the stress of dealing with real children and real problems weighed heavily on her. Added to this was the fact that she looked so young and was occasionally faced with parents wanting someone older for their child's nurse. I made a few suggestions, which thankfully she never tried to implement. She did well, acquired good reviews, and paid off all her student loan debt in a year. With her new Toyota 4Runner, she was on top of the world, especially after meeting the man of her dreams, Jerod Hicks.

Jerod was a great fit, and he entrenched himself immediately in our hearts. He fit in well with the parents, the siblings, and the nephews ... especially the nephews. The young man had his own successful business, was active in his church, was vocal and unashamed in his witness, and he was never afraid to admit he didn't know something and set out to learn. Everything he did was big—and fast. He drove a Mustang GT, had a speedboat, and drank so much Mountain Dew, an IV would have been easier. Most of all, I knew he would treat Katie well. I remember thinking once that our life was really coming together, and we were getting an idea of what the future would look like.

I heard Dr. James Dobson once speak about how each of us has a protective membrane surrounding us; it eventually is torn, exposing us to a pain we never knew existed (Paraphrased from *Focus on the Family* radio broadcast by Dr. James Dobson). Our family seemed to have escaped that type of pain, though we'd experienced our share of trials. The closest death had come to me was the loss of my grandparents, but there had been no untimely losses.

In the ministry, I had held family members at the bedside of a dying father, husband, or loved one. More than I had wanted, I had been summoned to accident scenes and emergency rooms to pray for the injured and comfort the bereaved. Professionally, it was something that suited me well and was appreciated by those needing comfort.

October 9, 2014, everything changed. The call was for *me* to rush to the trauma center where my daughter was being transported. Jerod's condition was largely unknown, but he was being airlifted to a different trauma center. Like white blood cells rushing to the infection, our family members sped to Grady Memorial Hospital in downtown Atlanta. As I drove, I begged God to spare Katie and Jerod.

That day, I was sure Katie had been handed more than she could ever withstand. Was I ever wrong! I have been blessed to have a front-row seat to one of the greatest exhibits of strength, grace, toughness, and tenderness I have ever known. But this is really her story, not mine. Katie Neufeld: my daughter, my friend, and another exhibit of God's amazing grace.

Kevin Neufeld

INTRODUCTION

I thought I knew pain after sitting through sessions in the dentist's chair with insufficient novocaine. Pain resulted in visits to the doctor when I played high school football at the hefty weight of 135 pounds. Pain and I were on a first-name basis after struggling through my first day at a new job in agony sandwiched between two emergency room visits that ended with an appendectomy.

Having experienced these and more, I can say there is nothing that hurts worse than watching your child suffer and being unable to do anything to change the circumstances, unless it is watching your child hurt for his own and neither of us being able to do anything to alleviate the pain. We have been through both in the last three years. Along with that, it has been a season of loss.

In the last six years, we have lost two parents, two jobs, one—and potentially two—careers, several close friends, a pastor, and we are currently praying that we do not lose a grandson. We know loss, and we know it too well. It has become a companion that we keep trying to leave behind.

We have learned much in these past years. Most of us possess a human trait of thinking that we know when we don't. I thought I knew loss. After twenty-eight years in ministry visiting the funeral home, waiting with family members as vital signs leveled, praying for members who had suddenly lost their income, and counseling those who had lost a spouse to infidelity or a young girl who had lost her childhood to molestation, I thought I knew loss. The discovery was that one cannot know loss until it becomes personal. This means a number of things:

1 One of the early responses to loss is to feel like no one has ever experienced this before, which creates an intense loneliness, even among those grieving the same loss.

1

2   No two losses are the same, no matter how much they look alike.

3   Loss is an on-ramp to the highway of grief where you find that you are not alone. There are plenty of companions, and no one chooses to be there.

4   Loss changes a person ... forever. There is no getting over it, past it, or around it. It is lashed to your back, and you carry it with you in varying levels of consciousness for the rest of your life.

Having entered the highway of loss, we have found ourselves in rush-hour traffic surrounded by on-ramps filled to capacity. I made it much further into life than many before entering the highway officially, but my daughter did not. My grandparents have all passed away, and it hurt but it wasn't devastating; it is the nature of time and life. Losing a parent hits closer to home and has not been my experience yet but is beyond my imagination. But, to lose as my daughter did is beyond my comprehension.

Being older, one is better prepared for such tragedies, if, in fact, it is possible to be prepared. Twenty-five years of age is extremely early to suffer such a devastating tragedy and its aftermath, but that is how old Katie was when she was in the horrific accident. It has been our pleasure, our pain, our joy, and our curse to take this journey with her.

As we've traveled this road of grief, we've noticed others who arrived before us. Some have joined us along the way, carrying their own suitcases packed with sorrow, and we've cringed at their entrances because they've carried us back to ours. It also became clear to us that there are many who have been on this road for years, many of them traveling in battered vehicles that seem to move along remarkably smoothly, while other dented travelers struggle with damages so great that travel seems almost impossible. Some of them amaze us that they are still moving at all.

The reasons for this book are as follows:

1   To gently tap new grievers on their shoulders, letting them know they are not alone, and to thank those who tapped us when we started our journey.

2

2 To share with those new to the highway what to expect and what we have learned. Hopefully, it will smooth the path for them.

3 To give hope. As a Christ-follower, my faith was tested by our loss, but my hope was tested more than my faith.

And please know that parts of this story are very raw, as we have included some direct and unfiltered quotes from the early aftermath from our journals as well as some of Katie's blog posts. We made the conscious choice to be honest about our thoughts and feelings with those around us. Far too often Christians froth at the mouth with pious platitudes and paint an impossibly rosy picture.

During my years in ministry, God used several people to change my thinking and outlook, and to them I will be forever grateful. One of them was a missionary who spoke very passionately about the need for leaders to be transparent. Oftentimes, it is easier to just state the ideal and act as if we have mastered it when, in fact, we have not. This truth was brought into clear focus one evening as one of my members shared with me that he wasn't sure he could keep up this Christian walk. Proceeding to tell me that I made it seem so easy, he was discouraged with how hard it was for him. The truth is that I was not being honest about the struggle. That day, I determined that if I were to be effective as a spiritual leader, I was going to have to be honest about things and admit more of my humanity than I had been apt to share. There are several reasons we write with the raw emotion and details that we do.

First, if we are to be real and helpful, we must be honest. I heard a spiritual leader proclaim once that he had not missed a day of devotions in ten years. Would that encourage or discourage you? Though I was quite faithful in that area when I heard his proclamation, it was more of a discouragement than anything.

Second, our culture does not suffer well. By that, I mean that our American Christian culture seeks to eliminate suffering, or at least suppress it, so we can project an image that the Christian life is working for us. As I read the Psalms, I find that sometimes the psalmists protest that *life stinks right now*. Often, by the conclusion of the chapter, the author has wrestled to a point of resolution, faith, and trust in God. There have been many times over the past few years that I would have to admit that life stinks. Faith admits that sometimes life stinks but also focuses on the joy set before us as Jesus did. Katie and I have both wrestled with God over the events of our lives, but we've come to the realization that He is God, and we are not, and that He is good.

Third, because of our tendency to put on the Christian mask, those who have not endured pain such as Katie did do not know what to say, how to act, or how to help. If by our transparency we aid someone in being a better comforter or supporter for someone in pain and grief, then our pain has been redeemed instead of repressed. Grief even with surrounding support is a lonely road; there are still things that Katie has not shared and probably never will share with us. Her attorney asked for her journal as he built her case, so he probably knows as much as anyone. A fine Christian man, he was still moved by the depths of pain she experienced.

Fourth, in order to appreciate the light one must know the dark. Pain has a way of deepening the valleys, heightening the mountains, and intensifying the sorrow while simultaneously multiplying the breadth and depth of the gladness. Joy and sorrow, we found, can and do co-exist. What God has done in healing and strengthening Katie will only be known if the depths of her sadness and pain are also known. This is at the heart of our reason for even putting her story in print. It is our desire that those in the dark night of the soul will find a fellow traveler and that those who struggle, wondering how to help the hurting, will be aided in understanding how to be a blessing to those who wrestle with unspeakable pain and loss.

"Brothers and sisters, we do not want you to be uninformed about those who sleep in death, so that you do not grieve like the rest of mankind, who have no hope. For we believe that Jesus died and rose again, and so we believe that God will bring with Jesus those who have fallen asleep in him" (1 Thessalonians 4:13-14). These verses imply that Jesus' followers do not get a pass on grief, but that their grieving is different, and it is different because of their hope.

4

After such a tragedy as Katie has faced, parents worry about their child's will to live, their capacity to function day-to-day, and their mental and physical state. We were also very aware that she was going to have a chance to either run *from* God or run *to* Him. To our great satisfaction, she has chosen the latter, even if it was sometimes to pound on His chest and give voice to utter dissatisfaction with the way life has unfolded.

My father, a pastor himself, used to say that any dead fish can float downstream, but it takes a live one to go upstream. I have added to the analogy that sometimes the current is so strong that a live fish can be carried downstream, or at best, hold its own. But, when that happens, it is evidence of life. To those whose faith is weak and hope is fading, may I suggest that the fact that you fight on *is* evidence of faith. We write this story to encourage you to keep on fighting.

We invite you to hear Katie's story. It is hers and, as her pastor says, it is her part in the story of God. Most of it will come from her, but I will add color to it from time to time. May God be praised and many helped in its telling.

Kevin Neufeld

CHAPTER 1

What Just Happened

Katie

A shrill and continuous scream pierced through the dense, smoky air. Where was the gut-wrenching noise coming from? I slowly came to an awareness as I began to realize what had happened. Everything was blurry as I opened my eyes. What was this lump of grit in my mouth? My gum was falling apart. There was a horn blaring continuously, but why?

Where was that horrible screaming coming from?

Once I became more alert and was lifted out of the twilight zone, I came to realize that those terrified shrieks belonged to me. They were coming out of *my* mouth! I've never screamed to that intensity or decibel in my entire life. It felt like a subconscious force was commanding continual shrieks to the surface.

I spit my gum out and began coughing up dust particles.

What a terrible smell! The mixture of gas and oil was nauseating.

Where was Jerod? There—to the right—still securely strapped in by his seat belt, yet hunched over with his head hanging forward and blood dripping from his nose and ears. I grabbed his arm and called his name. No response. My breathing quickened, and my heart pounded as the growing pit in my stomach threatened to swallow me whole. Desperation and fear overwhelmed me.

Is this really happening?

Almost four years of nursing experience flew out the window faster than any Georgia sports team chokes in the playoffs. Despite everything I knew about car accidents, I momentarily considered lugging him out my side of the vehicle with all the strength I could muster. No—not going to happen; I didn't even try. I started to hear voices coming from outside my vehicle. *Oh—they're talking to me.*

"Can you open your door?"

"Ma'am, can you get out?"

"Are you able to get out of your vehicle?"

Unsure of what to do next, I followed their lead and tried to open my door. My driver-side door opened enough to duck down under the deployed side airbags and slide down and out.

Everyone bombarded me with questions as they closed in around me.

"Is there anyone else in the car?"

"Miss, is there a baby in the back seat?"

They weren't listening or understanding me. *No! There is no baby in the back seat.* Were my words not making sense? Were there even any words coming out? *There is no baby in the back seat, but there is one in the front seat. My baby.* I pointed to Jerod. *Save him! Help him!*

I imagine my first steps out of my 4Runner looked akin to a toddler making his first attempt. My world was literally spinning. I realized that I was only wearing one brown TOMS shoe as I dizzily stumbled around to the passenger side of my truck and felt the rough pavement beneath my bare foot.

The 4Runner was crushed on the passenger side—totaled? Did I even care?

I fumbled back around the vehicle, assessing the scene, until I reached the driver's door. Jerod was still stuck inside and not responding. I reached back through the door, over my seat, and checked on him again. This time, basic nursing skills kicked in. I checked his left radial pulse. Life pumped through his veins. Racing and thready, but definitely a pulse. I held on to that—figuratively and quite literally. I didn't want to let go, as if my holding onto his wrist made any difference in his current health status.

Bystanders who had come to our aid must have heard the screeching crashes, smashes, and bangs of the accident, because they'd run out of their homes and out of the high school that was just a few steps away from where the accident happened.

Chaos surrounded me. Where was emergency personnel? Had anyone called 911? What was taking so long?

Sirens grew closer. *Finally!* A fire truck and ambulance pulled up, and EMTs jumped out of their response vehicle.

The initial shock had carried me through those first moments, but now pain shot through my body. Someone from the school brought out a chair for me, and a few ladies insisted I sit. I was not okay—something was wrong with me too. A few moments later, a firefighter stood in front of me, checking my vital signs and injuries.

Terrified for Jerod and his precious life, I heard a bystander ask if I wanted to alert anyone about the accident, then request a phone number.

"Seven ... seven ... zero ..." My voice shook as I heard it making sense for the first time, except I realized I was giving them my own number.

A few moments later, my mom was on the other end of a cell, but after asking a few questions, she told me to hand the phone back to them. She couldn't understand a word of what I was trying to tell her. Why did no one understand what I was saying? Was I speaking another language?

I sat surrounded by complete chaos. Cars were parked everywhere, except for the one that was flipped upside down. Paper and debris were scattered all over Campbellton Street. Gas and oil smells permeated the air. It looked as if a bomb had gone off. *Someone save my precious fiancé! He's my world! Save him! Get him out! Someone—anyone—*

My pounding head proved to be my worst pain by far. I couldn't take my dizzy, tearful gaze off my love. My left arm began competing for the worst pain. I forced myself to look away from Jerod and saw a significantly large burn in the crook of my left arm. My legs and right hip began aching and demanding their due attention.

It seemed like another short eternity before they started cutting Jerod out of my vehicle. I cried steadily as I awaited news on Jerod's condition.

A kind lady started running back and forth from my 4Runner to me, relaying updates about Jerod's condition as soon as she got them. "He has a pulse … he has a strong heartbeat …" She was an angel in human skin.

Her words gave me hope … until I saw an ambu bag flying through the air toward Jerod's general vicinity. He wasn't breathing. My living nightmare. Ambu bags are not a good sign; medical professionals use them to breathe for patients who cannot do so for themselves. I wept loudly in a stranger's arms. Those women—bystanders—were some of the best and most memorable comforters in my time of need. One held my head close to her chest with both of her arms and let me cry it out.

I thought I would be thrilled to see Jerod finally cut out of my car, but that wasn't the case as I saw a lady on top of him doing CPR as they rushed the stretcher to the nearest ambulance. I proceeded to wail inconsolably, so much so, that the firefighter helping me turned around to see what had caused my current spike in traumatic emotion. I remained inconsolable for quite some time as I watched them wheel my love away, wearing his favorite outfit, his blue plaid shorts that he wore to our engagement and his red Braves shirt. The ambulance rushed him to the nearest hospital. I was hopeful, since it was just minutes away.

They would be able to save his life, I hoped and desperately prayed.

CHAPTER 2

Divine Foundations

Katie

I consider it one of my greatest blessings to have been born into a family with many generations of faith passed down. I was raised in a Christian home, daughter to two godly parents and sister to two brothers, one older and one younger. I once told my mom that I wanted to put my second brother back where he came from and get a sister instead, obviously unaware of how things work at my young age. However, I believe growing up with two brothers has molded me into a well-rounded woman with a generous serving of grit and toughness, as well as femininity.

I was inducted into the preacher's kid (PK) club at birth. My dad pastored a small church at that time and throughout most of my childhood years. With all of our extended family—grandparents, aunts, uncles, and cousins—living hundreds of miles away, the members of my dad's church became like family, even serving as our emergency contacts.

I remember us kids being shuffled around late into the night many a time as my mom suffered some health problems during my younger years. Growing up in this church instilled in me a love for hymns, many of which I am listening to even now as I type these words. Most of my best friendships from childhood were also birthed out of this church family. Best and most important of all, I accepted Jesus Christ as my Lord and Savior at age five and was baptized by my dad in this church. And I remember swallowing some of the baptismal water—*yuck*!

I was not without my own share of medical problems as a child. Before I turned two, I was diagnosed with a seizure disorder that would cause me to stop breathing. My dad even had to perform CPR on me once. I remember a few times when I passed out and either woke up in an ambulance or in my mother's arms. She'd pat my face and urge me to stay awake. I don't recall every detail about these incidents, but it surprises me how much I do, and in such vivid detail too. It was necessary to take an orange-flavored seizure medication for many years until I grew out of the condition, as my pediatrician had predicted. So many of those fear-filled moments I would rather forget altogether.

Aside from medical problems, my childhood years were mostly full of joy and wonderful memories, with a large portion of that time being spent outside. I have always been a lover of nature and the deeper meanings behind things. I've always searched for the whys.

My older brother, Taylor, and I enjoyed playing in the woods, on the trampoline, or on our swing set. We lived within walking distance of Deerlick Park, and Dad accompanied us there many nights each week. Sometimes, we even took bread to feed the ducks—one of my favorite things to do there!

Taylor and I got along especially well; we played together, and we got spankings together. There's nothing like discipline to bond two kids. I believe one particular group spanking was after a spaghetti food fight. I always claim that I won, since I was wearing the most spaghetti!

My parents, my mom especially, raised us to be self-sufficient and able to make our own decisions. Painful lessons were involved at the time, but I am thankful now, as those lessons have served me well in my adult years. My decision-making ability was so lacking as a child that I would ask my parents what I should eat first when we sat down for dinner.

Fast forward quite a few years through two different private Christian schools to when I was entering into my high school years. My favorite subject throughout high school, though quite a challenge, was English. Every time I turned in a corrected paper, it would return with countless additional red marks for correcting. It felt like one correction turned into ten more. Unbeknownst to me then, the struggle in that class forged in me some of my greatest developing passions and talents—my love of writing.

High school had its challenges, but nothing like what I would face in college. I graduated among the top three of my class of thirteen and headed straight into summer semester to embark on my next journey—college. I'd always leaned toward healthcare, since one of my greatest passions is to help others in ways they cannot help themselves. After all, they say there will always be jobs for those in healthcare. It seemed like the perfect profession with my perfectionistic traits and my desire for a challenge.

Despite my introverted nature, I surprised my parents and went off to a college an hour and a half away, North Georgia College and State University. I completed my freshman year and was accepted into North Georgia's nursing school. Then, the real struggle began. Nursing school challenged me in more ways than high school could ever shake a stick at. It wasn't until late one night as I was studying that I realized nursing school had introduced me to one of my greatest struggles to date—anxiety.

My heart raced, and I was shaking uncontrollably as I rummaged around my dorm, frantically looking for my phone, or anyone's, to call my mom and tell her what was going on. I had no clue what was happening to my body. What I was experiencing was all new territory for me, and I didn't like it. I was unaware at the time that God would one day turn my greatest struggle into a strength, one I would be able to use in my favor.

Nursing school utilized intimidation tactics. One mistake could end the dream. My nursing career flashed before my eyes the day I failed a check-off. I had incorrectly drawn up two types of insulin into the syringe. We were allowed one redo on check-offs, and if we didn't pass that, we were out. No pressure, right? I retreated to my dorm room and cried the afternoon away in my bed. The perfectionist had failed. I thought my nursing career was over, but I didn't give up. This year, 2018, will complete my eighth year working as a registered nurse!

> *"I know how to be brought low, and I know how to abound. In any and every circumstance, I have learned the secret of facing plenty and hunger, abundance and need. I can do all things through him who strengthens me."*

—PHILIPPIANS 4:12–13 ESV

Katie – Living the Night Shift Life

I still work on the same floor where I started my nursing career, but my first nights were during our busy winter respiratory season. Talk about terrifying! I survived, and so did all of my patients. *Thank you, Jesus.*

It took a few years of working the night shift before I finally surrendered to the notion that I was not going to meet that special man any other way than the absolute least personal avenue—online. Since I wasn't one of those people who could flip-flop their entire world from work nights to off nights, I wasn't participating in life under the sun. I'm a creature of habit, and I found that I clocked my best quality and duration of sleep if I succumbed to the less-than-ideal sleeping patterns of being awake most of the night and asleep most of the day.

Fine, I thought. *I'll give it a shot.* I knew plenty of people who had met their special someone online. So, I thought, *here goes nothing.* I'd tried a few different sites with no luck and only laughs before I signed up for Christian Mingle. The guys on those other sites were so *not* what I was looking for, although they did provide the comedic relief I needed to continue my efforts. I didn't initially have much luck on Christian Mingle either.

I distinctly remember my continued cries to God in February 2014, reminding Him of my deepest desires for a godly husband and life partner that He'd planted in my heart so very long ago. I reminded God of that desire and told Him that I either needed Him to bring it to fruition or take it away from me completely. Those words were scary for me to pray, because I couldn't and didn't really want to imagine a world where I didn't long for a husband, but I'd reached a beautiful place in my life where I was ready for greater desires to flood my heart. After all, I have since learned that *marriage is not the goal,* and *singleness is not less than God's best.* God's plans have always proven to be way better than my dreams, and a man would never be able to fill that God-shaped hole in my heart anyway.

Valentine's Day, 2014, was spent alone in my Midtown apartment, and I penned the following that night in my journal:

"God, my heart sings to You. I feel Your presence as I sit in my apartment alone this Valentine's Day. No roommate. No TV. No boyfriend. Just You and me …

God I can't get over how truly beautiful and indescribable this night has been with You! I can't even journal how amazing it all has been. Who knew being alone at my apartment with no date on Valentine's Day, 2014, could be so incredibly filling to my soul! Only You, God, only You! I feel You near!"

Later, I shared about that night with my dad over the phone, and I stored these special words from him in my journal and in my heart. "Enjoy it," he said. "When we delight in Him, we are ready to receive His gifts. The same God who is working in you has His hand on whoever you are to meet, and you can trust His work there too."

I went on in my journal to note how truly joyful God had been making me in my singleness and that He is enough for me. The pain and misery of singleness is totally meaningful, and God will not waste one second of it. My final words were, "This has been the best Valentine's Day yet; thank You for that!"

One month and a few days later, on March 31, 2014, I met the man of my dreams! *Jerod.*

Kevin – Beneath the Foundation

Observing a finished building, the trained eye can get some idea of the foundation and its nature and composition, but only those who laid the groundwork know the details. Katie wrote about the foundation her parents and our church had created for her, but she wasn't around to see the building process. Growing up so far from family, she can't fully appreciate the support that was laid beneath her parents. Each of us stands on the shoulders of the previous generation.

One of the godliest men I have known was my father-in-law, Bill Green, who did not come to faith until just after my wife and I were married. His character, followed by God's amazing work in his life, made him one of my favorite coffee mates. Through the years, we spent hours over early morning coffee, discussing life and faith. Both Bill and Bev Green served faithfully for many years in their church and were some of our biggest fans and influences. They loved the Word of God, and anyone who spent time at their house was bound to see them faithfully having devotions with their Bible and *Our Daily Bread*. Pa & Nanny, as our children knew them, were wonderful grandparents and influences on our children.

On the Neufeld side, I know the foundation a bit deeper. At a family reunion a couple years ago, I stopped to visit the church where I first met the extended Neufeld family at my great-grandmother's funeral. The widow of the pastor who served with and knew my great-grandparents, "HT" and Anna Neufeld, dug out the church history annals and showed me pictures of their send-off in a covered wagon as missionaries to Montana. They faithfully took the gospel of Jesus Christ to Native Americans in Montana and Oklahoma for many years.

Their second oldest son was my grandfather, Abe, who with his wife, Alvina, served churches bi-vocationally in Oklahoma, Nebraska, and Colorado. I stayed overnight with them many times, and every morning was the same. I awakened to the smell of coffee and breakfast from Grandma's kitchen and always found my grandfather sitting reading his Bible or on his knees praying. Not once do I remember not seeing this scene, and it was his example that gave me my high view of the Word of God. His last words to me before cancer took him from this world were, "Kevin, it always pays to serve the Lord."

Their oldest child and only son was my father, Gerald, who served faithfully along with my mother, Jerry, for decades in several churches, but finally in the church he founded and pastored for over thirty-five years. It was from my father, though much more gregarious than I, that I got my love for people.

My mother taught me compassion. Her parents had moved to Colorado from Arkansas after her father's service in the armed forces. Ralph and Edna Mae Howard were faithful and active church members who loved to laugh and spend time with friends. Their house was always a place of joy and delight, especially when he wanted to relax and play the piano for what seemed like hours. Any time you rode with them in the car, you were likely to have a sing-along. One of the songs they used to sing was, "You Can Have a Song in Your Heart." That tune has been my companion during tough times in my life.

Kevin – Our Church Family

"Extended" family also poured into Katie's life for many years—Sunday school teachers, youth pastors, and family friends. In addition, they laid the foundation in good ground. Our daughter from her earliest days had a heart for God. She adopted her faith back in high school and didn't stray from it during her college years like so many do at that time. Even with the pressures of nursing school, a job, and a social life, her relationship with God has been a priority for a long time. It would take too long to thank everyone, but Gayle Wallace, Stanley and Ann Mason, Russell and Lisa James, and Ryan and Lisa Tyler were a few of her church family members who left their imprints on her life.

There's no way to place a value on this foundation that was laid years, even generations, prior to Katie's birth. It truly is one of the greatest gifts that one can give to his progeny. Further, it is a gift that can keep on giving if each generation guards it diligently. While it may change around the edges, if the core stays intact and each new generation connects not to the tradition, but to the God of the tradition, the foundation is laid deep, firm, and able to withstand strong storms.

This is the foundation beneath the foundation, and I am sure there is more of which I am unaware. Surely one of the joys of heaven will be to do a little substructure exploration. It also serves to remind me that *we* are laying a foundation day by day. I am so grateful that we had that legacy to offer our children.

CHAPTER 3

The Jerocuda

Katie

I have dreamed of the perfect guy for me since I was a little girl. I've condensed my list over the years to only include the necessities and the "would really like to haves," but my dream guy had to be a strong and growing Christian, a spiritual leader, a gentleman, have strong morals and values, treasure family and want children, have a funny personality, and be adventurous and outdoorsy. Jerod matched this list, plus some. My cup was overflowing. I had waited so many years to find this man.

We met on March 31, 2014, at 11:30 a.m. at Carolyn's Gourmet Café in Midtown—both thirty minutes early because we both hated being late. I thank God so much for giving Jerod persistence in his pursuit of me. He'd messaged me two times prior to the one where I actually responded with a "smile" on Christian Mingle. That's where our story began.

I'd just finished reading, *Real Men Don't Text*, by Ruthie and Michael Dean; Jerod was the poster boy for the book. He did everything traditionally and exactly how I would have wanted. He asked for my number and started texting me, but made sure to call me when he asked me on our first date. No texting that information. What a man! I had waited so long for this. That particular phone conversation was short in comparison to our couple of three-and four-hour phone conversations that lasted well into the wee hours of the morning. My first impression from that first phone call was that he talked fast! I thought he was just nervous, or maybe he was always that hyper and energized.

Jerod drove to Atlanta to see me the first couple of times; he didn't make me go to him. It was just *wow* after *wow* with Jerod! He made sure to pray and thank God for our food and for His faithfulness on that first date. That in itself spoke volumes to me. I had to chuckle as I considered how different and refreshing that experience was in comparison to a previous date with another guy. He'd asked if I prayed before eating, then bowed his head and waited for me to pray for us.

After lunch, Jerod and I meandered over to Piedmont Park where he decided he needed to perform a few pull-ups. He kept me laughing. Jerod held open every single door and ran up and stopped me in his silly little ways if I tried. He pursued me like I had always dreamed of a guy doing. I won't forget his parting words at the end of our first date that Monday, March 31.

He said something like, "I don't want to monopolize your time, but I would love to see you tomorrow, if you're free."

I initially was not sure I'd be able to handle his extreme level of energy and craziness. My roommate and I talked later. We agreed he was continually trying to impress me and that certainly made his energy levels a bit higher for a time. Once he knew how interested I was in him, he calmed down to a manageable level.

By the way ... I saw him the next day.

While dating, I'd become quite skilled at finding one thing, or many, to pick out and pinpoint long enough until it bothered me beyond what I was able to bear. I'd see a warning sign, then get ready to run. It was different with Jerod. I kept looking for something—anything—but *something* never came. The more I learned, the more I liked!

I won't lie to you and say that all of our dates were perfectly amazing and went according to Jerod's plan. During our second date, we had to search not one, not two, but three different sketchy convenient stores/smoke shops near Centennial Olympic Park to find a functional ATM in order to pay for the lunch we'd already ordered at Ann's Snack Bar. He didn't know that Ann only accepted cash. We were fortunate that nothing worse happened, yet none of that whole fiasco made me like him any less. It was certainly an adventure.

There was also the incident at the Braves game. A large drunk guy behind us plunged forward on top of me, knocking me onto the guy in front of me and then head over heels down to the ground with him falling on top of me, all while Jerod was gone on a bathroom break. I'll never forget his facial expression as he rounded the corner to walk back up to our seats. Jaw dropped. Eyes wide. By that time, an usher and two Atlanta police officers had arrived at my side. Some people around me who saw it happen said they didn't even know I was under there until the inebriated man got up, which seemed like forever. Jerod never left my side again that night. As annoying as it was that he made me get up with him every single time he had to use the bathroom, it was still a sweet gesture.

Dating Jerod forged an adjustment on my end. It was difficult at first, but I got used to the repeated embarrassment. I'm not one for making scenes, and it seemed like every next date brought with it more unwanted public attention. It was obvious that he cared less than I did what people thought about him. Jerod believed he could beat up anyone who ever made fun of him, being a third-degree black belt. Yelling, "Go Mets" on a MARTA city train en route to a Braves game was just not acceptable though. *Jerod didn't do that again.* Neither was yelling my name loudly while looking all over Ikea for me. Then, there was my self-inflicted embarrassment the time Jerod insisted I park his van and trailer at the lake while he got the boat into the water. We came back to a parking citation saying, "Use only one space please."

Eventually I glimpsed a serious side of Jerod, which helped me to accept and even love his silly and crazy side. Then we became more of a team, laughing together at his craziness and other people's uncertain reactions to his silly comments.

By the time he'd turned twenty-one, Jerod had started his martial arts business, Breakthrough Martial Arts. He impressed me early on with how he'd taken on such responsibility at a young age and with how wonderful he was with the kids there. He always wanted to know more and learn as much as he could about everything. Before he met me, Jerod wasn't a Braves fan at all. But it didn't take long before he got us season tickets for the 2014 season, just because he knew I loved following the Braves and attending games at the Ted (the old Braves stadium). Nothing was done half-heartedly; he jumped in with both feet. The man had even applied to compete on the show, *Wipeout*, but never got a response. Who does that? Jerod, apparently!

Jerod certainly had a silly side, but what I loved even more than that was his heart for Jesus and using what God had placed in his hands to advance the kingdom. He lived with open hands and an open heart. I was so impressed the day I came across the white board he kept at his business that listed his goals in three columns: business, spiritual, and personal. Like I said, the more I learned, the more I liked!

Katie – The Turning Point

Good Friday was a turning point for Jerod and me in our relationship. Up until that point, our dates had been a mixed bag of refreshing excitement and deep, meaningful conversation, along with the occasional embarrassment and sketchy venue. But I saw deep into Jerod's heart that night. We were actually late to buy our tickets and had trouble even finding any for the Passion Good Friday event at the Verizon Wireless Amphitheater. God provided for us. Jerod had found a pair.

It was a long drive and a cold, rainy night, but the Son was still shining, as Jerod put it. We didn't need the sun to shine when we had the Son shining through the clouds and the rain. Talk about some perspective shift! There was something so very special about worshiping together in our lawn seats under a shared umbrella in the cold rain. If there's one thing that attracts me to a man, it's seeing a heart on fire for God. That was Jerod's heart. He was after Jesus.

Jerod was beyond excited to share with me what he'd recently done at his school. He was led to share the gospel that Easter with all of his students, and he'd given them all their next belts—undeserved and without cost—to be an example of God's grace and gift of salvation from Jesus. He used this to make Jesus known in his business. He was bold and unashamed.

There was no turning back now. Jerod had won my heart. Simply stated, he had a heart for Jesus. He was very much a lifelong learner and searcher of truth, complete with a warm and welcoming spirit. He met no strangers, and all were always welcome—he was nonjudgmental.

Jerod was the spiritual leader I had so desired. When I met him, he was already heavily involved at West Ridge Church, specifically in their children's ministry. Jerod took on leadership so effortlessly. I knew early on that I would follow him anywhere. Except when he led us to the second row.

One of the first times we went to church together, Jerod chose to sit toward the front. As he left for the bathroom before that service started, I swiftly moved us back a few rows. I was never comfortable being up close and personal like that. I was never one for the stage either, but Jerod got me up on one of those as well.

One Sunday, he asked me to help with a lesson in Kids' Quest, the group full of elementary-age children, and while I had no speaking roles, he found a way to put me on the spot in true Jerod form. An impromptu board break. *No. No. Please, no.* But there was no getting out of it. Not with Jerod. I'd never broken a board, so I wasn't even sure that I could, but it was Jerod's silly little smiley nod right before my break that told me I could do it. I trusted him. I wasn't happy, but I broke my first board that day!

Jerod embarrassed, spoiled, and challenged me like I'd never been before. He was breaking through my tough, emotionless shell, bringing emotion out from the deepest parts of my heart. The process was obviously not always pleasant, but so worth it.

The activities kept coming that summer of 2014—the *best* summer! We were always out doing the next big thing. His mom, Carol, kept telling us to enjoy those fun and spontaneous days in life while we still could.

He'd bought a boat just before we met. Needless to say, we spent many a full day out on Lake Allatoona, soaking up the sun's warm rays and competing in water sports out on his fancy speedboat. Jerod always had to one-up me in skill and talent with watersports, and I was okay with that. Well, except for the time when he so effortlessly learned to slalom—water ski with only one ski—a skill I'd tried for years to accomplish.

Jerod always had to beat me in a competition, whether there truly was one or not, yet he was also one of my biggest cheerleaders. I lived exhausted between my thirteen-hour work shifts followed by late nights at Braves games to early lake mornings that turned into late lake nights. I bought Jerod a GoPro video camera for his birthday in August so we could capture our adventures and enjoy them for a lifetime.

I was a different person with Jerod. When I'd liked a guy in the past, I'd constantly look to the future and plan our entire lives out instead of living content in the present moment. But with Jerod, I was present-focused, enjoying all of our adventures. I didn't care what the future held, because I just knew he was in it. *He* was my future, so I didn't care where it led.

However, our relationship didn't experience the smoothest transition due to the fact that we were both extremely stubborn people by nature. But every time we had a disagreement—and we had a lot of them—we always felt better after talking it out and inviting Jesus into the equation. The process was sometimes fairly extended, but God was growing us together through those struggles. They made us stronger.

Katie – Our Future Together

It wasn't long before Jerod and I knew we wanted to spend the rest of our lives together.

On July 20, 2014, while riding into the city for a Braves game, Jerod started a conversation with the question, "How do you think we're doing right now?"

"Well, we definitely have things to work on, but we're doing okay." Not the most endearing reply, but we'd just come out of a fight from the day before.

Jerod had booked a behind-the-scenes tour of the Braves stadium before the game, so we proceeded to meet the designated staff member, Matt, upon our arrival. We each got a soft, reusable Braves bag filled with Braves memorabilia. That's what my bag had in it anyway.

The tour lasted roughly an hour, going behind the scenes where we passed by Jason Heyward, no big deal, among other players. He got away before we could get his autograph, though. *Bummer!* We were on our way to the next museum when I spotted my brother, Taylor, and his wife, Cori.

"What are you guys doing here?" I asked.

Taylor is in law enforcement and usually works traffic for the games. I've never heard of him actually attending one, especially on a Sunday. So, seeing him there was weird and unusual. *Hmm.* And where were their kids? Stranger than that was when they both sped off stuttering only bits of a reply to my question as Jerod tugged my hand along to keep us moving. He didn't utter a word as we continued into the museum. He didn't have to, though. His unusually sweaty hands were enough for me to know something was up. I didn't ask any questions. I was doing my own processing as my stomach knotted.

Somewhere along the way, Jerod became vocal again, and we headed out toward home plate after one more bathroom break for him, or so I thought. Neither of us had been out on the field before, so we began taking pictures. I followed Matt as Jerod sneaked away to get something out of his bag.

At the time, I didn't see any of that happening. Jerod quickly ran back over and joined us at home plate with a baseball he grabbed and held tightly against the palm of his hand. He performed an extended stretch with both arms up high toward the sky and held that pose for a few seconds. I don't remember that so clearly, but it's more obvious when I watch back through our videos. It was a secret signal. Jerod relaxed his pose and started to pretend like he was going to pitch the baseball but didn't right away. He finally threw me the ball, and as I was getting ready to toss it back, he walked over and looked down at the ball. *Did I miss something?* Apparently so.

Written on the ball were the following words: *Will You Marry Me?*

Next thing I knew, Jerod was down on one knee saying a few words before actually asking me to marry him. The funny part? At that point, I was so excited, I forgot everything he said to me in those moments.

"Yes!"

The answer was *yes*, followed by extended hugs and kisses and more hugs. The ring is so beautiful, and it's the exact one I'd picked out along with all the specific diamonds I'd liked. Jerod spoiled me. He tended to do that for those he loved. It took me a while to notice that we had an audience. All of Turner Field's early birds were cheering us on as we turned around to face Matt. I realized he'd been snapping pictures all along.

A few moments later, a large crowd made its way down to where we were standing. Both of our families, as well as friends, had been present the entire time! Jerod, in all of his generosity, had saved up our season pass game tickets to pay for all of their admissions into the game that day, and he'd set up everything necessary to make the inclusive proposal possible.

I would say it was seamless, but a small wrench was thrown into Jerod's plan when I saw my brother and his wife beforehand. They were under the impression that Jerod and I would be behind the scenes the entire time, so they thought the general admission areas were safe to stroll about. Nope!

The group photo we took at the end was truly like a scene in a movie. It's one of my favorite pictures, taken on one of the most magical days of my life. The cherry on top was being on the jumbotron for the first time, and with my new fiancé and our family and friends, no less! Not to mention the struggle it took to get us up there. We, along with all of the fans around us, cheered so loudly and jumped around like crazy people anytime they were panning the camera around the stadium, trying to make sure we secured our few seconds of fame. Success tastes sweet.

Kevin – New Man in Town

Jerod burst into the scene suddenly, yet it was as if he had been there forever. He never met a stranger and had a way of making those around him feel at home. Jerocuda, as one in our family named him, was swift but steady and always poised for action. That action began to take Katie away from our family and, to be honest, made me a little jealous at times. "Where's Katie?" became a common question.

Jerod was at our house quite a bit for meals, sitting around talking, and for 24. Ah, 24. We discovered that he and I shared a love of the action series on Fox, but he couldn't watch it due to his work schedule, which was mostly evenings. Upon finding out that we had a DVR, he asked if I'd record it for him and then asked if we could watch it together. It became a weekly ritual. It wasn't difficult to get to know him, but we became friends during our weekly "dates." On one occasion, Jerod proclaimed that if he and Katie didn't work out, at least he got me out of the deal. Those times were filled with episodes of *24*, followed by sitting and talking about a wide range of topics from theology to business, to sports, to life.

Occasionally, other events would postpone an episode of *24*, and we'd have to catch up the next week. It was on one such occasion that we jumped right into the episode knowing we had another to watch. Suggesting a short break before we proceeded to the next episode, he asked if we could postpone watching so we could just talk. At first, I wondered if he and Katie were having trouble, or if he was going to ask me for my counsel on understanding her, but he was a little too nervous for that, something that was unusual. I was quick to find out that it wasn't counsel he wanted—it was my daughter and her hand in marriage.

Laughter filled those times as well. During one of our *24*-watching events, he thought Katie was at work, where she often was until later in the evening. She'd hidden when he arrived and waited to slip into the room from behind him. As she slid down upon the arm of the couch and snuggled up close to him, he became noticeably nervous. With the discomfort increasingly etching itself upon his face, he attempted to politely move away until he could resist no more. Turning, he found Katie, and we all had a good laugh, especially when we discovered that he thought it was Katie's mother who had decided to sit on the arm of the couch.

Several other events from early on are prominent in my memory. We went to a Braves game one night, just the two of us. All the way there, we discussed faith, the Bible, and life. Question after question was launched in my direction. That was Jerod. Never was he ashamed to not know something or how to do it. He had the heart of a learner, a sponge looking to be filled and then wrung out for others, only to seek to be filled once again.

And he passed the nephew test. Brady and Mason, our grandsons, were attracted to him like iron shavings to a magnet. The time he brought his GoPro and chased them around the driveway will forever be a snapshot in my memory bank. Our other children were also drawn to him. Watching him play that night with our grandsons, I knew there would be years and years of that to come.

One of his instructors at the martial arts academy told of his first visit to the school and searching for the person in charge. Not finding anyone, he looked at the pile of children in the middle of the floor, only to find two adult legs protruding. The legs? Jerod's. It was easy to imagine a pile of my grandkids out on the grass, tumbling around with Uncle Jerod.

He was a special catch, and my daughter had hooked him. Katie had landed a Jerocuda.

CHAPTER 4

The Wait Continues

Katie

The week before the accident had been one for the books, probably one of my favorite weeks of ours to date. We were finally truly thriving and really functioning well as an established couple on the path to marriage. Jerod and I went apple picking with his dad in Ellijay where we captured one of my favorite pictures of us with me on Jerod's shoulders and an apple in his mouth, a true depiction of his silly side.

I had one unexpected day off work that week, and I used that time to visit Jerod at his workplace. Better than that, I'd finally learned to communicate well with Jerod. I was bubbling over with joy, and he could see and feel that. I kept telling him how much I loved him and how excited I was that I could spend my next two days off with him.

On October 8, I had told him, "You are very special to me, and I just adore you! You make me smile, and I can't wait to see you tonight! Just thinking about you a lot today!" I went on to mention the killer deal I'd gotten on fruits and veggies from a vendor at work. We could take them with us on the boat that Friday.

Later that same day, Jerod sent an e-mail asking me about going to a Braves season ticket holder play day later that month. He ended the e-mail in a way he never had before. He said, "I love you forever." It captured my attention even that day. He'd told me plenty of times before that he loved me, but never coupled with the word *forever*.

The deal was that we would spend Friday on the boat if we got a lot of wedding errands done on Thursday. We both agreed. Thursday, October 9, 2014, arrived, and it proved to be absolutely the most beautiful and perfect morning, sunny and not a cloud in the sky. Jerod was wearing his blue plaid shorts with a red Braves T-shirt; I was wearing denim capris, a T-shirt, and my brown TOMS.

We debated which vehicle to drive. It all depended on whether or not I wanted to pick up the vintage farmhouse doors I'd had my eyes on and wanted so badly to use at our wedding. A fun DIY project, I'd envisioned them opening as I walked down the aisle to my man. I decided against those particular doors and instead continued searching for the perfect pieces at the right price. We wouldn't need to drive his work van after all. My 4Runner would work for the day.

Jerod and I got an early start and met to drive down to Douglasville to register for our wedding at Bed Bath and Beyond at the mall. We'd also planned to meet his mom and sister at Firehouse Subs, his favorite fast food place, for lunch.

After breakfast at Chick-fil-A, we stepped into a few stores on our way to Bed Bath and Beyond, and as usual, Jerod had many of the employees laughing as he shopped. Yep—I'm with him! Registering for our wedding proved to be a test to our relationship; we didn't agree on much from silverware to the popcorn maker Jerod insisted on scanning. I looked down at my watch—12:29 p.m. Time to leave so we could meet his family in Hiram for lunch. We held hands on the way out to my 4Runner and discussed how our registering adventure had gone.

Our ride to Hiram started out fairly quiet compared to the usual steady conversation we'd have along the way. He was on his phone looking something up as we were turning left onto Chapel Hill Road.

We continued north on that road as it merged from four lanes down to two. We were slowing down at the stop sign on the south end of Douglas County High School on Campbellton Street when we were blindsided by a massive force that came upon us from behind, changing the trajectory of both of our lives as we knew it, totaling my 4Runner and shattering my innocence.

Noises jumbled into one loud conglomeration of smashes, bangs, and horns, but the one that will forever be burned into my memory is the ear-piercing screaming. *Mine.*

Glass, debris, gas, oil, and all of our wedding plans were scattered all over Campbellton Street. Cue the traumatic scene that I have lived and relived in my memory thousands of times.

Katie – Meet in the Middle

One phone call to my mom from the accident scene set a number of things into motion. She left work immediately. Word of the accident made it around quickly to my immediate family and some extended family as well. It was like what happens when the body endures an acute wound: all of the white blood cells and other properties flood the site of injury to support and begin healing the wound. We had yet to know the extent of our wound, though.

The paramedics and firefighters seemed to be trying to decide who was worse and which hospitals everyone needed to be targeted to. Per emergency personnel, the accident scene looked like a war zone—complete chaos. Jerod and I had been hit from behind so fast that the black box on the vehicle that hit us couldn't even recognize the speed, meaning the driver was going over ninety miles per hour at impact.

Although the car hit us from the back, the greater damage was done to the passenger side where Jerod sat, causing us to smash into the vehicle in front of us on our passenger side, then land at a screeching halt head-on with a red truck on the opposite side of the road.

I don't even remember seeing a car in front of us as we were slowing for the stop sign before the impact. We basically served as a pinball in the middle of vehicles crashing. My mom made it to the accident scene before they sent me out in an ambulance, but she couldn't get in because the entire road had been blocked off due to the severity of the accident.

Emergency personnel helped me onto a stretcher, and they initially decided to send me to Wellstar Douglas Hospital. The C-collar was administered next. I never knew those things were so uncomfortable, yet they could never be as uncomfortable as the wait to learn of Jerod's condition, which felt absolutely excruciating.

I spent the entire ambulance ride to Grady Memorial Hospital's trauma unit in tears. They had rerouted me once they learned the critical condition Jerod was in. Any passengers in that type of accident automatically earned a visit to a hospital with a certified trauma unit. I was completely unaware of where they were taking me, and I had no idea if anything serious was wrong with me, but it wouldn't have mattered because I was far more concerned about Jerod than myself. The paramedic in the ambulance with me updated me as she received any news. Jerod was critical but stable, she told me.

Upon my arrival at Grady, I was wheeled down the hall, and as a doctor came alongside me, his first words to me were, "Why are you crying?"

Did no one tell this doctor of the torment I have just endured? His words made me want to cry all the more.

I was placed in what seemed like a holding area for a few minutes before the first familiar face in that cold and dreary place walked up to me. My older brother, Taylor, a police officer, held my hand as he began talking to me. The comfort he unknowingly brought with him was palpable. Taylor was the only family member allowed to immediately come back to see me since he was in uniform, a small piece of the divine preparation for this moment. Gratitude abounded. Thank You, Jesus.

Slowly, more family began trickling in and taking their places by my side. My mom was the next person to join me in the hall where I still lay on my stretcher.

The following minutes were all a blur as I was quickly wheeled from test to test in order to evaluate any potential internal damage. I was finally awarded a room of my own. My nurse walked in and introduced himself. *Jared*. For more reasons than one, I was rendered speechless. Cue more tears. Jared was taking care of me as my Jerod lay fighting for his life. Only God could have orchestrated the raw and painful beauty of that moment.

I realized once the initial rush of testing was complete that I had a strong urge to pee. There's nothing more humbling than relieving oneself in a bedpan during that special womanly time of the month. I was mortified, not knowing what extent of bodily content Jared would be disposing for me, becoming a monthly reminder of the extensive trauma I had faced that day and the trauma that was still to come.

My dear friend, Katie, who I'd met in 2007 during my first year of college, left work early and arrived at my bedside. I'd lost my phone in the accident, so I had no way to contact her. She'd seen a post about the accident on Facebook and messaged my sister-in-law, Cori, for the details, then just showed up. Her act of selfless love that day continues to inspire me. Katie is the true friend that every person longs for and desperately needs. I have prayed on many occasions that I would have opportunities to be that type of support for someone else. Katie stood by and held my hand as the wait continued. My dad and younger brother, Caleb, were also at my bedside.

My mom left the room and made her first phone call to Megan, Jerod's sister, for updates on his condition. Her report: Jerod had since been life-flighted to Kennestone Hospital. Speaking from her ICU nursing experience, she thought it was a good sign that they didn't rush Jerod right into surgery. That was all we knew until my mom left the room again a few hours later to call for the next update. The wait was utterly agonizing. During that time, the team at Grady addressed the burn on my left arm, applying cream and wrapping it with gauze.

Thirty to forty-five minutes passed, but that stretch felt like an eternity. I asked Katie repeatedly if she thought it was a bad thing that it was taking my parents so long to come back with an update. She did her best to comfort me with her words in the midst of uncertainty, but her calming presence was enough. Sometimes in life's hardest moments, that's all you can give anyway—your presence, your full attention, and your time.

Eventually, Katie walked out into the hall to see if she could find out any news for me, but she returned saying that there was nothing new. Years later, I learned that what Katie had told me wasn't true. She knew something was very wrong, simply from seeing tears in my mom's eyes as she stood out in the hallway, trying to get my dad's attention to join her. My mom isn't a crier, but it wasn't Katie's burden to bear my mother's grief. Shortly after Katie returned, my parents reentered my room together. It felt like everything and everyone around me moved in slow motion.

What followed is difficult even now to put into words. However, the mental picture and emotional toll of what took place next are still quite vivid in my memory, turning out to be one of those defining events in my life that has replayed over and over in my head like an obnoxious broken record—one that won't stop. It was one of those moments that stakes its claim so deep into your Georgia clay that the only way you tell time forevermore is before or after that mark in history.

Mine arrived on *October 9, 2014.*

"Jerod didn't make it," my mom said through tears. Straight to the point. She said they were keeping him on life support until I was able to get there and say my good-byes. The doctor planned within the next twenty-four hours to do final tests to evaluate what brain activity, if any, Jerod had left.

Katie – The Beginning of the End

"Are you kidding me?"

My already traumatized brain couldn't process my mom's words, much less the severe weight of them. But I knew it was far from her to joke about any such thing—that would be the cruelest form of emotional torture. Shock resounded, and within seconds turned into disbelief. *This can't be happening.* God had sent Jerod to me, and we believed our relationship was all from Him.

God! What is going on?

Shock and disbelief were there to stay but were soon married to a sudden heartbreak so overpowering that not only did I feel it through my entire body, many people and rooms around us did as well. I'm sure the guttural cries and wails that blasted from my trauma room for quite some time could have broken any heart, even the most unknowing.

I'm a natural-born peacemaker and have never been one for making any kind of scene, but upon receiving any type of life-shattering news, emotion takes over a body and forces its release, whether authorized or not. There really was no clear cognitive thought in those initial moments of lament, only heartbreak so overwhelming that an outsider could almost touch it. But of course, no one would dare do so for fear that any wrong move on his part would be the straw that shattered anything that had survived the initial crushing blow.

There really aren't enough letters in the alphabet or accurate words in the English language to begin to describe the level of pain I felt in response to the devastating words that had reached my once-innocent ears. I'm convinced that the few people who fully understand the suffocating weight of traumatic loss are those who have unfortunately suffered that type of loss as well.

God bless all of our wonderful family and friends who showed up and even drove some of my family to Grady—due to unstable emotional states—and stood with us, prayed with us, and carried some of the weight of our pain.

Once we'd confirmed there was nothing more to be concerned about regarding my current health status, my mom began talking to nurses and doctors and anyone else she could find to rush the discharge process. It truly was one of our first miracles that I was not hurt worse physically. I was wheeled out of Grady with a large burn to my left arm, aches, pains, cuts, bruises, gashes, and a mild concussion. According to emergency personnel, if the initial collision had taken place a few inches over, I could have lost my life.

While I wished for many, many months that it had been the end for me as well, God met me right there in my darkest valley and began carrying me. He can handle the weight. He knows the pain. I felt Him hurting and crying right along with me, and honestly, that was some of my favorite comfort. To know that God loves each of His children so dearly that our pain becomes His. It breaks His heart just like it breaks any parent's heart to see His child in pain. Jesus wept. He grieved with Mary and Martha over the death of Lazarus knowing fully what He was about to do. That He was about to raise him back to life!

Jesus is our perfect example of how to best comfort those who are grieving any type of loss. Shared tears over a loss bring two people together like no other thing can. "When Jesus saw her weeping, and the Jews who had come along with her also weeping, he was deeply moved in spirit and troubled ... Jesus wept. Then the Jews said, 'See how he loved him!'" (John 11:33, 35–36).

After discharge papers were completed and signed, my family and I began our mad dash to Kennestone Hospital where we would join Jerod's family, hoping irrationally and against all odds that some sort of miracle had happened in the time it took for us to get there. My friend, Katie, drove my mom and me to Kennestone, since neither of us had our vehicles. I'd arrived via ambulance, and a dear friend of my mom's, Rebecca Vincent, had driven her to Grady.

The ride from Grady to Kennestone was one of those out-of-body experiences I'll never in my life forget. It was the longest, yet shortest, ride of my entire life all at the same time. How does one prepare his mind for something like that? For what was to come in all too short a time? How does one come face-to-face with a broken love—a shattered dream—knowing there's absolutely nothing short of a miracle that can be done to repair the damage?

Prayers continued to be spoken. If I'm honest, my heart had the most difficult time putting words to any prayer, and I'm convinced that Jesus understood that.

"In the same way, the Spirit helps us in our weakness. We do not know what we ought to pray for, but the Spirit himself intercedes for us through wordless groans."

—ROMANS 8:26

Kevin – That Day

The day began like any other with morning activities and the ride to the office in Kennesaw, Georgia. I worked in an office of forty loan officers for American Advisors Group, and things were going well. My view was even better on the third floor with an exterior glass wall overlooking hawks, squirrels, and other wildlife in the woods outside. The position had been awarded to me as a result of my production. Life was good.

Most days were spent in my cubicle with a headset on my head and a computer in front of me. I'd work my way through follow-up calls and handle incoming calls inquiring about reverse mortgages. My cell phone was always set off to the side, and between calls, I'd check for messages or spend a few moments in light banter with my fellow cellmates, as I jokingly called them.

Shortly after one p.m., my cell phone rang and I turned to find my youngest son's name and number on the caller ID. Puzzled, because he normally didn't call me at that time, I answered. What I heard next made time stand still.

"Katie and Jerod have been in a bad accident, and you need to go to the hospital."

Immediately, I began to pepper him with questions, but he didn't have any answers. As I ended the call, I turned to see all eyes on me. "My daughter and her fiancé were just in a bad car accident," I told my coworkers. "I have to go."

From then on, it was a blur as I grabbed a few belongings and headed for the elevator. I don't remember much about the trip, except that I was going as fast as and praying as intently as I could.

Repeatedly asking God to spare Katie's life, then intermittently turning my prayers to Jerod, I was heading to Wellstar Douglas Hospital when my phone rang again.

My oldest son, Taylor, informed me that Katie was being taken to Grady's Trauma Unit. It seemed to me that she must have been worse than I thought, so I asked if he knew anything more about her condition, but his answer only confused me more. He said we should probably pray harder for Jerod; he was probably in worse shape. As a police officer, he knew what I didn't. Protocol in a possible fatality is for all members to go to a trauma unit, regardless of the degree of injury. Jerod was being airlifted to another trauma unit at Kennestone Hospital.

My course turned to Grady Memorial Hospital. We'd regularly made thirteen-hour trips to Michigan over the years, but the frantic dash to the hospital seemed much longer. Finally making it to Grady, I went inside to look for Katie and found that she wasn't listed as a patient. After going in and out several times, I made my way to the row of ambulances, still not finding her.

"Dad," I heard a familiar voice say. My son had arrived dressed in police uniform, and soon after, an ambulance arrived with Katie. His uniform got him past security where he met Katie, but I wasn't allowed yet. Other family members and several friends arrived as we waited to enter the area where Katie was taken. My wife was driven to the hospital by a fellow teacher and good friend, Rebecca Vincent, who waited with us doing what friends do best—being present.

Another good friend was Katie Van Horn (Lovesy). A fellow nursing student, she'd been there for my daughter many times during college. She was there again that day. Arriving at Grady Hospital, she kept Katie company in her room, drove us to Kennestone, and once again waited there with Katie on the darkest day of her life. One does not forget such kindnesses and their givers.

My friend, Dan Hultquist, came to see if there was anything that we needed and to offer his support. Other friends from our various churches came to offer support and pray with and for us.

40

Much of our initial time there was spent in a blur, but eventually we were escorted back to join my daughter, and I saw her injuries for the first time. Externally, she didn't look like she'd just been in a horrible accident. Cuts, bruises, and burns from the airbag were visible, but she didn't appear in great discomfort, except for her questions about Jerod. I wondered if she were afraid to ask. Looking back, after what she saw at the accident scene, I can imagine there was some of that. We kept checking for updates on him as we waited for her to have some internal imaging done to make sure there were no further internal injuries, and we met her nurse ... Jared.

Katie was taken out of the room for a CT scan, and we took the opportunity to visit the waiting room to greet a few friends who had come. We also wanted to check on Jerod, and it was there that we received heartbreaking news. He was on life support with little hope for recovery, and after one or two more tests, it would be clear if any brain activity still existed. How were we going to relay that information to Katie? After a short deliberation, it was determined that we should do it sooner rather than later, so we headed back to her room, carrying the dreadful news.

Standing around Katie's bed, we prepared to share the heartbreaking update with her. That scene remains clear in my memories. Informing the nurses of what was about to happen, they alerted the chaplain who joined us, and the nurses respectfully excused themselves for our privacy.

This father looked on as his little girl, his sweetie, the apple of his eye wailed so loudly and so continuously that I feared we'd be escorted to a more remote part of the hospital. She was inconsolable, and I was speechless. What do you say to someone who just a couple hours ago was working on a wedding registry but was now facing a funeral? The death of her beloved, her hero, her knight in shining armor, and the death of her dreams, her hopes, and as it seemed, her future? There are no words to adequately describe those moments. Reminiscing brings me once again close to tears. As I looked at my daughter lying in the middle of her shattered dreams, I saw her as if in every stage of her life from infancy to adulthood, and I felt so helpless.

God had spared her life, but what kind of life would it be? After receiving test reports and being treated for her injuries, she was discharged just six short hours after her accident. We headed to Kennestone where she joined Jerod's family in their vigil.

After that, everything runs together again in my memory. Jerod's family and friends waited and prayed, hoping for a miracle, but fearing the worst. Our pastor stopped in, as did several pastors, but I'll never forget Paul Richardson's ministry to the Hicks family and to those of us gathered in the waiting room. If there had been a camera rolling the next few days, it would make for great teaching material for seminarians training for ministry. Paul was the model of what every family in this type of situation needs, and I will be forever grateful to him.

In Scripture, there are several accounts of time standing still. October 9, 2014, it stood still for us—for several days. Time is divided, or used to be, into BC and AD, Jesus being the one splitting time. There are a few days in life that become such time markers, and that day was one for our family. Everything is referenced as "before the accident" or "after the accident." Life changed that day, irreversibly, and each of us is forever changed.

Katie

It was dark outside by the time we made it to Kennestone. My mom found a wheelchair and wheeled me, my one TOMS shoe, and my broken heart up to the green tower where the appropriate ICU wing was located. We were directed to the large ICU family room where all of Jerod's family and friends were located.

As soon as I made it into the room, Carol and Megan—Jerod's mom and sister—got down on their knees, and at my wheelchair level, hugged and loved all over me with tears in their eyes saying, "Thank God you're okay. Thank God you're okay. Oh, thank God you're okay."

We all shared a few moments together in the family room before I saw Jerod for the first time since the accident. I knew what to expect but didn't. At that time, I'd been a nurse for four years, but no amount of nursing experience could have prepared me for that moment or any that followed.

There he lay—quiet. My Jerod. My Love. Lying in a hospital bed, lifeless, a far cry from Jerod's usual high-energy self. He was hooked up to so many machines, monitors, lines, and drains. Seeing him like that crushed me. He looked and smelled like some of the patients I'd seen in my nursing career. That thought alone wrecked me. I just wanted to fix him so badly. All of that nursing knowledge under my belt, but that's all it would ever be for Jerod, just knowledge. Only God holds the power of life and death.

So much of that night is now a big blur in my memory. Countless tears were shed. Hands were held. Prayers were sent. Friends and family drew near. The waiting room at Kennestone overflowed with people who knew and loved Jerod and wanted to support Jerod's family and mine.

In the wee hours, my parents had tried to convince me to go home with them, get some sleep, and return to Jerod later in the morning. They assured me they'd drive me back to the hospital as early as I wanted, but I didn't want to leave him. What if something happened? What if I missed something important? The unknowns were too much to bear. Nothing was going to keep me away. I agreed to leave with my parents, but only to get a change of clothes and a few other personal items, take a shower, and then return to my Jerod. There was not much sleep to be had that night, only silent sobs and aches.

The miracle we so desperately prayed and wished for had still not happened by dawn of October 10, 2014. I don't remember how many brain activity tests the doctor performed, but Jerod proceeded to fail every single one of them. I suffered through watching only the one where the doctor injected a syringe full of cold water deep into Jerod's ear canals, hoping for a response. *Any* response.

Nothing.

No response.

They did something with his ventilator that should've caused him to cough, but he didn't. Only my mom could endure the last test. They paused his breathing machine to see if he would take a breath by himself. *Nothing.* Jerod could do nothing without mechanical assistance.

Is this all a nightmare? If so, someone please *wake me up!*

I found a few minutes to have some alone time with Jerod, not knowing what he could hear or of how much he was still aware. I opened his eyelids and asked him if he wanted to build a snowman like I used to do when he'd be trying to take a nap. *Frozen* was our favorite movie at the time. It was hard to come up with any words to say really, but I just kept doing things that were special to us, like the eyelid lift and other Jerodisms.

I held his hand, rubbed his arm, adored his unique divot and mole in the middle of his chest, itched his nose and fidgeted with his hair like he used to, and kissed his lips around the ventilator. And were those lips still as soft as ever.

I'm not sure whose idea it was, but I wanted to lie next to him one last time, in the hospital bed. My mom asked the nurses to help make that happen, and they happily agreed to assist. They repositioned the ventilator equipment and got me situated next to my love, and I snuggled into him. My mom stayed in the room for those tender moments and proceeded to lift Jerod's left arm up to my back like a hug he would've given me if he were at all aware of his surroundings and capable of doing so himself.

It didn't seem like long before my *almost* alone time with Jerod was interrupted by someone relaying the message that it was time to talk to Life Link about organ donation. *Say what? Organ donation? This nightmare is still happening, huh?*

Much to my dismay, I was still not waking up from that living nightmare. Talk about emotional whiplash, going from registering for an upcoming wedding one day to planning out organ donation the next. That agony cut way deeper than any physical pain ever could.

The anguish of canceling every remaining part of my future with Jerod, one by one.

My family began making phone calls to cancel the wedding venue, the photographer, and the beautiful bridesmaids' dresses that were coming from across the world in Singapore. We got every nonrefundable deposit back, except for the money we paid for the actual wedding dress, which is still hanging in my closet, along with my veil and other accessories. A huge thank you to Spring Lake Events and Mike Moon Photography for agreeing to an exception, due to those extreme circumstances, and refunding all of the money from our nonrefundable deposits. That was such a weight off our shoulders during those most unfathomable days.

My mom made the phone call to the floor where I work to update them on what had transpired over the last twenty-four to forty-eight hours. Word of the accident and Jerod's condition spread rapidly. Many people had reached out to offer their words of love, support, and prayers, although I wasn't able to see any of that until a few days later, since my phone was initially lost in the rubble of my totaled vehicle. I probably would have been too overwhelmed to communicate with anyone anyway. Traci Sullivan, one of my mom's police friends, was so kind to go back through the accident scene and find as many of my personal items as she could, like the mini stuffed talking Olaf that Jerod had surprised me with one day.

After Life Link finished talking to us about organ donation, they gave Carol, Megan, and me white porcelain heart necklaces to symbolize the life-saving gift that someone would receive in accepting Jerod's precious heart. That was *my* heart. It beat with love for me. Those were *my* lungs that breathed sweet words to my ears and kept me laughing. His organs and mine were supposed to live as one in holy matrimony until we were old and decrepit. It felt like I was leaving my own heart that day as my family and I walked out of Kennestone without Jerod. How does one just walk away, looking at his entire future filled with the most magnificent of dreams through the rearview mirror?

45

Katie – A Dark Day

A post I had shared on Facebook on October 12, 2014, sums up my
sentiments on those first days of grief rather well.

> "First of all, I want to thank each and every one of you for
> your calls, texts, messages, comments, food, and all the over-
> whelming support and love I have received the last couple
> of days. It has meant a lot to me during these trying times.
>
> I am not even sure what to say. All I can come up with is
> *why, God, why?* I keep telling Him how I just can't see the
> good in all this and how Jerod just could not have been done
> on this earth because he was doing so much to further His
> kingdom.
>
> I have not been able to compose coherent sentences or make
> any decisions, big or small, over the last forty-eight hours.
> I don't know what I want to do, what I want to eat, if I even
> *want* to eat, if I could keep the food down that I would even
> try to eat, who I want to see, or the bigger questions of where
> I am going to go from here. It still just doesn't seem real to
> me. It seems like my sweet Jerod should be walking through
> the door any minute, texting, or calling me.
>
> I love every fiber of Jerod Hicks and who he was and still is in
> my heart. He was so special to me. Jerod was just so different
> from anyone I had ever met, a true one of a kind treasure. I
> really admired how he never cared what anyone thought of
> what he said or did—he was his own person for sure!
>
> He was always so generous and had such a heart of gold. In
> the middle of these last couple of nightmarish days ... nights
> ... or whatever this mess is, I have heard countless stories
> of things I never knew about that Jerod had done for other
> people. These stories melt my heart. I feel like we really found
> a way to cram a lifetime into six very short months. Jerod

has forever changed my life. I learned so many valuable life lessons from him, even though that process wasn't always easy. I am so very thankful for the refining process we had to go through to strengthen our relationship.

It doesn't even seem right that I am typing all of this right now. I just want to hear his voice and feel his tight hugs and sweet kisses again. I want to tell him about my day. I want to tell him what great family and friends he had and what a support system they all are. I can't even get my thoughts out coherently, so bear with me. Everyone is asking how I am doing. I have cuts, bruises, abrasions, a large burn, achy muscles, and bad headaches, all things that will eventually heal. My heart, however, I am not sure will heal. Or at least it feels that way right now. This year has definitely been the very best and absolutely worst year of my life. It is hard to know a relationship is so right in God's eyes and to move forward planning on a lifetime commitment together only to have it ripped violently out of my hands.

Life is precious. Jerod is so precious. I miss him. I love him deeply. I want him back. I need him. I want to feel his embrace. I want to see his eyes light up again when he is excited about something. I want to laugh with him again. I want to hear him rave about all the things he loved: Firehouse subs (turkey bacon ranch with no onion—peach Mellow Yellow with no ice … or Mountain Dew … still with no ice, of course), Baja Blast, Panda Express, the Braves, days on the lake. The list goes on. He really knew how to live life like there was no tomorrow, always packing his days full.

This takes me back to one of my favorite verses through high school: 'Be very careful, then, how you live—not as unwise but as wise, making the most of every opportunity, because the days are evil. Therefore do not be foolish, but understand what the Lord's will is' (Ephesians 5:15–17). Jerod lived this

47

verse. As a matter of fact, Jerod lived out a lot of verses. You could definitely see Jesus in him.

I feel like I go from numb to inconsolable in 2.2 seconds these days. None of it seems fair, and I feel desperate to have Jerod back. I ask why a lot. None of it makes sense. I (too frequently) have flashbacks of those moments right before the accident to the sheer terror, screams, bangs, smashes, horns, shock, etc. of the accident. And then there are the images of Jerod I have from the accident, which are forever burned into my memory. Those I cry over almost constantly at times. I am not sure how I will make it through these next days, weeks, months, and even years without him, but I know it will definitely be a moment-to-moment process. It seems like things that help me one day hurt me the next, so there is definitely no consistency during this whole thing. I take that back. One thing has been consistent. And shocking. Chocolate has never tasted so bad.

I love you sooooo incredibly much, Jerod, and always will. God, please tell him this."

Extended family from out of state began trickling into town over the next few days to offer support in any way they could, and we needed their love and support then more than ever before. The weather we experienced during the first two weeks after the accident only accentuated our loss; it rained for two weeks straight. In a way, the rain brought me comfort. It matched the anguish in my soul, the deepest parts of my being.

The day came—October 14, 2014. Jerod's service was to be held at West Ridge Church, where he faithfully served for some time. How was I ever going to survive that day? My body still ached, and my head was pounding, but my heart felt the worst pain by far. I was taking medicine around the clock to relieve some of the discomfort from my external wounds, but what could possibly touch the unspeakable hurt inside?

One of the most poignant memories of that entire day was my initial entrance into the auditorium and seeing the casket in front, which reminded me again of the finality of my traumatic and unexpected loss.

I'd always dreamed of walking down the aisle to my Jerod, adorned in a breathtaking white gown, hair all done up, makeup on, nails polished, the whole bit. Except in my dreams, Jerod was standing down front in his gray tux, hands clasped in front of his waist, grinning from ear to ear, and possibly with a tear or two leaking down his face as he watched his bride walk down the aisle to take her place by his side. I'd waited years for that moment and had so dreamed of seeing the expression on Jerod's face when he first saw me walking down the aisle. My dad and I shared unforgettable tears that stung their way down my face as I shared that heartbreaking revelation with him.

The estimated three thousand-plus people who attended Jerod's service were a testament to the kind of life he lived and the incredible legacy he was leaving from his short twenty-eight years on this earth. He'd finished well, even though he was just beginning, in my opinion. But, God had other plans.

I sat in front with Jerod's family as I watched the receiving line continue to grow until it reached the back of the auditorium, around those doors, and all the way outside of the building. West Ridge is not a small church. The length of that line and the way it never got shorter made me feel like I was about to have a panic attack. People were so genuine and so kind, offering their deepest condolences and prayers. They said they were so sorry for my loss. I wondered if I could be sorry for my own loss. Because I was. I was so sorry it happened. I was sorry I couldn't keep my sweet fiancé safe. I was sorry we had to be productive with planning and register for the wedding that day. I was just sorry.

Many of my coworkers made the long drive to attend the service, and for that, I am so grateful. I had to take a few breaks for snacks and pain medication. Some people were really good huggers—too good. Every next person who squeezed my neck made me feel like my head was going to pop off from the pressure and pain left over from the accident.

The service itself was quite touching, as painful as it was and as little of it as I remember now. Many people accepted Christ as they heard about the way Jerod lived his life and who he lived it for—Jesus. A large number of Jerod's martial arts students were in attendance and all sat together. Toward the end of the service, they all stood together and did one last formation. There was not a dry eye in the room. It is one thing to deal with your own grief and tears, but to watch those kids perform what Jerod had taught them with tears streaming down some of their faces and painful expressions on others was too much to bear. Childhood is a time to have heroes who prove to be invincible, withstanding all foes. Jerod was a hero to many. I know he was to me.

A word to the wise—don't pick your favorite songs to be played at a funeral. Just don't do it. When we sat down a few days beforehand to discuss song choices, we had chosen "Lay Me Down" by Chris Tomlin and "Oceans" by Hillsong. "Oceans" had been a favorite song of mine and Jerod's at the time but has since haunted me for years, even though the lyrics turned out to be something providential for our circumstances.

I have certainly been called out into deep waters where feet fail and fear surrounds. This song demands to be felt, and any resistance on my part is futile. Once the initial chords have reached my ears, the flashbacks have undoubtedly already begun. While the flashbacks from this song are less brutal and gruesome these days, the second most poignant memory from the day of Jerod's service, and the first scene of the continuous video reel of traumatic scenes in my head when I hear this song, is Jerod's family and me and mine walking out behind the casket to the tune of "Oceans." Like I said, providential. And wickedly painful.

The second longest day of my life ended at graveside. I remember thinking, *I don't know how I am going to do this.* What I didn't understand then was that I didn't have to know how. I just had to trust God with that and watch Him faithfully lead me through my darkest valley.

CHAPTER 5

Sorrowing

Katie

October 25, 2014, 4:55 a.m.

So many long nights. So many unanswered questions. So many nightmares. So, so, so many tears. So many memories. So much love. So much selfish longing to have you back with me. I know you are now where you were ultimately made to be. Just too soon, it seems. It just isn't easy to come to peace with losing such a priceless treasure. I miss you more than words can express. You will forever stay deep in my heart. I will love you forever, my Jerod, my love.

What was I supposed to do now? My perceived purpose and future had died brutally and instantly with Jerod on that dark day. How was I going to survive beyond my shattered dreams? A devastating loss so crushing and deep that it broke me to my core, to places I didn't even know existed within me. How was I supposed to live when all I wanted to do was die?

I didn't know. But I felt like that for months beyond recollection. Time was passing whether I was ready and wanted it to or not. Time was dragging me face down through the muck of my lowest valley, and I was too weak to put up any fight against it. That's a laugh—fighting against time. Grief is the furthest thing from anything logical.

I spent the first days going to follow-up doctor appointments and physical therapy, despite my ... resistance. Mental resistance anyway. Any opposition on my part was futile; I was far too weak to win any battles. Physical therapy seemed pointless. I could've done so much of that myself in the comfort of our own home. In hindsight though, physical therapy forced me to get out of the house and gave me a small dose of the life that was still very much going on around me. My time continued to stand still, regardless of what I did or didn't do and where I did or didn't go.

I'd moved back into my parents' basement per their recommendation so I wouldn't be left alone. They feared for me and what the darkness could birth in me. At that time, I couldn't have cared less about essentially anything. The darkness could have its way, if it were up to me.

To be transparent, I prayed on a few occasions for cancer to ravage my body and take me out, or for a plane to just fall out of the sky so my death would be quick. I just wanted relief from my life, from the nightmare. I wanted out of here. The truth was that I desperately needed my family's support whether I admitted it or not. I hated my life, yet I had no idea how much darker it would get before I would see the dim glimmer of light shining through the ash that was now my life.

Katie – The Gift of Anxiety

As it turned out, the crippling anxiety that I'd come to know all too well in nursing school turned into a strength in God's hands. My college anxiety had taken me to a darker place than I had ever been up until that point, and it became a divine preparation for what was to come. It forced me to come face-to-face with my mortality and question if I was going to act on any of my scary thoughts. I never had an action plan but was just overcome with fear of the new and undesirable me and ... what if?

The anxiety I experienced in college wasn't from unforeseen circumstances, but rather mainly from the stress I knew would come along with starting nursing school. It was late one sleepless college night when I came across an infomercial about a program that helped equip me to fight my battle with anxiety. The program was too expensive for me to buy in college, so I just signed up for the free trial, and over time and through that program, Jesus changed me.

First, the program helped me understand how many people deal with exactly the same thing. Secondly, and I will never forget when the instructor said that if you're scared of something you might do, or just scared of yourself, but didn't have a plan, then you were going to be okay. That advice may not work for everyone, but it did for me. Jesus used it to break down the fears that ravaged my mind. The instructor got into the *what if* thinking, automatic negative thoughts, expectations as well as self-talk, scary thoughts, and stress management.

I didn't know it then, but the anxiety Jesus led me through in college became a blessing in disguise. He turned that pain into power. Because I'd learned those techniques and conquered anxiety with Jesus once already, I knew it was now just the enemy infusing fear into my heart, jumbled together with the trauma and every other emotion you deal with in grief. And thanks to my prior *win* over anxiety, I felt confident that even though it didn't feel like it, I wasn't going to act on it. I still wouldn't have minded if something had transported me to Jerod and Jesus, though ... whatever it took.

Katie – Oh, My Aching Heart and Body

I slept in my parents' bed with my mom for the first month, but I didn't really sleep. Nights were mostly spent writhing around in tears, trying to find a position where I could get comfortable, and then staring into the darkness and crying some more. Everything ached. I couldn't cough, sneeze, or take a deep breath without pain. My ribs hurt for quite a few weeks. The burn on my left arm was painful and unusually itchy. It was a few days before I looked closely at the label and realized I was allergic to the main ingredient in the cream the doctor had prescribed to treat the burn.

My stomach was constantly upset for months, and I lost ten pounds. I was really only snacking at first, but eventually I was able to get two meals down a day. I'd wanted to lose a few pounds and gain some tone, but not at the price paid. I would've rather done it the easier way. It's sad to think that shedding blood, sweat, and tears at the gym *is* easier.

I started seeing a Christian counselor within a few weeks of the accident who helped guide and support me along grief's disorderly path while alerting me any time she saw yellow or red flags. Per her assessment, I was initially exhibiting an acute stress reaction, as expected of course, indicating that my irritability, emotional instability, flashbacks, nightmares, numbness, and seeing myself outside of my body were all normal, considering the trauma I'd experienced.

According to my counselor, if the acute stress reaction had not resolved within four to six weeks, it was then labeled PTSD, post-traumatic stress disorder. Hearing that news felt like an out-of-body experience. Maybe she mixed up the diagnoses between me and another patient? I would never have imagined my list of diagnoses would include PTSD, but the acute stress symptoms didn't subside and showed no signs of even letting up in the slightest. I began to startle easily with even the mildest triggers from e-mail notifications on my phone to people laughing unexpectedly around me.

The triggers would cause an immediate spike in my heart rate, followed by intrusive and vicious flashbacks that relentlessly haunted me. I would see myself sitting in my 4Runner as the accident was happening, then move to Grady when I learned of Jerod's condition to Kennestone where I hugged and kissed his body for the last time. The flashbacks would continue to "Oceans" being played at the funeral and beyond, like a morbid movie reel running nonstop through my brain. And there was no stopping them once they started. A smell could set them off. A sight. Even nothing at all sometimes.

I often felt hypervigilant, as well as extremely irritable and outright angry. Any combination of those symptoms or triggers would set off the entire bomb of physical manifestations, and much of the time, there was no rhyme or reason to it. My emotional outbreaks weren't predictable. I wasn't expecting the level of exhaustion that was married to grief. When I actually became a participant in the land of the living again, I'd feel exhausted after simply getting myself ready.

Flashbacks were haunting and persistent. As expected, they happened the most and the worst when I was driving. If at any point I was afraid someone was going to hit me, I'd start having flashbacks to the accident scene so vicious that I'd start to have physical manifestations. I could smell gas and oil, hear the screeching and smashes, and feel the initial overpowering impact from behind all over again, which led to short ten-second headaches that left as fast as they arrived. My head would sometimes even fall forward to absorb the imagined impact during those scares while driving. It was all so bizarre and unpleasant.

The flashbacks were not limited to driving time, though. One of the drawers on an isolation cart at work got stuck one day and instantly my mind flashed back to the accident scene. Jerod was stuck in my car. The whole scene proceeded to play out in my mind, part of the disturbing video reel I couldn't delete from my memory. Cue the ambu bag toss and the CPR and the rest of the memories.

I became so angry, and it wasn't even me trying to get the cart open. And then the images and feelings of being so insanely scared and worried, bawling my eyes out in my front row seat as I waited for them to cut him out of my car. That led to everything else I saw as I sat there in that chair with a stranger's arms around my pounding head. And my aching body. Oh, my aching body. I was washing my face one night in the shower, eyes closed, letting the water run down over my face, and instantly I started visualizing blood running down my face. It was so startling that I jumped back and had to calm myself down.

It wasn't long before I started experiencing the most disturbing and distressing nightmares. I would see Jerod die in countless ways over and over again. Before the trauma of the accident, I used to wake up from a nightmare to the sweet relief of reality, knowing that it was all just a bad dream. But after the accident, I would wake up from my gruesome nightmares of Jerod dying just to find out that the living nightmare continued. I couldn't escape it.

I have always been one for vivid dreams and nightmares over the years, but they were on another level entirely after the accident. I had journaled that by the time this was all said and done, I will have seen Jerod die a thousand times in my nightmares. I just didn't know how to process this level of pain, so it would seem that some of it had to happen on the subconscious level during what sleeping hours I could get.

For a while, the only way I knew I was getting sleep was if I was dreaming. Diamonds fell out of my ring. Jerod was under the ocean somewhere, but I wasn't able to stay. Planes crashed with me in them. My name was on the front page of the newspaper for some felony. I was lying on some sidewalk dying. Knives were coming at Jerod out of nowhere. Jerod was mad at me and didn't want to be with me anymore. I witnessed decapitations, as well as mutilations, in motorcycle accidents. You name it—I dreamt it. Most of the time, Jerod was not himself in my dreams.

Many times I would be driving like the fast and furious through chaos and accidents happening all around us, trying to get Jerod to a safe place. In one dream, I tried to hide him in my nanny's bathroom from guys hunting him with guns, but when I turned around, he was already dying in the tub. In another, I was in the car driving by the same place looking for him over and over again. I never did find him. And then I woke up to a world where I would never find him again. But, the opposite type of dream was just as bad. Jerod and I would be enjoying time together somewhere, but once again, I'd wake up to my bitter reality without Jerod.

Some dreams made more sense than others. In one, Jerod left me alone to walk a road that went on for miles. Yeah, that unfortunately turned out to be real life as well. I've walked this path of suffering alone, or without Jerod anyway. But no matter how many people surrounded me, I still felt completely alone. I used to be mad at Jerod for leaving me, even though I knew it made zero sense, since it wasn't his conscious decision. I just wanted to be with him.

I came to a point where I accepted the fact that dreams or nightmares were as close as I would ever come to Jerod until I was able to tackle him in eternity one day. I would take the good with the bad just to see him one more time on earth, even if it was only in a dream.

Hollywood could've made some sell-out horror movies from my nightmares. Oftentimes, I woke up gasping for air or physically crying, my face already drenched in tears. I'll never forget the bomb scene. People were after my coworkers and me, and at some point, one of them held a knife to my neck. I knew he was going to snap my neck if I didn't answer the question he'd asked me. During one dream, we were all forced to hide in the walls of a building from people who were after us. I had journaled once that I woke up with a heart rate of 108! I was so worked up in the dream that I was fat burning, according to my Fitbit. My usual sleeping heart rate is in the high forties and fifties.

Nightmares or not, ten hours or two hours, regardless of all sleep-related factors, I woke up exhausted. *Jesus, come quickly*, I would pray.

Every day felt exactly the same, like I was stuck on some sort of tragic Groundhog Day. I just wanted to wake up to a day before Groundhog Day ever started. I wanted to wake up to a day when Jerod was here. That feeling was only accentuated by my almost nightly watching of my newest favorite movie, *P.S. I Love You*. I watched that movie most nights of the week for many months.

Before the accident, I absolutely hated that movie; it was depressing and mopey the entire way through, just a sad story about a woman whose husband had died and left her to grieve his loss as he left her letters helping her to start living again. Why would anyone like that film?

I was dealt the brutal answer to that question. The movie became my anthem. What I loved most? *Hope.* I loved that the story showed so much of the dark and mindless chaos of grieving while still painting a beautiful picture of hope at the end when Holly, the main character, considers love again. I laughed. Of course, I cried. But more than that, I felt understood. Someone out there had to know exactly what I was going through to have made the movie.

My worst moments were during evenings, nights, and weekends. Understandably so, as these were times when Jerod and I spent the most time together, evenings and weekends anyway. He worked a different schedule with his martial arts business, so most of his free time came late at night after classes were over and on weekends.

I became so apathetic about everything. I didn't care if I ate, if I slept the days away, if I ever exercised again, if I showered, if I died from dehydration, if I lost fifty pounds. Nothing. Not a care. Anger became an unstoppable force when it came to my moods. I would snap in a split second and sometimes for no obvious reason at all. Angry at God. Angry that Jerod was not here with me. Angry that God didn't save Jerod like He could have. Angry at how it felt like my dreams were in ruins. Angry at how my life constantly felt like a living hell. Angry at everything. Angry at nothing. Angry.

There were moments when I wanted to roundhouse kick Jerod in the face for leaving me here to deal with life by myself. I cried daily, sometimes all day, for seven straight months. I could count the times I genuinely smiled on no more than two hands. The shock factor of it all alone took months to subside. On one hand, the accident felt fresh, like it had just happened. Yet, on the other hand, it felt like I'd been without Jerod for years.

It wasn't long before I realized that all forms of social media, and especially the radio, had to become off limits. Engagements and baby announcements were far more than I was able to bear, especially the posts about people whose weddings were around my supposed-to-be wedding. It made me feel like everyone was out living their "best" lives while I was stuck sitting in the ashes of my dreams, as an extended family member put those terms so well. I felt like I was walking around without half of myself, so empty and lost, stumbling around in the dark abyss of this new and highly unwanted life.

After the extreme emotional pain would subside slightly, numbness would set in, which was a scary place to live, because I knew extreme pain was following shortly behind again, just waiting for its opportune moment to rear its ugly head and blindside me. I became too familiar with what I call the reset button.

The Reset Button
by Katie Neufeld
June 15, 2015

Imagine. You're stuck outside. In the middle of a terrifying storm. One hundred mph winds. Torrential rain. Damaging hail. Ground-shaking thunder. Electrifying bolts of lightning. Ear-piercing sirens. Walls of water slamming against you on all sides. Fear. Stumbling around in the dark, green, blurry chaos. Creaking. Breaking. Smashing. Loud noises. Car horns. Screaming. Air bags. Smoke. Debris. Blood. Tears. Mental images. Burned. Forever. Into. My. Memory. When will the storm ever end? I don't know. But I do know that it gets better once the nine-minute-and-one-second ride is over.

The song "Oceans" by Hillsong transports me from wherever I currently am and places me in something like the above scenario, usually including flashbacks from the accident scene, but only after taking me back, once again, to the very last day that I ever laid eyes on my love. The song was played at the funeral as I walked out of the sanctuary behind the casket of a lifeless man—the man I was supposed to enjoy the rest of my life with. This song will always mean pain and traumatizing flashbacks for me. It was played at church a few times recently. I was ambushed. I was also trapped in the middle of a row full of people. Even if I could have escaped the room, I couldn't have escaped the flashbacks that had already begun haunting me the second I recognized the beginning notes of the melody.

It surprises me sometimes what things do and what things don't bother me. Those I expect to completely wipe my feet out from under me are sometimes not so bad, and the things I expect to slide right past the radar without a blip end up setting said radar off completely, making me lose all control in one short moment. Aside from the pain of *all things wedding* during this season, there have been songs, comments, memories, and other wickedly painful things that I have endured along with all of the "normal" grief stuff. Even happy memories with Jerod still hurt so much. Honestly, I feel like I am in such a weird phase of grief right now anyway. I am unsure how to even begin describing it.

Something I am able to describe quite well, due to my extensive history with it over the last few months, is the reset button. Just when I start to feel I have found my bearings. Just when I start to think I can see the light in this dark and scary grief tunnel. Just when I start to cry less. Just when I think I have a handle on my grief. Just when I'm starting to feel encouraged—that's when the reset button is pushed.

Some trigger will start the rollercoaster over from the beginning. Some unexpected and seemingly insignificant thing will make its appearance. A smell. A song. A face. A sound. A picture. Words. A car accident. A dream. Food—sometimes a restaurant. Sometimes it's something that didn't even seem like a big deal to me before. I don't understand it. No matter the trigger, or lack thereof, it always brings those intense initial emotions back to the surface. The reset button has not only wreaked havoc on my grief, but it has also set my spiritual life in a whirlwind. I feel like my walk with the Lord has not only taken a plunge into some deep, yet refreshing places, but it has also been stripped bare. Stripped down to the basics. I've found myself on a journey to learn to trust God again. Or to truly and completely trust Him for the first time. The loss I've endured has torn down the veil that was once before my eyes. I feel like I've entered into a whole new level of being—one where I'm able to see God everywhere some days, yet nowhere other days. One where certain passages of the Bible now scream at me.

The story of Lazarus has never meant so much to me. Even though Jesus knew of Lazarus' imminent healing, He loved His friend so deeply that He joined Mary and Martha in grieving the "loss" of Lazarus. He was "deeply moved in spirit and troubled" (John 11:33). Wow. Reading of Jesus weeping over a friend's death as I weep over my own loss has opened some new doors for me.

Even though I know Jesus loves Jerod so much, He still allowed his earthly death and, consequently, my emotional torture and suffering. I am finding that even though He may not have caused this, but rather allowed it, He still loves me too, even though I sometimes just don't really feel like He does, knowing what pain this would cause for me.

I love in the book, *The Shack*, the profound conversation between God the Father's character and the main character, Mack, who tragically lost his daughter. God explains that He doesn't cause all the heartbreak in the world. Sin is the root of evil. He is God, though, and can bring good out of any and every circumstance. Furthermore, God doesn't need hardship to show grace. Grace stands alone. It can be found in the middle of heartbreak in countless ways (Young 2007, 185).

In His grace, God has continued loving me even in my most unlovable grief-stricken moments. In fact, He loves me enough to arrange for my eventual healing, even though full healing won't happen until I reach heaven. Before the world even came into existence, God placed my full healing into His plan, arranging for some to take place here on earth, but ultimately, for full healing to come to completion upon my arrival into heaven. He's doing the same for you, dear reader!

How good is God! He shows His love by speaking to me through His word and through different experiences I have had with people and also by myself through nature and other venues. He shows His love by renewing me day by day. He shows His love by sustaining me in this storm. And though the fact that I'm even still here and breathing sometimes feels like punishment, I am learning that this whole thing is not even about me. It's not about Jerod either. It's about Jesus.

It's about the impact that Jerod made here and all of the people's eternities that were affected by his testimony. Lives forever changed. It's about Jesus rewarding Jerod with his new home and what Jerod had lived for—and for so many years. Jerod met Jesus! I can only imagine the level of excitement he was expressing in that moment. ❤ And even though Jesus declared that this was Jerod's time to go home (way too early, in my opinion), I am still so thankful that I was able to be a part of his journey here on earth. That we were able to enjoy and make the most of his last months here. He is now complete. And perfectly happy. Content.

I miss you, Jerod. ❤ I love you! ❤ Until we meet again ... never soon enough.

> *"Therefore we are always confident and know that as long as we are at home in the body we are away from the Lord. For we live by faith, not by sight. We are confident, I say, and would prefer to be away from the body and at home with the Lord."*
>
> —2 Corinthians 5:6–8

> *"I am hard pressed between the two. My desire is to depart and be with Christ, for that is far better. But to remain in the flesh is more necessary on your account."*
>
> —Philippians 1:23–24 ESV

Katie

One of the painful lessons I learned in the midst of deep sorrow was that while grief and sorrow may have painted dark colors on the canvas of the tragic parts of my story, they are absolutely meaningful when placed in Jesus' hands. And just because the painting looks dark now, it doesn't mean it will stay this way forever. Experiencing the darkness contributes to a profound appreciation of the Light, our Savior, who experienced the ultimate darkness so that we can become heirs of the Eternal Light, having hope beyond any grave or bad news in this broken world. Deep sorrow expands the capacity for greater joy.

Brushstrokes of Hope
by Katie Neufeld
May 13, 2015

Wow. I *finally* noticed it. I saw something so differently in a painting that I'd seen possibly hundreds of times before.

A few years ago I went with some work friends to a fun paint party. We spent the evening painting a beautiful landscape of the Atlanta skyline, including many of the major landmarks of the city we call home. As I was painting, I remember getting a glimpse of what I see so clearly now. I remember thinking something like ... *Wow. This is super ugly and disorganized. Something is supposed to come out of this? There is just no way that this will turn out pretty enough to put on my wall. Can I start over?*

The teacher had a plan, though. She knew where each stroke of the paintbrush was leading. She knew the beauty that was coming. Each of us in the class had our own style, our own choice with color and technique, though, so no two paintings could ever be exactly the same. And who would want that anyway?

During the painting experience, I had to make sure to keep my attention on the instructor. Whenever I wasn't paying attention,

65

or when I went off with my own ideas, things got ugly fast. A few minor creative strokes turned out okay, but overall I found things went the smoothest, and I stayed most on track, when I was following the instructions given to me by the professional painter. Of course, whenever I got off track, all I had to do was ask for help and she would help me fix whatever messes I had made.

Once everything started to come together and my painting started to look presentable, I glanced to the person on my left and quickly saw that my painting did not appear quite as good anymore. The same happened when I peeked to the person on my right. My painting was looking pretty good until I surveyed everyone else's. I kept at it, though, hoping that in the end it could be something beautiful in itself. And wow, did it ever surprise me in the end! It went from being a big blob of dark, mismatched colors and smears to my own personal version of the beautiful Atlanta skyline.

It all seems so clear now, thinking back. I vaguely saw the parallel to my spiritual life that night, but now it's crystal clear. The painting symbolizes our lives. Each of our paintings can look very messy and just plain hideous during certain seasons we go through. Thanks to God, though, that they don't stay that way and that there is hope for redemption and beauty from the rubble. We just have to acknowledge where we are, face the ugly truth, and ask for help. I'm still in that season where everything looks hideous and dark, where I would rather start over and see if I could do better next time. But see, that's the thing.

It is not about what I can do. It is about what He can do. The pressure is off.

So, now there's no need to start over, even though I'd still like to return to October 9 and begin again. I just need to stop grabbing the brush out of His hand. He alone can make my painting beautiful. I just need to keep my eyes fixed on Him and trust that He sees where this is all leading and that it can be beautiful again.

The dark colors of my painting seem to currently be the dominating force, but when I start to feel the spirit of despair, I hear His tender and loving message to me. "Just be still in My presence and

66

trust." Trust Him to lead me to that point of restoration and regeneration. Trust Him to give me those much-needed cleaning breaks to cleanse my paintbrush of the dark colors and keep going even when I can't see. When I absolutely can't ... and won't ... see the potential for future beauty. Even when I would rather chuck my painting, give up, and start over. Trust Him that those dark colors in the painting aren't meaningless. That they won't last forever—even though it surely seems like some form of forever that they are claiming right now. That they are working to make the painting, as a whole, beautiful and so unlike any other painting.

And for my own sake, stop looking at the paintings to my left and my right. My painting is no better or worse than the next. It is beautiful in its own way with its own contrasting shades of light and dark colors, with some parts of the painting particularly darker or lighter than the others. But as they say, and I also believe, comparison is the thief of joy. I must focus on my own painting for now, because it's requiring quite a bit of focus and hard work. But, beauty will come. It seems it may be years and years from now, but I have a growing hope that my painting will not always look as miserable and dark as it does right now. I just have to keep my focus on the Master Painter and trust that He has a plan to work this messy and chaotic canvas into a magnificent masterpiece.

> *"And I am sure of this, that he who began a good work in you will bring it to completion at the day of Jesus Christ."*
>
> —PHILIPPIANS 1:6 ESV

Kevin – The Grief Tree

We have a tree beside our house that I've watched for over thirteen years. It was damaged by the landscaping work done when the house was built, and I've observed the transitions over the years. Day to day the changes are unnoticeable, but there have been a number of stages through which it has transitioned during our time in this house. My interest was casual at best until recently when I considered my observations and the parallel to grief. The lessons from nature are mind-blowing when you're attentive enough to see them. The Creator has put hints all around us that point to Him and help us understand spiritual principles.

The base of the tree was no doubt disrupted during the building of the house. When we first moved in, I wondered just how much damage was done to the root system, and it became evident fairly quickly. The damage exposed the heart of the tall oak on one side, as well as cut some roots. The first sign of trauma was the running sap and random dying branches, and later, whole limbs. Also, the bark was stripped away from one side, exposing old wood, which drew woodpeckers. The woodpeckers hunted for insects in the tree, perforating it with a myriad of holes.

As time passed, the dead limbs began to rot, and after being soaked by rain, would fall in bits and pieces, sometimes quite large. For probably ten years we picked up dead limbs and branches regularly in the yard. They were a nuisance when mowing, but they were also an eyesore, protruding out like a skeleton from the healthy parts of the tree. Finally, this past year I noticed that all the dead limbs had fallen and the leafy part of the oak finally had a nice shape and looked alive.

The trunk went through a transition of its own. From exposure of the deepest parts of the tree to woodpecker damage and missing bark, it began to heal. At one point, I thought the birds might kill it with so many holes. Each year the bark wrapped itself a little farther back around the tree like a blanket. It didn't happen fast, so it was almost negligible. One day I noticed (I had been looking but not seeing) that the bark had grown completely back around, and now the only visible evidence remaining is the sagging bark.

While riding with my daughter one day, it struck me as we talked that this tree was our "grief tree." Let me explain. Grief starts with a loss, hurt, deep disappointment, heart-wrenching pain that goes to the root and heart of who we are. It exposes our very being in a way that was never intended, and if continued without healing, it could prove fatal. The initial wound is bad, but the damage is not completely known or understood immediately. Many observers will rush to the support of the initial damage and render aid. After a while, the caregivers and well-wishers are gone, but the full damage is not known.

As the griever tries to just stabilize life, collateral damage becomes evident. In reading stories and accounts of grief, it is almost universally true that the initial pain is not the worst. At first, shock sets in for preservation, but as the anesthetic of shock wears off, the pain crescendos. The dead limbs show up, dry up, rot, and eventually fall off. The timing of this phase is different for each person, but when nearly everyone around wants the griever to move on, the griever is still coming to grips with all the ways his life has changed. Like the dying, falling limbs, grief changes the shape and character of the one who mourns.

Healing is slow and almost unnoticeable, but about the time one thinks progress is being made, another limb falls, sometimes taking healthy parts of the person with it and doing further damage. Other parts of the person are compromised by the invading birds. Life happens. There is no reprieve from the normal frustrations and pains of life while healing takes place. Storms come, bills pile up, seasons change, friendships fluctuate, birds poke holes, and irritations are magnified.

But, if passersby or even the griever will notice, the bark is beginning to grow and in time will enclose the tree. Over time, there's usually decreasing exposure as more and more of the tree is enveloped and protected. The tree begins to take on its new shape just as the injured person finds a new normal.

Our tree is not finished healing, but the bark has grown back and now just appears to sag. For most, this hides the scars, but for those who shared the journey, the damage remains, though unseen. The sealing bark locks in small bits of pain and reminders, and yet it locks out new friends and passersby from the unseen damage. Over time, that sagging will be less visible, but to the arborist, it will always be evident that there was a traumatic event in the history of the tree. The tree is forever changed, just as the damaged human can never be the same. That is not to say that the tree is not beautiful. Ours has a beauty that it's never had since I first laid eyes on it. So the wounded human, though forever changed, has a beauty never possible before the loss.

And I can't help but wonder if, during the quiet nights, the trees do not knowingly recognize the beauty in other damaged trees. So the fraternity of the grieving offers a knowing glance and timely words each time a new member is ushered into the association, thereby joining the band of wounded healers.

To those who might doubt that there is a Designer in this world, I ask, "Is it harder to prevent pain or to redeem it?" For me, the answer is obvious. The eyes of faith see the order and struggle with the chaos, while the eyes of unbelief focus on the chaos but have no explanation for the order. The grief tree has been a thirteen-year lesson leading to a fuller understanding of the events of our lives these many years later. And though it doesn't explain our loss, it tells us that our loss is not unnoticed by our Creator who sees, cares for, and redeems our pain.

CHAPTER 6

Who Turned Out The Lights

Kevin – Fog of Grief

I was sitting in the conference room at a real estate closing waiting for the closing attorney. As we spoke casually among ourselves, my client asked how Katie was doing. After listening to my update, the realtor asked a few questions and then proceeded to mention that he and his family had experienced a tragic loss twenty-five years ago. His daughter and his other daughter's fiancé were both killed in the same accident. He had my attention!

After answering a few questions about details, he proceeded to make an interesting statement. "I thought I was going crazy for the first couple years ..." What helped him through was a support group he'd found of others who had gone through similar losses. The description resonated with me profoundly. My history is one of stability. I served as pastor of a church in Lithia Springs, Georgia, for fourteen years. Two other churches where I was happily serving and wanted to continue were cut short by pastoral resignations of the senior pastor. My tendency is to stay long ... sometimes too long.

In 2011, when my staff position was cut due to financial difficulties and the recession, I was self-employed for two years and then transitioned into the mortgage industry. It was a good fit and the work was enjoyable. The company where I worked had tabbed me for potential management prior to the accident. After the accident, my focus turned to my daughter and my job became unbearable. After attempting to fight my way through the pain, a better job opportunity opened up and I moved. Besides the side work, my resume for 2015 included the job I left and four other employers.

To several close friends, I confessed that I had never been so confused in my life. Grieving with and caring for my daughter, wrestling with my faith, and dealing with the normal struggles of life became crushing weights on me. Physical, mental, and emotional fatigue wore me down, and the way forward was as clear as mud.

Robert McNamara was featured in a documentary titled, *The Fog of War*. The phrase describes the chaos encountered in the midst of military conflict. While I have gratefully not experienced the fog of war, I have experienced the fog of grief, and I cannot tell just how long it will last. Even now, though the haze seems to be lifting, it has become difficult to determine whether my sight is clear or ever will be. Katie has experienced fog of her own as she lost what appeared to be her desired and anticipated future and now has entered the waiting zone. We believe there is a future, and we can even hope that it is good, but we cannot connect the dots from here to there just yet. We must use some of the strategies of driving in fog.

1 Slow down.

2 Don't use the high beams.

3 You may need a different color light.

4 Find someone to follow ... but not too closely.

5 Use the right edge of the road as a guide.

6   If necessary, stop, rest, and wait.

7   Ask for help.

8   Beware of patchy fog.

Let's look at how these principles apply.

Slow down. This can be difficult. The world around us does not stop or slow down to accommodate our pain; it barely finds time to pull over out of respect for the deceased. While stuck in traffic behind an accident, I now find myself wondering about who was driving, who is getting *the* call, and how lives are suddenly changing. It seems a bit selfish to fret over my inconvenience when it may be the end of the road for a fellow traveler and the beginning of an unwanted journey for friends and family.

If and when possible, get over to the right and travel as slowly as it's safely possible. Many evenings in the months that followed, we found ourselves sitting together in the living room doing nothing in particular other than just talking, doing menial work, grading papers (my wife), doing light reading, or watching a movie. We weren't necessarily trying to accomplish great things; we were just enjoying today. With the freshness of loss foremost in our minds, enjoying those we still had became extremely valuable. As a family of very independent people, this was a change and a good one.

Don't use the high beams. We use high beams to see better. More specifically, we use them to see farther. That's not possible or even necessary during early stages of grief. In my thinking, high beams equate with understanding. We were created as inquisitive beings and that sets us apart from other creatures. One of the sure responses to loss is the attempt to make sense of it. Why? What if ...? When? How could ...? I should ... There are a myriad of tormenting questions that call for the high beams, but beams don't turn corners, and they become useless in the circular valley of grief.

As we seek understanding, straining only wears us out; it doesn't bring clarity. For me, the tensions of God's sovereignty and man's responsibility wrestled in my head and brought no resolution to the questions that plagued my mind. God is sovereign, but did He make the driver go over eighty-five miles per hour in a school zone? Is He responsible for the design and manufacture of vehicles capable of such speed? Could He have prevented it? Each question only led to other questions or a dead end. In the end, we must either bend the knee and admit He is God and we are not, *or* we stiffen our necks and assume His role. The movie *Bruce Almighty* humorously shows the futility of such an endeavor.

I learned to ask questions, accept the understanding that I could gain, and release the mysteries to the loving hand of God who came personally into this world of pain and endured it for the joy set before Him. There's also the fact that some light will be available later, but I can't see it from my present location or situation. So we slow down and move cautiously forward within the light that we have without demanding to see further down the road. This is much easier, in my opinion, for me than for Katie due to the nature of her loss. It's also the reason I stand in awe at the transformation taking place in my amazing daughter right before my eyes. That's worth a slow passing.

You may need a different color of light. Cars equipped with special fog equipment often have fog lights. These different-colored lights reduce the fog's effects on one's vision. It doesn't remove the fog, nor does it change the unseen or obscured obstacles out in the fog. It casts a different light, and it requires a change of perspective.

All of us operate on a foundational belief system. Times of pain, uncertainty, and confusion cause us to question and even open us to the possibility that our perspective may need adjustment. The wise king in Ecclesiastes 7:2–4 (ESV) states, "It is better to go to the house of mourning than to go to the house of feasting, for this is the end of all mankind, and the living will lay it to heart. Sorrow is better than laughter, for by sadness of face the heart is made glad. The heart of the wise is in the house of mourning, but the heart of fools is in the house of mirth."

Sometimes it is a small adjustment that's needed; other times it's an earth-shaking transformation that's demanded. Thinking and thought patterns change and *need* to change. True values emerge, and old values are exposed as being of lesser or little value, or they're affirmed and solidified. All of these revelations are made possible by the change in perspective, the color of light illuminating our lives.

Find someone to follow, but not too closely. Initially, we were surrounded by friends and family who rushed to our side, but as time passed, sympathy subsided, as it should and must, and we were left to travel this road with a smaller group. Our convoy was made up of family, friends, our church small group, and new acquaintances on the road of grief. Of special value are those who are on a similar journey, but ahead of us.

After all the initial support wanes, one can find himself very much alone. It can be like driving across the deserts of the great Southwest where you never let your gas tank get below half full for fear that you won't find gas for two hundred miles. One of the things we did was to move Katie into our basement so she wouldn't be alone. We also made sure that we actively sought out support. Katie has seen a Christian counselor who has been a great help to her, and we've found comfort and wisdom from friends who lost their sixteen-year-old son suddenly to an unknown physical defect. Various others have made themselves available, and still others have reminded us that they pray for us.

When driving through fog, I've found it helpful to make visual contact with a vehicle ahead of me. On many long night trips to visit out-of-state family, it was an eighteen-wheeler, due to the number of lights on the truck. This is both good and bad. It gives additional time to react to what the person ahead reacts to, but it also assumes that the other driver can see. It's proven effective to me if a safe distance has been kept between the two vehicles.

No two griefs or grievers are the same. The losses are different, the angles on the loss divergent, and the duration variable. Every vehicle has its own limitations and challenges, so when following in the fog, we can follow, but we must not follow too closely. One's ability to maneuver can be very different from another.

After Katie's interaction with several people who came into her life, the observation was made that we can learn from everyone—what to do and what not to do. Great insights can be gained with less pain if we can learn from the experiences of others.

Unfortunately, with grief, some turn inward and shut everyone out. They place themselves on the Wilderness Road in the fog with no other travelers in sight. This is so unnecessary since there are so many others trekking the same road. In fact, one of the surprises on this journey has been that so many were already ahead of us, and we had no idea until we entered the highway.

Use the right edge of the road as a guide. One of the dangers of fog is the inability to see road markings, especially lane markers. I remember reading an account of a driver maneuvering through London fog who had rolled down his side window, allowing him to extend his head outside the car and see better. Unfortunately, an oncoming driver had the same idea causing a collision of ... wait for it ... heads. When driving with limited vision or into blinding lights, it's good to have a reference point, and a point to the right will keep one from being blinded.

For us, there were some foundational truths that guided us when there was so much other confusion. Though we live in a world that increasingly believes that truth is relative, life teaches us that this is foolishness. Our world is filled with absolutes and operates by them. It is what makes chemistry, physics, and math possible. We need a reference point in the fog; God's truth is that reference point.

If necessary, stop, rest, and wait. There are times when fog gets so thick and has so wearied a driver that the best course of action is to get some rest. Each of us has a unique ability to tolerate stress, but none of us is indestructible. One's perspective can become clouded and responses hampered after pressing forward in weariness. Numerous times in the past fifteen months we have wanted to jump ahead and get on to the next thing, but part of grief is experiencing the whole loss instead of just rushing though it. Taking a breather often feels like no progress is being made, but we need rest. We need to take time to smell the roses even when we're surrounded by thorns. Only stopping will afford us that possibility.

I'm reminded of an experience I had as a sixteen-year-old. Three of us had gone to the mountains to go water tubing and had found a nice, swift, turbulent stretch of the Platte River to explore. After shooting down a few times and being thoroughly exhilarated, I was attempting to aim for certain parts of the rapids. To get there, we had to ease by a large rock on the right side. Unseen at that rock was an undertow that took me and my tube under and separated us, propelling us into the rapids. Having no life jacket, I was sucked under and kept there as I traveled down the rapids, fighting to get my head above water.

Somewhere in the midst of the rapids, I was able to gain my footing, stand, and see my location. My position was precarious at best, and there was no safe or easy way out, but those few moments to catch my breath and survey my surroundings gave me needed perspective when the rapids finally won the struggle. I was pulled under again, but I had an idea, as I once again fought for survival, of where I needed to get to exit the torrent alive. It seemed like an eternity later when my hands finally found a rock out of the rapids, and I pulled myself out of the water on the edge of the river. Scared to death, I made my way to the car and called it a day, but I doubt I would have made it without the breaths I'd gained in the middle during the few brief moments of respite.

In the same way, stopping, resting, and waiting can give a chance to renew energy, regain hope, and prepare for the next challenge. Grieving is long and healing is slow; pauses have made it bearable. We've scheduled big events on days we knew would be bad. March 22, 2015, was to be the wedding. Rather than sitting around, moping, and thinking about what could or should have been, we traveled to Michigan to be with family. My sister-in-law suggested a family gathering on March 22, where we paused to acknowledge the loss.

Family time was a wonderful idea, and I think it did all of us some good. The next morning, my son and I headed home to Atlanta while Katie and my wife headed to New York City to meet friends who had suffered a loss several years prior. They spent several days enjoying the sights and sounds and taking a break from grieving. It was a needed respite, but it was also followed by the pain of re-entry into reality when they returned.

Ask for help. While I've had some training in counseling, as it was part of my job as a pastor for many years, we knew right away that we were in unfamiliar territory and in no position to be counselors. We'd have our hands full just being parents and going through the fog *with* our daughter. Early on, we sought out a good Christian counselor for Katie. The truth is that we might have been advised to see one for ourselves as well, but we didn't.

Seeking counseling for Katie was one of the best decisions we made in this process. As her parents, we were processing our own grief. Somewhere between nine months and one year after the accident, I began to think about what I had personally lost when Jerod was taken. It had never occurred to me that we'd been so focused on Katie and her loss that we hadn't grieved our own.

A counselor can give a perspective from a distance and can often see things in the fog the griever cannot. It's almost like having radar. Training can provide the counselor an anticipation of what is likely to be hiding in the fog ahead and the best way to approach it.

Further, due to the necessary and built-in professional disconnection, this helper can speak the truth without the strings that attach a family member or close friend. To be sure, family members and friends are important, but an outside professional perspective is invaluable. It also gives validation to messages the family is sending that the griever may be struggling to accept from family. In my perspective, the counselor serves a bit like a doctor making rounds or doing follow-up visits. The family and close friends serve more like nurses who keep close contact with the patient.

Others who have been a help for both Katie and our family are friends who have experienced deep personal losses themselves. Sometimes, just knowing there is someone who "gets you" is such sweet comfort. Other times, it is a phrase, a thought, or a moment in the midst of just being together that becomes a source of strength that can empower for days and weeks and can sometimes even be life-changing.

A couple weeks after our loss, a good friend who had suffered a tragic loss told me something profound. He looked at me and said, "You don't realize it now, but you're in shock." He proceeded to tell me that while we felt like we were in horrible pain, the hurt would get worse before it would get better. Only someone who had experienced this kind of loss would know that and have the courage to say it. Today, we're grateful for those words. They weren't offered as a pat answer or the need to say *something* to fill nervous silence; rather, they were words of truth and light in the fog for us.

Beware of patchy fog. One of the most dangerous times in treacherous driving conditions is the entry and exit, but more often the exit. After enduring a strenuous drive through the fog (or ice), the conditions clear up, and after a bit of clear sailing, we can assume we're out of it for good when we're not. Grief is the same. What we're finding now is that certain stories on the news or posts on social media can re-open wounds and send you back to the beginning.

Recently, we got word that a friend had just lost her son in an accident. He was attempting to pull someone out of a ditch with his tow truck when he was struck and killed. It snatches you back. You remember the first call, the frantic rush to the hospital, the tear-filled prayers, and the denial of reality. You re-live it over and over again.

When nursing students at Georgia Southern were killed by an eighteen-wheeler in South Georgia, it sent Katie back. That time I think it was the fact that they were nursing students that hit so close to home for her. It can be a common bit of information from a totally different situation. For us, it could be a fiancé, a nurse, a

79

totally senseless death, or some other piece of commonality, but it ambushes and drags you from your state of recovery and thrusts you back into the beginning. Knowing that it can and will happen is a large part of being able to handle the situation when it actually does take place.

Making your way through grief is a lot like fog. Leaving it is also similar. For us and for many who have spoken to us, working through it is also very similar to leaving bad road conditions. You believe that it's better, but you live with the ever-present knowledge that there are still foggy valleys ahead.

Kevin – Summary

I give this parting advice to those who know someone who has suffered sudden and/or great personal loss. Many would ask out of genuine concern how Katie was doing. They wanted so badly for us to say "better." Due to the wandering and cyclical nature of grief, "better" can be short-lived as can "worse." It's very difficult to quantify how a griever is doing. It's a three-steps-forward, two-back or two-forward and three-back environment. Some days are better than others and others are worse. Furthermore, we found that Katie wasn't always telling us exactly how she was doing. One time I mentioned that she seemed to be doing better. She responded that we don't see her when she's driving in her truck or alone in her bedroom or even in the shower.

It's now almost sixteen months since the accident, and I can honestly say that she *is* doing better. The progress is very erratic and hard to trace from day to day and even week to week. It's my counsel to those who care for the grieving that they remember the fog analogy and understand that when you're in a fog, you can lose all direction and reference points. Often, there's no right answer to how one is doing.

For us, the answer to such questions is best answered in relation to our faith in God. We still believe that He is God, He is good, and

He can make even the worst tragedy turn out for good, though right now we cannot see how. We have hope that Katie will heal and will one day thrive again because of Him, and that today, in her pain, she is running *to* Him and not *from* Him. That doesn't mean that we haven't suffered great loss. This world is a worse place without Jerod. There's a hole in our hearts, and there will always be scars, but *there will be a day* when the hole will be filled. Eternity's perspective, and nothing less, will bring the final healing.

> *"Because we know that the one who raised the Lord Jesus from the dead will also raise us with Jesus and present us with you to himself. All this is for your benefit, so that the grace that is reaching more and more people may cause thanksgiving to overflow to the glory of God.*
>
> *"Therefore we do not lose heart. Though outwardly we are wasting away, yet inwardly we are being renewed day by day. For our light and momentary troubles are achieving for us an eternal glory that far outweighs them all. So we fix our eyes not on what is seen, but on what is unseen, since what is seen is temporary, but what is unseen is eternal."*
>
> —2 CORINTHIANS 4:14–18

Katie – Fog

There were many times in the fog of early grief when I'd come to a complete stop at a green light. Other times, I'd try to find something quick for dinner, pull up at the drive-through, and forget where I was entirely.

"Can I get a chocolate frosty and a soft taco with no lettuce and a side of cheesy biscuits?"

My brain just couldn't compute. Many times, I'd have difficulty calculating even simple math. Multiplying three-times-three was a mental workout. Months drifted by. Years even, at this point. Where did time go? It certainly wasn't waiting on me to catch up, a painful reality as well as an unexpected blessing, since each passing day brought me one day closer to Jerod and Jesus. I'm 1,388 days closer even now to seeing Jesus and to experiencing that glorious reunion with Jerod.

I believe the fog of grief is one of God's protective mechanisms to help humans endure suffering and loss. I would not have survived the tragedy leading to what I call my quarter-life crisis had I been completely aware of every little detail during this time.

The fog is akin to a protective cushy layer around our feeble hurting minds and hearts. There were many times I would sit alone, weep, and wonder if you could die from a broken heart. I thought if so, my time was coming very soon. It truly felt like I could have broken in half or spontaneously combusted from the intense level of anguish I was experiencing. How long can the body endure this level of pain? I could hear my broken heart still beating; Jerod's absence in my life so overwhelming that it felt almost palpable.

It surprised me how smells affected my mood and my stress levels. I don't remember exactly how aware I was of the odors of the accident during those particular minutes, but there are a few specific smells that bother me to this day. My response to these scents is much milder than it used to be, but introduce my nose to that stuffy hospital aroma or the pungent mixture of gas and oil, and the memories flood my mind like a fresh wave of grief.

The odor sometimes even makes me sick to my stomach. These smells used to initiate the vicious and morbid mental video reel of tragic flashbacks, but now I have better control over the effect they have on me. Not only have scents had a negative impact on me, but they also bring back happy memories of my time with Jerod, which depending on the day can be a good or bad thing.

If I came across Jerod's deodorant or cologne scent at the right time, I would feel him so near, like I could reach out and hug him. Those are the times I'd find myself talking to the empty space around me, hoping Jerod could hear what I had to say to him, all the stories and things I never got to tell him. There was a time when I would get irritated with the way Jerod seemed to douse himself in cologne, especially on his neck. His pungent, yet agreeable smell, would give me a headache and cause me to complain, but it turns out that the smell itself helped keep those memories alive—the times I would hug Jerod and get a nose full of his scent. His bear hugs. The sweetly soft skin on his neck.

Talking to Jerod usually led to me giving God an earful, frequently ending in my screaming and crying. Most of these moments happened while driving in my new truck. I wanted a vehicle that I felt safe in after surviving such a horrific accident. A bright blue F-150 was just the ticket. This blue was "Jerod Blue" or "Breakthrough Blue," as I called it, the main color inundating his martial arts business.

Driving became such an emotional rollercoaster for me. I never would have imagined how useful Jerod's screamo music would become. I'm certain many fellow drivers who saw or heard me going completely nuts in my truck probably thought I could've used an admission into a psychiatric ward as I proceeded to scream at the top of my lungs, kick the floorboard, bang on the steering wheel, and pound my head at the headrest with all I had in me at the moment.

Once, I took my hands off the steering wheel to come back down and bang the wheel. I came down with just one hand making my truck veer into the lane on the other side of the road that, might I add, would usually have oncoming traffic. In God's mercy, it currently didn't have any. God knew I wasn't paying attention to those *minor* details.

It became a morbid competition of sorts, to me anyway, of who could scream louder and more convincing—me or Jerod's screamo music. It was a surprising avenue to release my anger and sorrow; tears just didn't cut it so much of the time. Too much emotional pressure would build up from day to day, and that was my way of letting it out.

Usually, those scream fests evolved into violent cries, coughing, and gagging, which made it difficult to breathe. In those moments, it's impossible to regulate all the fluids coming out of your face (just being transparent). Tears. Saliva. Snot. Sometimes pre-vomit. It ain't pretty, but it's necessary to release the emotion and ride it like a wave.

I'd get so choked up and cough uncontrollably that I'd end up having to take my inhaler to catch my breath and open my lungs back up. Yes, that all happened while driving. I know, not safe, but I didn't have a care in the world. My truck was my haven, a refuge where I knew I could let it all out without judgment or the overbearing concern that was sure to follow if my parents ever witnessed any of those violent fits I had frequently, especially within the first seven months.

Somehow I started driving again only two weeks after the accident. In God's providence, my brother Caleb had taken the semester off from college even before my accident happened. My family took me anywhere I needed to go up until that point, but I just needed my alone time after that.

Driving time didn't seem significant during those darkest days, but looking back, driving moments were holy. Anointed. Flooded with God's presence, and I was aware of His presence even then. How could I not be since the time I was driving was mostly spent crying out to God and screaming *at* Him and *to* Him about the circumstances of my miserable life? I reminded Him for months that He'd forgotten about me, like the typical middle child, and that I still wanted to die. I thank God for His mercy often, for not always giving me what I think I want or ask for.

Those moments were truly holy ground. It was during one particular drive home when, as David exemplifies in the Psalms, I started out screaming at God about why He took Jerod from me, yet it was after a string of tear-streaked negativity and complaining at and to God that I came to a deep surrender (again) and genuinely thanked Him profusely for the cross and what Jesus did for me so that I could see Jerod again. *I had never been more thankful for the cross.*

And if it took that living hell I was stuck in to draw nearer to Christ, then so be it.

It wasn't and still isn't my choice, but I learned to lean into the pain and submit to His will and His plans for my life. I don't always see or understand it, but His ways have always been better and much higher than mine. And they always will be.

I came to the realization that He was God and I was not. That He is good at being God, and He *is* a good God, whether or not I felt it at the moment. It stands true apart from my feelings or beliefs.

This was one of those mantras that I came to repeat over and over in my mind, and out loud some too. I repeated it until I believed it, as I often had to do when enduring heavy grief, since my head and my heart were often on different pages.

He is God and I am not.
He is good at being God,
and He is a good God.

In my cries to God, many of my unanswered questions flowed out of my mouth like word vomit. Sometimes, they even turned into angry screams.

Where were You?
Where are You?
Where were You when I needed You?
Where were You that day?
Why didn't You save him?
Did You know You let someone You so cherish die?
Will You ever be there for me again?
I need You!
What are You doing?

I doubted things I knew all my life to be true. Was God really near? Near to the brokenhearted like His Word says in Psalm 34:18? Did He really love me like I'd heard all my life? Did He love Jerod? Was all this really working for something good? Could He have really prevented that wretched accident? Why didn't I die too? Wouldn't that be merciful to me?

You could've taken me instead. Why did I have to live through the accident? You forgot me! We were a package deal, God. You gave me these desires for a godly husband and led me to a wonderful man who I knew was from You.

It was painful to have my unfulfilled desires for a husband survive the accident along with me. A year after the accident, I started praying that if God was not going to bring those desires to fruition that He would take them away completely. It would be easier to not have them at all than to keep mulling over all those questions and all of the ways I felt God had wrecked *my* dreams and *my* plan.

Why, God, did You give me these dreams if You weren't going to see them through? Why did You put Jerod in my life to only rip him out of it as quickly and violently as he entered? And he was doing so much for Your kingdom! It just didn't make sense to me.

It came to the point where I had to throw away all of my wedding planning magazines that I'd accumulated over many years. I've dreamed of marriage for I can't even count how many years, but it was more than I could bear to see any of them anymore. My dream had died its tragic death. Tossing those magazines felt like throwing away the ashes of my dreams that had disintegrated in the fire started on October 9, 2014. The fire was still burning. Why should I care about my dreams anyway, since it seemed like God didn't either?

I sometimes wondered, what if Jerod and I had never met? Would he still be alive then? What if we'd driven Jerod's work van or his Mustang instead of my 4Runner? If he'd never met me, he probably wouldn't have been going to the mall that day and never been in the accident.

Pondering those *what ifs* brought up more questions in my mind than it answered. This next question was painful to journal. I questioned directly if it was my fault that he was dead. The thought killed me a little bit more on the inside. I may have been breathing—my heart may have been beating—but what was inside of me felt very dead.

On those impossibly heavy days when I was desperate for help, this prayer has stuck with me ever since. "Help me to live when my heart feels dead." Those words pierced through the pain to the deep-est, most broken parts of my soul. I felt dead, yet I was breathing. My heart was beating. Those words eventually became a prayer of my heart that God would resurrect my shattered heart and make it a holy exchange for something beautiful, something He could use to help people going through suffering and loss. And I knew it would take an act of God to make this exchange.

Why could we not have shared more of the injuries? I always came back to the fact that the outcome, as bad as it was, could've always been worse. We could've both been killed, although that sometimes sounded appealing. We could both be brain dead lying in a hospital bed somewhere, a burden to our families. Jerod would've hated that; it's not living. I just know I would've taken so much physical pain and suffering to have my Jerod back.

It was during my grief when I first realized the way I'd placed Jerod above Jesus in my life. It was a painful but honest revelation. Jerod had become an idol in my life, even though I believe he *was* a gift from God. It dawned on me that even God's most precious gifts to us could become idols in our lives when we focus more on those gifts than on the Giver of all of our good gifts.

The deep life questions plagued me too.

Why do evil people prosper? What about good people?

I'd finally found my one. My match. You sent him to me. I didn't settle in my search for my guy. Instead, I did just like I thought You wanted.

Now what?

Is heaven really all I've heard it to be? Who could really tell me anyway? No one has come back.

Can I trust You if You can't even save Jerod like I've heard You're capable of?

Why did You lead us to each other if this was going to happen? Why would You build us up to fall?

I was brutal in my questions to God, but as I was told then and believe even now, He can handle it. He welcomes our questions and would rather hear from us any way He can than not at all. He desires our hearts. It was in the asking of these gut-wrenching questions that my relationship with Christ deepened and matured. The struggle itself proved to be *faith* in the good God I had placed my trust in so many years ago. I was only realizing just then in all of the overwhelming pain just how much opportunity my trust had for growth.

I have unanswered questions to this day, but I have peace in the fact that some questions will never be answered on this side of heaven. I learned that these questions often became a prison where I found myself trapped for months at a time. I was focusing more on the whys than on the Who. More on the problems than the Problem Solver, the Answer. I learned from *Glorious Ruin* by Tullian Tchividjian that since we can't understand the mind of God, we may never have the answers to our questions. So instead I replaced those *whys* and *what ifs* with the *knows* of God, the promises of God that I knew to be true (Tchividjian 2012, 25). Focusing on all of the unanswered questions led me down the same dead end over and over again and delayed my healing, but somehow it was still such a significant part of my recovery.

John 9:1–3 came alive as the words jumped off the page and into my broken heart. It shed a little light on my unanswered questions. "As he went along, he saw a man blind from birth. His disciples asked him, 'Rabbi, who sinned, this man or his parents, that he was born blind?'

'Neither this man nor his parents sinned,' said Jesus, 'but this happened so that the works of God might be displayed in him.'"

Those words opened up new doors for me and introduced me to the beginnings of shifts in perspective I would come to know and love. Maybe the accident didn't happen because of anything I did or didn't do, but rather that the work of God's hands and His power be shown through me. Wow! Sorrow turned into honor. Use me, God!

I realized that even if I did find out the whys and the answers to my questions, that knowledge most likely would not heal my broken heart anyway. As Tullian Tchividjian explains in his book, *Glorious Ruin*, looking for those answers can actually become a replacement for faith (Tchividjian 2012, 150). Faith that the God who led me this far won't leave me here to fend for myself. Faith that He is God and He is good, that He is good at being God. That He loves me more than I could ever fathom, and that He has already gone long before me to plan healing into the pages of my story. I had to just hold on and trust that my pain was not wasted and that 1 Peter 5:10 is true. That "the God of all grace, who called you to his eternal glory in Christ, after you have suffered a little while, will himself restore you and make you strong, firm and steadfast."

There really is so much freedom in trust. I liked the way Tchividjian explains this concept in his book. Here I was trying to figure out how to overcome, all the while forgetting that Jesus has already overcome. Because Jesus is strong, marvelous, and victorious, it takes the pressure off of us. It's okay if we are weak. If we are ordinary. If we lose. If we fail. Jesus' sufficiency more than covers our lack (Tchividjian 2012, 169-170).

Within the first months of residing in my parents' basement after my loss, I found myself down there scouring the Psalms. The fact that I was even living local was entirely thanks to God and His mercy. Jerod had moved me with his work van from my Midtown apartment in Atlanta into a duplex he'd rented out in order to spend more time with each other and also save money as we planned for our wedding. This turned out to be one of many divine things already in place after tragedy crashed into our lives. Anyway, I digress ... back to the day in my parents' basement. It was during those days as I was scouring the Psalms that I pieced together truths that I knew. I learned to repeat them, even when I didn't feel them, until my heart believed them and overflowed with their beauty and the beauty that is Jesus.

What I know is that God is love.

"Whoever does not love does not know God, because God is love."

—1 JOHN 4:8

What I know is that nothing can separate me from the love of God.

"For I am convinced that neither death nor life, neither angels nor demons, neither the present nor the future, nor any powers, neither height nor depth, nor anything else in all creation, will be able to separate us from the love of God that is in Christ Jesus our Lord."

—ROMANS 8:38–39

What I know is that He makes everything beautiful in its time.

"He has made everything beautiful in its time. He has also set eternity in the human heart; yet no one can fathom what God has done from beginning to end."

—ECCLESIASTES 3:11

What I know is that He will never leave me nor forsake me.

"The Lord himself goes before you and will be with you; he will never leave you nor forsake you. Do not be afraid; do not be discouraged."

—DEUTERONOMY 31:8

What I know is that He is nearer to me now than He has ever been. He is near to those who have a broken heart.

"The Lord is close to the brokenhearted and saves those who are crushed in spirit."

—PSALM 34:18

What I know is that He does all things well.

"People were overwhelmed with amazement. 'He has done everything well,' they said. 'He even makes the deaf hear and the mute speak.'"

—MARK 7:37

What I know is that He is the God of *more*.

"And I pray that you, being rooted and established in love, may have power, together with all the Lord's holy people, to grasp how wide and long and high and deep is the love of Christ, and to know this love that surpasses knowledge—that you may be filled to the measure of all the fullness of God. Now to him who is able to do immeasurably more than all we ask or imagine, according to his power that is at work within us, to him be glory in the church and in Christ Jesus throughout all generations, for ever and ever! Amen."

—EPHESIANS 3:17–21

What I know is that He is *not* the God of the dead, but of the living!

> *"But about the resurrection of the dead—have you not read what God said to you, 'I am the God of Abraham, the God of Isaac, and the God of Jacob'? He is not the God of the dead but of the living."*

> —MATTHEW 22:31–32

What I know is that if I believe in Him, though I die, I will live.

> *"Jesus said to her, 'I am the resurrection and the life. The one who believes in me will live, even though they die; and whoever lives by believing in me will never die. Do you believe this?'"*

> —JOHN 11:25–26

Through all the questions, I came to the conclusion that I just wanted God and *only* God to get glory from this ugly tragedy. Only He could obtain glory from all of this mess. I continued to wonder why God chose me to go through this horrific heartbreak, but I knew if I had to choose, I would've still wanted to meet and love Jerod and would've done it all over again. My sorrowful heart welcomed the complete honor to think that God would handpick me to bring joy to Jerod's last six months on earth. It thrilled my heart and soul to hear his mom, Carol, say that Jerod had been the happiest she'd ever seen him, and to realize that I was granted that special opportunity to make his last days his best. Thank you, Jesus.

I eventually started to pray, "God, I want You to get all the glory and praise from whatever good comes from this, even though right now it just seems that no good will come. My head and part of my

92

heart know that You can clean up this mess on aisle nine. You can make something beautiful from these ashes."

Katie – Justice Found

It's actually a miracle that I'm still alive. A few inches over and there would've been two funerals. While I wished for months that I had died too, or in Jerod's place, Jesus had been healing my heart ever since and developing my new-found purpose: helping the hurting. I wasn't killed in that accident because of a plan far greater than I could ever dream of or imagine. I'm completely honored to be playing a small part in a story far bigger than me.

There's another facet to my story that exacerbated my grief: court dates. We were in and out of court for one whole year. That experience was pure torture. It always felt like a losing battle, and there were always tears. It felt like there would never be any justice or any good thing that was going to come out of the legal side of things. Honestly, there wasn't much good that came out of it except that it was just one more thing that pushed me to Jesus. I realized that I had to change my perspective in order to be able to survive the outcome of the judge's decision. I had to let go of my desires. I had to give them to Jesus, unwillingly and with tears. Always with tears.

But once I shifted my perspective, I was able to see how justice would come. And with justice came more healing. I found purpose in sharing Jerod's story, my story, and the one we shared together. Redemption came with using this impossible pain and tragedy to make Jesus known. It came by telling people what Jesus had done, picking me up daily out of the dark prison of grief and comforting me once again.

Psalm 71 became a favorite. I especially love verses 20 and 21: "Though you have made me see troubles, many and bitter, you will restore my life *again*; from the depths of the earth you will *again* bring me up. You will increase my honor and comfort me *once more*." I love the fact that these verses are a reminder that no matter how many times we are desperate for help in the midst of our suffering, the Lord is faithful to comfort us *once more*. His mercies are unending and new every morning. And thank You, Jesus, for a brand new day. There is something comforting and refreshing about having the chance to have a fresh start every day, every week, every month, and so on. It's the chance for a new beginning, for restoration, and for the redemptive power of Christ to invade our lives in the best of ways.

> *"Because of the Lord's great love we are not consumed, for his compassions never fail. They are new every morning; great is your faithfulness."*

—LAMENTATIONS 3:22–23

CHAPTER 7

The Questions Remain

The Cocoon
An Analogy of Grief
By Kevin Neufeld
February 2015

A caterpillar crawls slowly along amidst a myriad of dangers to its life, apparently oblivious. Birds, human feet, boys, car tires, pesticides, and lawnmowers all lurk in a constant world of danger. Time is not even an afterthought; the idea that there is a world off the ground more than a few feet has never entered the realm of options for this creature. Its Creator has colored it to blend into its environment, its only real protection. It is slow, exposed, and vulnerable.

Then it happens. *It* happens. An event. An irresistible urge to climb, attach to a limb, and begin surrounding itself in silk. What color, mobility, and life it had comes to an end. Soon, the cocoon is complete, attached and once again camouflaged to its surroundings. It is an airborne casket. Life as it has been known is over, and to the watching eye, there appears to be nothing happening. It seems to go on forever, stuck in this colorless, cold, unchanging, boring existence.

Unseen to the keenest observer is the transformation going on inside that dark shell. There were rumors back in caterpillar world that there was a strange phenomenon that takes place in a caterpillar's life if he survives the birds and the boys. The butterflies used to tell about it, but how would they know? They aren't even caterpillars. They fly around, bouncing from bloom to bloom, dancing to an unheard rhythm far above caterpillar world.

One day the creature inside the cocoon feels its surroundings getting a bit cramped. With that feeling of confinement, the prisoner grows increasingly dissatisfied with its situation. I wonder if it ever wishes for rescue from this prison. Finally, fed up with waiting, it begins to fight its way out. Scientists tell us that this fight is absolutely necessary in order to have the strength necessary to fly and survive as a *butterfly*. What emerges from that cocoon has a resemblance to what went in, enough to identify it as being related. At the same time, there is a beauty never imagined and a glory totally different. The caterpillar lived in black and white; the butterfly exists in HD colorful brilliance.

Birds and boys still present risks, but the butterfly is not confined to the ground any longer. Travel is abundantly quicker. And casual passersby cannot escape the brilliant beauty of a creature that can no longer blend in for its colorful, symmetrical splendor.

This process has aligned with our recent encounter with grief. We were sailing along headed for a wedding. Our daughter who had patiently waited and waded through several prospects had found the love of her life. She fell fast, and she fell hard ... and she fell good. Her fiancé fit our family with ease. The grandkids loved "Uncle Jewod." Katie's brothers loved his boat and got along well with him. He was like another brother. He had become more than a future son-in-law to us; he was a friend and frequent guest in our home. He and I watched the whole season of *24* together. It was after watching an episode that he asked me for Katie's hand in marriage. The date was set and preparations were underway.

Then *it* happened. October 9, 2014. A day devoted to wedding preparations changed all of our lives forever. Jerod ended in heaven; Katie was bruised, yet thankfully alive, but we buried her dreams. Her world, Jerod's family's world, and ours changed in an instant.

I know of no one more ready for heaven than Jerod. Had God told him in advance His upcoming plan, as much as he would have wanted to stay for Katie and his loved ones, I can actually see him saying to God, "Your will be done." That is the kind of man he was. Katie, along with her dreams, on the other hand, was sealed up in a dark, colorless existence. She had entered her new world, the cocoon.

A cocoon must be a place of turmoil as much as it is of metamorphosis. From the outside, we are helpless to do anything much to change it. She is being changed from the inside out. Many times physical death would be a relief. Cocoons look dead. Over the years, I have found them and wondered if anything lives inside. There have been times I wondered if Katie would ever emerge from this nightmare, and if she did, what would she be like? There are days when I still wonder. That's the thing about cocoons; they look dead and they look as if nothing is really happening.

Another difficulty is the yearning to rip the cocoon open and rescue her ... but from what can I rescue her and to whom can I take her? I can't bring Jerod back. I can't take away the memories, and I can't take away her love for him and wouldn't if I could. All we can do is *be there*. Sit there outside the cocoon, letting her know we are there and wait. That must have been the hardest part of the three days between Jesus' crucifixion and resurrection. It is the hardest part of change. It takes so long; meanwhile, time flies. But we dare not disturb the cocoon. To do so would be to tamper with God's work, and it would destroy the final product.

Recently, we have seen glimmers of what is going on inside the cocoon. One night, as I prayed for her and with her, I asked God to make Himself known to her in a very personal way while simultaneously wondering if she even wanted to know Him at all. I have prayed like that with other grieving believers in my years of ministry, not knowing what it is like to feel raw betrayal as the God who could have changed the script chose not to. She has chosen to run to Him ... sometimes to scream and pound, sometimes to cry, and other times to rest. But she has run *to* Him and that is what matters.

She has moved from being comforted, which she still needs, to seeing value in her story and its usefulness in giving hope to others. She was recently prompted to share it with her group at a recent Passion 2015 weekend. She said she felt God say, "This is where I want you to tell your story." She obeyed. Others have dinner with her to encourage her or spend time with her to be a blessing and walk away saying how much she blessed them. I know the feeling. She amazes me too.

She carries with her Jerod's indomitable spirit. He impacted her life in six-and-one-half short months with inspiration that will propel her further than she would have otherwise gone. I see a growing calmness and peacefulness about her that is surely a work of God through this process. She remains more than just friends with his family and both gives to and receives support from them. Her fear of death is gone and her hunger for Scripture is voracious. Yesterday, she and a close friend climbed Kennesaw Mountain and sat on the mountain and read the Bible together.

No question, we are still in the cocoon ... the between. We hope this is not the norm for the rest of her life. She so looked forward to being a wife and mother, and she cannot see that with anyone but Jerod at this point. That is part of the process still to come, and we are placing that in God's hands. If God chooses to grant that desire, she will be ready when and if that time comes. For now we keep checking the cocoon. We can hear things going on inside; we get a glimpse now and then. We wait with eager anticipation to see where this road leads.

Meanwhile, we almost missed the cocoon in which each of us individually is being changed into a new creature. Second Corinthians 5:17 (ESV) says, "Therefore, if anyone is in Christ, he is a new creation. The old has passed away; behold, the new has come." May I be as cooperative as my faithful daughter.

Losing Trust
A Journal Insert from Kevin
February 21, 2016

For those who are believers, this topic may be difficult. For many years, it has been my aim to be honest, and in my writings about our loss, that has meant some very raw emotions. Faith, as I understand it, is not the absence of doubt but the pursuit in spite of it. Over the years, I have observed Christians who say all the right things in the face of loss or tragic pain but bottle up their doubts. It is neither honest nor edifying to acknowledge one without the other. Faith and doubt are both realities of life and they were that for us.

Upon seeing the wreckage and considering what could have been, we realized we had cause for thanks. Many reminded us of the fact that we could have easily had two funerals and not just one, and we know it is very true. That is still a sobering thought. In the midst of watching our daughter go through the loss of her fiancé, we tried to thank God for sparing her. Let me explain what could have been.

Katie owned the Toyota 4Runner that was involved in the accident. Jerod owned three vehicles himself, any of which they could have been driving that day: a Ford Mustang, a Honda sedan, and a fifteen-passenger van. Katie was driving at the time of the accident, but she did not always drive. Had Jerod been driving her car, she would have been the fatality. Had they been in either of his cars with the impact of an SUV doing 80+ mph with their stopping car, we would have had a double funeral. Had they been in the fifteen-passenger van, they may have been better off, but she would have been the passenger and would have taken the greatest impact and most likely would have died.

In my analytical mind, all of the "what ifs" tumbled over and over. All scenarios ended in the loss of our daughter. We should be grateful—period—we have been told. Herein lies the problem. Before I could say amen to end the prayer of thanksgiving for God's protection of Katie, my thoughts would always go to Jerod. Why was he not spared? Where was the protective hand of God for him? There have been plenty of times that Katie has thought and even stated that she wished she had died too. What kind of cruel Protector spares one life but not the life of the object of that one's deepest affection? Could He not have spared both? Such thinking usually ends up in the dead end of the triad of: Does God love? Does He know? Or is He powerful enough to intervene? There is no end to the circles that can be turned in this cul-de-sac of confusion. Some days my faith was strong, and other days it was not so much. There was a mixture of trust, distrust, self-trust, self-doubt, anger, pain, and a myriad of emotions.

After turning enough circles one has to make a decision: either stop and give up or go back the way you came. For me, there are anchors to which I retreat in moments of confusion. These anchors are akin to the memorials that God instructed Israel to leave along their wandering path so that the generations to come could hear the stories of the living God. Creation is one such anchor for me. I have never had enough faith to believe in randomly increasing complexity. Any order in this world is by design. Disorder and decay is the natural result of non-intervention. The radical changes that God made in people, like my father-in-law at salvation, are a testimony to His power and intervention as well. The common graces of life given to all are a reminder of God's attention to our tiny spinning sphere we call Earth.

Yet, the questions remain. And they haunt. Occasionally, I have confided to close friends that my prayers have changed. When asked to pray for someone's safety, I find a slight pause in my spirit. Does God do that? How does He determine when? No doubt, the same doubts ensue for those who have lost someone to illness, accident, or circumstances beyond their control. Not knowing how to pray has sometimes caused me not to. At times, my trust has given way to my desire to order my own world. It has seemed so out of control and in total upheaval at times. Unknown to those around me, I've experienced nights when sleep has been peppered with worrisome dreams or interrupted with thoughts of panic for a world outside of my control.

Being human means having the ability to reason. Along with the ability to reason comes the desire to make sense of events around us. When they do not add up, each of us has the inherent bent to some degree to trust our own ability to understand and decipher our circumstances. It is then that we bump up against Isaiah 55:8–9 (ESV) where it says, "For my thoughts are not your thoughts, neither are your ways my ways, declares the Lord. For as the heavens are higher than the earth, so are my ways higher than your ways and my thoughts than your thoughts."

What I found underneath my pain was a stubborn heart that wants my own way and my own kingdom. Our pastor has a saying that he repeats often that goes something like this: "This is God's universe and He does things His way. I know that I have a better way of doing things. My problem is that I do not have a universe" (Ken Williams, former pastor of West Cobb Church). In John 6:66–69, it tells us that at one point many of Jesus' disciples went away due to the difficult teachings. In other words, it didn't add up to their held value system. He looked at His closest followers and asked them if they were planning to leave as well. Peter, as he was prone to do, answered immediately with a question of his own: "What other option is there?"

There are times in my life that I have remained a follower of Jesus Christ not because of great faith but because of lesser options. Do I deny His creation or redemptive work in human lives? Do I ignore His apparent hand in the past because I cannot presently see it? Where will I turn for the answers which I so crave? As I survey the secular nonsense around me it becomes clear that the problem really lies within. There is a desire within this still-human heart to ascend a throne that is not mine, to assume the scepter reserved for the King of kings, to understand things that are beyond human understanding. A decision is demanded of me. Will I bend my knees in worship or bow up my back in rebellion?

This has been a struggle of mine in these months since Jerod was taken from us. It has been more of a struggle beneath the surface than a visible one. There may be less that I would claim to know for sure, but there are some things of which I am now more sure of than ever. One of those is that I have not seen Jerod for the last time. My heart longs, as do many others, for that grand reunion that has been purchased for us by the Author and Finisher of our faith who has gone before us to prepare a place for us and left us with the promise that we will some day be reunited with Him.

Until then I will live with the mysteries. I do not know why; it makes absolutely no sense. I may never know why. There will probably always be that ambush of pain that catches my breath from time to time. There are some questions that have no answers and it will be my aim not to answer unanswerable questions for myself and even for others. God has given us hints of faith all along our path, reasons to believe, but at the end of the path there is always a chasm that requires a leap of faith. And it is no different for the atheist, the secularist, the pantheist, or the narcissist, except that their leap is a lot longer and the fall a lot harder.

CHAPTER 8

It's Okay to Not be Okay

Katie

October 21, 2014, 4:48 p.m.

I miss you every day. Every hour. Every moment. I need you. I love you, my Jerod. I will love you forever. You were my dream man. My true love. I am so eternally grateful that in Christ we have power over death and that you are with our Savior now as we on earth suffer and mourn your loss. The world is such a different place without our Jerod "Dusty" Hicks. I feel like this pain won't go away or let up. Every day is brutal. I just need you so much. You were my comfort, my supporter, truly my rock. I miss the bright excitement I'd see when we locked eyes. I miss all of our moments.

I so wanted and was looking forward to our life together. We were so close to starting that phase. I ache inside thinking how badly I wanted that with you and only you. I wanted little Jewods running around and driving me crazy every day. I wanted to raise them to be just like the man you are. I wanted to make their ouchies all better with a kiss and a ninja turtle Band-Aid. I wanted to tell them to never be afraid— Mommy and Daddy would always be there for them no matter what trouble they got into.

I was so proud of you and all your amazing accomplishments. Sorry I didn't tell you this more. You deserved to hear it constantly because you were so amazing. I would do anything to have you back. You have no idea how desperate I have been. I hope you are able to see and hear some of the things I'm saying to you and doing for you. You've changed me in so many ways for the better. Actually, you've changed my entire family. I adore you, Jerod. I will always love you.

Katie

It was just over one month from the accident before I returned to work at the hospital on November 15, 2014. My counselor thought it would be a good idea for me to visit the floor where I work a few days before I actually had to report for duty. That way, I'd be able to simply dip my toes in the water of life reentry before jumping in completely. My sister-in-law, Cori, went with me to visit my work family. I was so thankful for her company, as well as the countless ways my coworkers and managers accommodated me in those first days back.

There was so much fear infused into my return to work. Would everyone already know what had happened during my month away? *Surely so*, I thought. How would I be received? Would I smell or see anything that would cause me to crumble at a moment's notice? Would I be able to take the best care of the patients and families who were relying on me and my expertise?

I made it a point to pray before I entered each and every room. Pray that God would get me through the task at hand. Pray that I would have a clear mind to safely care for each patient and answer any questions that arose. Pray that I wouldn't break down in tears for any reason in the rooms. Ever since that day, I have prayed every day on my walk in to work that God would keep my patients safe, and that despite my foggy thinking, I would do no harm. I would pray for clear thinking and a smooth shift. I have since started praying for God to use me and my story wherever He pleases, to place me in the rooms and the paths of the people where He wants to use me the most. I am willing.

My manager was so wonderful, offering me the key to her office that first weekend in case I needed to step away for a moment. Just knowing I had that option was such a comfort. I will never forget the not one or two but *three* fire alarms that ended up going off during this first day back. I thought, *really, God?* They all startled me, especially the first one, because I thought, *no, not a code blue! Please don't let it be my patient!*

After the alarms, my coworkers made it a point to check on me and make sure I was okay. Their caring gestures brought me so much comfort and will be forever appreciated. A dear coworker, Jane, actually called my phone many times that day just to check on me and see how I was doing. Jane wasn't someone I was initially really close to. But she called me from her cruise ship to let me know she wanted to go to lunch with me when she returned. I thought, *wow, that's so nice, but that'll never happen.* Not because Jane isn't completely amazing, but just because generally speaking, people tend to say things like that and not follow through. Jane did, though. She called me once she returned, and we ended up meeting quite a few times; she even accompanied me to Shane Co jewelry store to try to help clear up the stresses that my unpaid wedding rings brought with them. What a friend! I have since prayed to be a friend like that to someone else in need.

My dad drove me in to work on that first day back after my one hour of sleep I got the night before. (My parents actually woke up with me every single workday at five in the morning for months to keep me company and see me off to work.) We'd received a Life Link letter about Jerod's organ donation that Friday evening before, bringing on the flood of tears lasting well into the early morning. I was distraught and unable to sleep after reading the letter. Having my dad along for the ride helped keep my mind busy and kept me from crying the entire time, especially since Jerod would usually call me during my drive in and talk to me to help keep me awake. I was already crying before we left the house, just thinking about the memories. What love—waking up at 5:30 a.m. for no other reason than to call your love and talk her through a portion of the forty-five-minute commute to work.

A sweet coworker, who lived on the complete opposite side of Atlanta, offered to take me to dinner if I wanted, as well as drive me home that first day. I agreed. Before we left, a group of my work friends were waiting for me with a wrapped gift in hand. They had me wait to open it, since it would probably make me cry. It was a wooden picture frame with the precious picture of Jerod and me dancing at a friend's wedding with these words painted below, "Perhaps they are not stars in the sky, but rather openings where our loved ones shine down to let us know they are happy." That gift warmed my heart and lifted my spirits. People I didn't really even talk to much at work asked if I needed a smile and proceeded to help me forge one on my face. Have I mentioned how I love my work family so very much?

I came to learn that I adopted a work mode per se where I was able to block a large chunk of my life out while caring for my patients. Most days, it was a break from the life that I knew and hated so much outside the doors of the hospital. Every day as I left work and walked to my truck, an ocean of tears would rise to the surface and flood down my face. It was like my heart knew when I was okay with it crying, even though I did in fact shed tears in bathrooms and closets at work.

I learned how to release emotions while staying professional at work. One time, I was going into the linen closet to get a clean gown for a patient, and I turned my work phone on silent for a moment as I proceeded to bang my constantly beeping and ringing phone on the pile of linens on the cart, looking like a crazy person I'm sure. It was surprisingly one of the most therapeutic things I remember doing to survive my first days back to work. It was oddly relieving.

After my first day back, I remember thinking that day felt like my second first day as a nurse, completely discombobulated. I did many an air-headed thing at work before the heavy fog of grief wore off, thankfully none of them being serious. I once poured Pedialyte into a feeding bag that wasn't open, spilling liquid all over the floor. Thankfully the parent did not question my credentials or my competence as she offered that she had done the same thing many times at home. It was always a relief to be able to walk out of the hospital doors at the end of a shift knowing I had kept all of my patients alive and safe throughout my shift, but to what was I leaving? What better place did I have to go? I didn't want to return to my life, to my brutal reality.

Katie – Surviving the Holidays

Whether I liked it or not, the holiday season was quickly approaching. I came across a post on Lysa TerKeurst's Facebook page that resonated with me about the season. She mentioned that it can be rough during the holidays when everything shouts "happy" or "merry" when all you feel is lonely and broken (Paraphrased from Facebook by Lysa TerKeurst). That was my exact sentiment as an endless number of people wished me a Happy Thanksgiving and a Merry Christmas. It's such a difficult and sensitive thing, because people really do mean well and want you to be happy, but I learned it's completely okay to not be okay. I was not okay, especially during this first holiday season. And I didn't have to be okay. It was a special card from a fellow griever who had lost her fiancé many years ago who granted me the permission to *not* celebrate if I didn't want to. Not that I needed permission, but it sure was a relief for someone further along in the healing process to tell me that and take some pressure off from following traditions.

It broke my heart to have such a broken heart during such a usually happy time of the year, but there was no avoiding the raw and overwhelming pain that was still very much a part of my daily life during that time. I found myself sad that I was unable to enjoy all of the Christmas songs I used to love so much. They were simply too

107

painful to endure. I was heartsick about not being able to put up decorations and my cute little Christmas tree. I normally enjoy those things but knew I wouldn't want to see them out. It would make it even more painfully obvious that Jerod was not here to celebrate our first Christmas together. He should've experienced it all with me. The lights. The decorations. The family time. The gift exchanging. The love. It is just so exhausting trying to pretend these big days don't exist. It's draining trying to protect my fragile emotional state from any more trauma than it has already endured.

The days and weeks leading up to big, significant days were usually worse than the actual day itself. I experienced supernatural peace that first Christmas Day. I tried to treat it just like any other day. The things that brought me the most smiles and laughter surprised me, though. While I was spending time with Jerod's family, we wrapped up some tissue paper from the presents we exchanged and bounced it around, trying to keep it from hitting the ground for probably about an hour. Mindless, lighthearted fun. Sign us up! We all laughed probably the most that we have since the accident. His family has been so good to me, always including me in their family time and acknowledging what Jerod and I had together.

I actually skipped all major holidays for the first two years after the accident. No Christmas music. No driving to see lights. No parties. Nothing. Hands down, the best gift I received that first Christmas was from my younger brother, Caleb. He took the time to search through my computer for a particular video that Jerod had sent me where he was being so silly and telling me he loved me in a variety of octaves and tones. Repeated "I love yous" were the only words in the video. Caleb recorded this clip and surprised me with a ninja turtle from Build-A-Bear. Press the turtle's hand and the clip played. More tears, but thank you, Caleb, for giving me the opportunity to shed them. Ninja turtles now have a special place in my heart, as so many of my favorite shirts of Jerod's were his silly "turtley awesome" shirts. Caleb's gift was the only one that first Christmas that even acknowledged Jerod's existence in my life, and for that I was thankful. I knew it was an awkward time for gift-giving, since no present could fill the gaping hole in my heart and in my life, but my ninja turtle Hudson was the greatest comfort. He now joins me on all of my travels and has already seen Italy, Germany, Las Vegas, the Grand Canyon, New York City, Michigan, New Zealand, and soon he'll add the Half Dome hike at Yosemite National Park to his list! He's also been skiing in Colorado with my dad and me. He got lots of attention and "cowabungas" from ski lift operators as I carried him with his face sticking out of my backpack. *Cowabunga, dude!*

I felt so relieved once the major holidays were over, but what I didn't see coming was the way I didn't want to start a whole new year without Jerod. I didn't want to experience any firsts without him. I decided, though, that Jerod *was* coming with me to 2015. Not in the way I wanted, but in my heart, I am bringing him with me always. God really did carry me through the holidays. I felt Him so near. I could sense His tight embrace so many times, almost like things could maybe be okay. One day.

January brought with it not only an unwanted new start, but also my first pneumonia. I had never been that sick with a respiratory illness in my life, not that I remember anyway. I was ill for a few weeks with this, especially since my immunity was most certainly down. I also noticed lots of little sores popping up all over my skin. I still don't really know what they were, but I assume something also related to my lowered immunity status.

The next unwanted and dreaded day—Valentine's Day. It turned out to be the opposite of what happened at Christmas. I'd experienced some lighter days of grief prior to Valentine's Day, but that night all hell broke loose again. Not to lose sight, though, of the sweet memory my coworkers created for me on Valentine's Day. I worked that day and was surprised to walk into the staff lounge and find a whole table of Valentine's gifts just for me. Flowers. Candy. Stuffed animals. Mugs. Everything red and hearts.

My work family had spoiled me rotten, wanting me to feel loved since my love was not here to do so himself. They succeeded! In hindsight, I realize how God had placed me in this particular work family, knowing I would need every ounce of the love and support they have given me in order to help me through the darkest valley of my life thus far. I love you all! Following is a snippet from the blog post I shared in regards to that first Valentine's Day after Jerod's passing.

Can We Just Skip This Day?
by Katie Neufeld
February 14, 2015

Everything is red. Everything is flowers. Everything is cards. Everything is balloons. Everything is chocolate. Everything is love. I have tried to avoid all of these. All but the chocolate, of course. Four months ago, I would have thought I'd have quite different emotions in regards to the day devoted solely to love.

Love. Love. Love. That's all I've heard about and seen this past week. It's on television. It's on the radio. It's in advertisements. It's in conversation. It's in commercials on Pandora. It's in e-mails. It's in jewelry commercials. It's apparently even on *Disney Junior* and news talk channels too. It's in the air. Love is in the air. However, the air surrounding me has grown stale. Smoky air filled with the debris, sadness, and fear that are left over from October 9. I never really got into all of the Valentine's Day hype. It's always been just another day for me. I've actually been single for most of them. And it didn't really bother me until the last couple of years. Even then, Valentine's Day just consisted of a few moments of wishing I could finally find my guy, my forever love, after waiting "patiently" and holding my standards so high for so long.

I looked back into my prayer journal from Valentine's Day last year and felt so encouraged again by those words I'd written just one short month before I met my sweet Jerod. I'd felt God's presence so near that night as I spent time in the Bible and in prayer. The same God who pursued me and loved on me that night in February 2014 is still holding onto me so tightly and tenderly even now. I have felt His love so strongly over this last week. I think He must know the dread and

110

loneliness that I have in my heart as I prepare to simply survive the weekend. It has not specifically been Valentine's Day that has bothered me. Well, it has in a way. But all the festivities and preparations that I've seen people take for this one day of love have directed my thoughts, something like an intense form of tunnel vision, to March 22, the day I was supposed to marry the love of my life and the most amazing man I've ever met. That's when the pain hits so hard, pulling me under an enormous wave of grief with no hope of coming up for air. Suffocating me and any hope, peace, or positivity I had fought so hard to build up.

This week brought with it not one, but two very big, dark clouds, two very heavy burdens—the four-month mark *and* Valentine's Day.

Can I just skip this week? That'd be great—thanks!

No. God apparently has something bigger for me, so I must endure. In spite of the week's storm clouds, He has shown His love to me in such big and personal ways. I've been learning that the more I'm able to lean into the pain, and the more I surrender it to God and focus on Him through the pain, the more I feel His presence and grip on my life. The more I see Him turning my loneliness into love. His satisfying love. Great love. It really is a constant struggle to keep moving in this direction. Most of the time, loneliness still prevails. But it's amazing to see what can happen when I truly am able to hand it over and let God exchange it for something so beautiful.

God has sent multiple friends my way this week who have been such an encouragement to me. They've really helped me stay busy and have also helped me turn my eyes back on Jesus, the only One who can rescue me from these enormous waves of grief. Virginia is one of these sweet friends of mine. We enjoyed such a great time on top of Kennesaw Mountain digging into the Bible. That was such a filling and peaceful time.

Another thing that God gave me this week was great amounts of love and support in response to the launching of my blog. It was truly overwhelming and just so awesome to see how God used it to touch so many people. I totally didn't expect this because I just feel so empty and like I don't really have anything to give.

God impressed upon many people to send multiple cards and gifts to me this week. He used coworkers, other friends, previous nursing students that I have precepted at work, and even families of patients at work this week. Some of these things were sent to me with such impeccable timing. One of the gifts I received was actually supposed to be given to me last December, but I think it's no coincidence that it just so happened to get to me this week.

One of the coolest things, though, happened at work on Wednesday. A coworker had asked me if I was ready and able to take on a nursing student yet. I said yes, but jokingly (and kind of seriously) said, "It better be a good one or else!" What she didn't know was that God had used her to assign this particular student to me. It was no accident. Through talking to the nursing student, I quickly found out that she is closely connected to one of the people who encouraged me through her own painful story so early on in my grief. The divine thing is that I felt encouraged and touched by this lady's story even before my own tragedy came about.

After talking more with this student, I came to find out that she also goes to my church and even occasionally attends the community group I recently started going to through the church. How neat! We connected on countless other things, but we both felt like the day was just a continuous blessing. I left work feeling so loved, so known, and so seen by such a big God. How cool that He would connect me with this sweet girl in this way in the place I least expected.

God has also given me a very sweet moment in one of my dreams recently. In the dream, I saw Jerod from afar and ran fast to him and jumped up high into his arms, hugging him and loving on him. I remember wrapping my arms around him and hugging him for so long and telling him, "It's been too long since I've been able to do this." How overjoyed I was to *finally* have another sweet dream about my Jerod, for they now come all too infrequently.

But how heartbroken I was waking up and realizing that it was only a dream. Early on, all I had was nightmares—while I was sleeping *and* when I was awake. The nightmares while sleeping have slowed down tremendously. These sweet dreams just don't happen enough. As painful as it was to wake up from this one, I'm so thankful for it. Through that dream, God answered one of my recent prayers. I had asked/begged Him to please, please, please let Jerod meet me in my dreams.

I truly believe that God gave me all of these moments and gifts to make sure I felt loved, as so much of the rest of America was preparing for their own day of love. How fulfilling true love really is! True love of course with my Jerod, but more importantly true love from the Lover of my soul, my first and greatest love.

In all of these things, God is really taking me back to the basics and teaching me to trust. To believe that He will take care of me and provide for me in this drought. When I start to worry or dread, I am not trusting. As messy and ugly as the circumstances of my life are right now, I know my God, and I know that I can count on Him. Now to just trust ...

> *"'For my thoughts are not your thoughts, neither are your ways my ways,' declares the Lord. 'As the heavens are higher than the earth, so are my ways higher than your ways and my thoughts than your thoughts.'"*
>
> —ISAIAH 55:8–9

> *"... for love is as strong as death, its jealousy unyielding as the grave. It burns like blazing fire, like a mighty flame. Many waters cannot quench love; rivers cannot sweep it away."*
>
> —SONG OF SOLOMON 8:6–7

Katie

Days were hard. Nights were harder. March arrived. I was hoping by some off chance that we could just skip March altogether. March 22 was the day Jerod and I were to be married. What was to be the happiest day of our lives was now a looming day of darkness, consumed by death and disaster. Knowing the day was coming, regardless of my sentiments, I decided I wanted the chance to at least wear my wedding dress once more, the gown that hung in my closet for a man I will never see again on this earth and for a wedding that will only happen in my dreams. I put on my dress, veil and all, and wept. I knew it would be a profoundly painful thing to do but felt I owed it to the day, and I'm actually glad I put it on. My hope—if I released my tears then, maybe there would be less on the actual day. Unfortunately, that wasn't the case.

"One Fit Widow," a lady's encouraging page on Facebook, inspired me to use what could be such a dark time, the wedding day, to do something enjoyable or something that we both had wanted to do. I'd never been to New York before, so I thought that could be a new, exciting adventure. Our family friends had wanted to go there as well, so we made a girls' trip of it. Those few days in New York City were some of the lightest days of grief that I had experienced up until that time. Thank you, Jesus, for that priceless gift.

Following is the blog post I shared on the wedding date at the exact time we were to start our wedding.

The Day That Never Was
by Katie Neufeld
March 22, 2015

I have been dreading this particular day for quite some time now. Since October 10, 2014, to be exact. I've thought about it a lot. I've cried and screamed countless times. I've been stuck for days at a time trudging through the thick range of negative emotions that are and probably will forever be leeched onto this day, sucking dry every drop of energy I have as I persistently strive to find the positive in the midst of the abyss where my past, present, and future have been lost.

I've thought about this day, obviously, when I've seen anything wedding or bridal-related, but also less obviously (to the public or specifically to anyone who has not personally experienced loss of a loved one) when I am waking up, when I am eating, when I am getting ready, when I am driving, when I am sleeping, when I am dreaming (having a nightmare), when I am working, when I am shopping, when I am with friends, when I am alone, when I am sitting on the couch staring at the wall, when I am laughing, when I am crying, when I am silent, when I am talking. *When I am breathing.*

I've had plenty of time recently to consider what a compounding loss this has been. This makes me sad to consider, but I haven't been able to avoid it. In losing Jerod, I instantly lost my fiancé and very best friend. I lost my (future) husband and father of our children. I lost each one of those precious unborn children. He wanted four. I lost our sweet little (future) family and the big family get-togethers that would have followed. I lost my spiritual partner. I lost my date, my hand to hold for big (and small) events: church, weddings, concerts, Braves games, dinners, date nights, lake days, etc. I specifically lost some of those fun events—for a time, at least. I just can't picture myself going to the lake or to any Braves games ever again—at least not for a very, *very* long time. I lost my snuggle buddy. I did gain one thing, though—the haunting and tormenting thoughts of what could have been, what never was, and what never will be.

pause for tears

A few times here recently, I've felt like we, as Christians, are on the brink of hearing that trumpet sound. I never thought I would so desperately long for the Lord's return before my lifetime ends here on earth, but many days I feel completely ready to hear that sweet sound, that heavenly melody that will bring my Jerod back to me (or rather take me to him) so we can finally start our forever together. I have recently found myself looking at the concept of time quite differently. Many people dread birthdays because it makes them one year older and (morbidly thinking) one year closer to their own earthly death. *Instead, I have been counting each increment of time as just one more moment that brings me that much closer to seeing my precious Jerod again.*

Growing old is a privilege denied to many, as I have once heard and now know all too well and in a very personal way. I'm not sure yet, but I imagine myself one day experiencing my birthdays quite differently than I had before the accident. Growing old just doesn't seem near as glamorous as it once did. I know aging is not glamorous in and of itself, but having the man of my dreams here with me for the process was a dream to me. Growing older accompanied by a bruised and broken heart was certainly not my desire. My dream has actually changed over time.

Some years ago, my goal was to have this amazing wedding, one I had envisioned for years and years, with less of the focus being on the man I would be marrying and more of the focus on the actual day. I had almost every detail of *my* wedding planned out in my head … and in a PowerPoint. That was during a time in my life when I had felt so desperate to be in the next stage of my life, a time I had been so tired of just waiting and waiting (and waiting) for this amazing guy to come into my life. I'd thought my wedding would be the day when my life would truly begin; the focus had always been on the *day*.

Well, *today* should have been that day for me. Instead, my heart is shattered in too many pieces to count. Today is not the celebration that it should have been. But what I really want to focus on instead is the man I am so blessed to have come into my life at the perfect time, although I keep wishing it had been much sooner and lasted so much longer.

When I met and fell in love with Jerod, something beautiful was happening. My focus was changing. *Yes*, I knew early on that he was the man I wanted to marry and spend the rest of my life with. *Yes*, I dreamed of our wedding day and being married to him quite often, but my focus was not on the actual day. What a beautiful transformation that was! The weird thing is that I'd never even really planned much of the details of our wedding out in my head like I'd always done in previous relationships. That was so unlike me.

I believe the difference was that I knew with my whole heart that Jerod was the man God had made just for me. He had every single quality I'd searched for in a guy and then some. In hindsight, this was totally a God thing because I was able to fully enjoy and cherish our short time together instead of being pushy for the proposal and for our future to begin.

Well, actually being the type of go-getter Jerod was, he never really gave me time to be pushy! Four months in and we both knew. He popped the question on July 20, 2014, and we still enjoyed every day for the day it was. Our focus was on today, the here and now. We didn't have every detail of our future lined up and planned out, although we did have our big ideas. I can't even begin to explain how much I love that man! I never knew you could love someone as much as I love Jerod. And I didn't care too much where or how our future took us as long as it kept us together, where we belonged.

In spite of all of the pain and torment associated with this disaster, I want to somehow learn to live, to *fully* live and not just exist, in honor of my Jerod and all of the living that I personally think he had left to do. And boy, would he have lived. However, Jerod is still living it up even now, just not in the way I had dreamed of for us. I can just see him tearing it up in heaven, so beyond excited to be there with our King, who just happened to have quite different plans than our own for Jerod's, mine, and our families' futures. And to think I ever had any control! Ha! So, I am going to try to live—for Jerod, of course, but also for my God who apparently still wants me here, as evidenced by my miraculous survival of this so horrific accident from which I should not have walked away. And without any serious injury too. As much as I have wished at times that that had been it for me too, I can clearly see that God still wants me here. So, I am going to try to fully live in honor of my God who has so lovingly been pursuing me these last five-and-a-half months.

One thing I have always known, but never in such an intimate way, is that God has always been available to me in the good times and in the bad. As I always knew, it was me with the problem. I so often was not looking for Him. I did not hunger or thirst for Him anywhere near as strongly as I do now. But now that I have reached out to Him in such a state of desperation, I find that I now crave time with Him every day, sometimes almost constant interaction. The more intimate our relationship grows, the more I find that I crave that time with Him.

I have truly felt God's presence in such a real way in my life. I now see Him so much more often in my every day. I cherish those moments that I feel God so near, sometimes as if I could almost touch Him. I have felt His peace at times, though it seems to be just not often enough. He met me in the middle of the mess that is now my life and has been rescuing me daily. I have found Him at the very rock bottom of this dark free fall just waiting to catch me in His loving and tender embrace. He was ever so patiently waiting on me and has been gently and lovingly leading me through this whole grief process, never forcing anything, as true love never does.

> *"Have mercy on me, Lord, for I am faint; heal me, Lord, for my bones are in agony. My soul is in deep anguish. How long, Lord, how long? ... I am worn out from my groaning. All night long I flood my bed with weeping and drench my couch with tears."*
>
> —Psalm 6:2–3, 6

> *"Restore our fortunes, Lord, as streams renew the desert. Those who plant in tears will harvest with shouts of joy. They weep as they go to plant their seed, but they sing as they return with the harvest."*
>
> —Psalm 126:4–6 NLT

> *"For I am about to do something new. See, I have already begun! Do you not see it? I will make a pathway through the wilderness. I will create rivers in the dry wasteland ... Yes, I will make rivers in the dry wasteland so my chosen people can be refreshed."*
>
> —Isaiah 43:19–20 NLT

Date at the Braves game

Rays on the River date

Blustery day at Brasstown Bald

Father's Day 2014

Ahoy matey, Jerod and Katie!

Smiles for days!

YES!

Go Braves!

The proposal

I would say yes to you forever.

Us. Jerod's and my family and friends.

a Sundial birthday dinner

Love these three dearly! Jerod, his sister, and his mom

Dressed up for a friend's wedding

Thank you, Jesus!

Having an apple-pickin' good time!

Heaven-sent healing

Just a grampaw (Kevin) and his granddog

My furever valentine

Dusty's first trip to the beach

My not so lionhearted dog

My siblings

My family

So thankful for these wonderful ladies, Jerod's mom and sister

Jerod loved what he did and he was good at it. The kids loved and looked up to him.

Jerod in his element

Chief instructor Jerod Hicks, forever in our hearts

CHAPTER 9

The Art of Tears

Katie

My rings became a source of additional stress and tears as we discovered that despite the unforeseen and tragically unusual circumstances, the bank was still making us pay them off completely if I wanted to keep them. That was not even a question. Those rings were mine, and I would do or pay whatever it took. Or I would beg my mom to help do whatever it took, because I had no patience or persistence for that sort of thing, as I was still so weak physically and emotionally. I eventually paid for the rings with the settlement I received from the insurance company.

I didn't expect the uncertainty that plagued me as I wondered how I should wear them. I chose to continue just wearing the engagement ring until I could decide if or how to wear the wedding band, since we were never technically married. My heart was already committed though, which complicated my decision. I certainly didn't want to answer every unknowing person who was sure to ask about my husband and how long we'd been married or about the rings when they saw them in all of their sparkling beauty.

There were days I wore both and owned it like I was a happily married woman, knowing on the inside what a façade that was. I wanted to see what it felt like. I didn't wear them both publicly very much though because of all the questions they would elicit, but it didn't take long for me to decide that I was no longer comfortable with that anyway. It became a reminder of the painful reality I was living every day of my new life.

I went through a phase where I would only wear the wedding band on the ring finger of my right hand, and I liked the feel of that for a while. After that phase, it was back to the original and truest form. I wore my engagement ring on the appropriate ring finger for I can't even remember how many months. I just couldn't take it off like our engagement never happened; I wasn't ready, and I knew that was okay.

I prayed quite a few times that God would prepare the heart of my "Chapter 2," my second love, to meet me while I was still wearing my engagement ring from Jerod, because I told God I was absolutely not taking it off. In hindsight, that's all a laugh, because I obviously wasn't ready for that next step anyway.

Kevin

One of the ways that we made it through the pain of sudden loss in those months and years post-loss is one that is still a bit uncomfortable for me. Our family was not one to express itself emotionally through tears. Outside of the natural crying of children who have fallen or injured themselves, tears were a rare occurrence. That has now changed. Please understand that we've reached a point where we are not likely to be found crying a great deal, but we no longer have an aversion to tears. We've learned so much about them.

Discussing this recently with Katie, she mentioned that she was seven months post-loss before making it through a single day without tears. She was quick to clarify that she was still crying internally, but it took that long for her to cry herself out. One of the hardest times for me was passing the place to which so many memories of Jerod had been tied. My drive to work took me past Jerod's business, and initially, I chose a different route, finding the pain too great. Once I reverted to my normal route, it took several months before I could drive past Breakthrough Martial Arts without breaking down, or at the very least, becoming teary-eyed.

We discovered that there are numerous ways to cry. The inconsolable wails that poured out of the examination room at Grady will remain with me as long as I live. God bless the chaplain and caregivers who stood there with us as our world suddenly went dark; their job is an unenviable one.

There were the quiet sobs and the single tears squeezed out of parched tear ducts that had emptied all the tears humanly possible. We had our community tears as we would cry together, and each of us had our private tears known only to ourselves. Sometimes those tears were dash-pounding, screaming tears, and sometimes they were pull-over-because-I-can't-see-to-drive tears. Often, we remained secluded until we could regain our composure to be out in public without becoming a spectacle. Crying publicly makes onlookers uncomfortable and is often met with attempts, often futile, to assuage the pain by subduing the tears.

We each had our safe places to "lose it." Sometimes they would intersect. What do you do when you retreat to the basement to check on your heartbroken daughter only to hear her wailing in the shower or sobbing as she lay on the floor of her bathroom? You cry. When the worship team at church sings about the church being like a bride awaiting her groom and you turn to see a bride whose groom was never—the finality of it was paralyzing—*never* coming back for her, you cry with her. You cry with her, for her, and for others who must also carry heart-crushing pain. You cry because there is nothing you can do to change it. You cry because the worst pain in the world is to see your child hurt and know there is absolutely nothing you can do to change it ... now or ever.

One of the lessons we learned was that it wasn't our job to stop her tears. The Bible says to weep with those who weep. Oftentimes, we attempt to stop the tears of others, but this, though well-intended, turns out to be more about our own discomfort with tears than the one who sheds them. In those initial days, there were many times when we would wrap our arms around Katie and cry with her. Stand and cry, lie beside her on the bed and cry, talk together and cry, sit together as a family and cry. As we did, we became more comfortable welcoming our reluctant friend, tears. I recall very clearly the day that Katie cheerily announced to me, "I had a good cry today."

We shed tears for different reasons. At first, we cried because we hurt, and then we wept because we knew the pain was not going away. We cried because of what we would never have as we mourned the loss of dreams never to be fulfilled. We learned tears were our Creator's means for pain to discover a pressure relief valve.

When one has a head injury, it's sometimes necessary during the first hours and days following to provide a means for the pressure created by the brain's swelling to be relieved. A shunt may be inserted to drain excess fluid or a portion of the skull removed to accommodate the body's reaction to the injury. In much the same way, tears provide an initial relief valve. After some time, the acuteness of the initial pain subsides, and tears will be needed less frequently, but they remain available. Occasionally, during an ambush of pain, they will arise suddenly like a geyser and then quickly subside.

We've learned that tears are good. We no longer try to suppress them in ourselves or in others. When they come, they come. If they come, they come. The best thing we can do is either cry with the mourner or at least sit quietly and just be present. In some ancient cultures, it was tradition for someone to provide a vessel in which tears would be saved. It was called a tear bottle. Psalm 56:8 (NLT) speaks of them when it says, "You keep track of all my sorrows. You have collected all my tears in your bottle. You have recorded each one in your book."

The history of tear bottles is a bit vague as to the specific details, but it seems that there are several very likely uses. They are reported by many to have been used by both those who mourned and those who joined them. In some cases, the tears were collected in a bottle, and the duration of the mourning was determined by how long it took for the tears to evaporate. There is also evidence that the bottles were sometimes buried with the grieving (Tear Bottle History). Several lessons can be learned from these practices:

1   Catching the tears and not stopping them was the work of those who accompanied the hurting. Acknowledging and validating the pain are priceless gifts to the grieving. After a period of time, many no longer want to hear about the pain and often want someone to "get over it." Each of us needs at least a small circle of friends who are there to catch our tears as long as we need to release them. God gave us such friends, and for that we are eternally grateful.

2   The intense pain will eventually be assuaged, though how soon is often unknown. When it is, the tears will evaporate. The bottle may serve as a memorial, but the tears will be dried. God granted us friends with empty tear bottles who acknowledged our pain but also came alongside us to show us their empty bottles, assuring us that this period too shall pass. We will be forever changed, but there is life post-loss, though the timing is unique to each loss.

3   Some losses will continue with us to the grave. There are some losses that will not be passed. Life-changing, path-altering losses. We are learning that though the loss may describe us, we must not let the loss define us. As followers of Jesus Christ, we are complete in Him. He makes up the lack in our lives and fills up our sufferings with His sufficient grace.

"But he said to me, 'My grace is sufficient for you, for my power is made perfect in weakness.' Therefore I will boast all the more gladly about my weaknesses, so that Christ's power may rest on me. That is why, for Christ's sake, I delight in weaknesses, in insults, in hardships, in persecutions, in difficulties. For when I am weak, then I am strong."

—2 Corinthians 12:9-10

Tears do not come nearly as often these days, but we're often reminded of what we have lost and the pain. We acknowledge it, we strap it on our backs, and we move forward. We still have a "good cry" from time to time, but we've also learned that there's something else that can accompany tears … laughter. We do that now too, though there have been times when we thought we might never laugh again.

Katie

I wouldn't learn this until later, but tears proved to be an invaluable gift from God, a way for me to lower the intense pressure building up inside me. Tears are sacred; God cares about and sees each one. Tears became an unusual and often awkward enemy turned into friend, a surprising gift in the midst of deep suffering.

I just never knew before the accident that releasing tears could be such a violent, full-body workout. I often found my entire body was sore and tense after a "good cry." And just when I thought I'd run out of tears, I'd always find more. Though, one time I cried on my way to work, but no tears flowed. It was so odd. I didn't even know it was possible to feel such strong, negative emotions on the inside and experience the physical aspects of crying without tears. Had I run out? That answer is no.

Another time, I saw something that made me want to cry, but then I realized that I was already crying. Grief is so unexplainably bizarre and often makes no sense whatsoever. There's no sense in trying to make any sense of it either, but just to recognize that no two grievers will respond identically, and that's okay. Oftentimes my mind would tell me that if I wanted him back badly enough, maybe it could happen. There was the time when I drove by his business on my way home from dinner and saw all the kids sitting on the mat, listening to their teacher while he walked around the room. My heart so wanted him to be my favorite instructor. My mind, even. I did a double take trying to see who he was, hoping beyond all logic and reason that the man was my Jerod.

After a while, I got quite proficient at the art of tears, and sometimes it was a conscious choice if I wanted to cry or not. Although, putting the tears off often led to their inevitable return, but with a vengeance. I never knew that cries could sound so confused, even to the crier. Those sounded awful, as if I cared. My variety of cries meshed together at times—angry cries, whimpering cries, moaning cries, throat-screeching cries—all together in harmony, such sorrowful harmony.

There was a time within the first year of losing Jerod that it truly felt like something had died inside of me, inside my soul. There honestly was no possible way for me to stay the same after experiencing such a life-altering tragedy, nor would I want to stay the same. My tears became healing waters that seeped down into the darkest places in my soul, what I thought had been buried under the ruins of my loss. I learned later that what I perceived to be the death and burial of my soul had actually been the planting of greater things to come.

While the old Katie did have to die to survive, the dark soil of grief is remarkably fertile ground. With God's divine work in my life and my healing tears, my parched soul began to find the strength to fight through the soil and wreckage, to wrestle with my biggest questions, to bust through the rock solid cement of loss and start to see the beginnings of the light. I had not been buried, but planted.

CHAPTER 10

But Not Without Hope

"And now, dear brothers and sisters, we want you to know what will happen to the believers who have died so you will not grieve like people who have no hope. For since we believe that Jesus died and was raised to life again, we also believe that when Jesus returns, God will bring back with him the believers who have died."

—1 Thessalonians 4:13–14 NLT

Katie

The date was April 5, 2015. The day arrived with a chill in the air and partly cloudy skies. I honestly wasn't sure what to think or expect going into Easter weekend 2015. This weekend a year before was such a memorable and exciting time for Jerod and me, as we were in the beginning of our developing relationship. Good Friday 2014 turned out to be the night when I could no longer keep looking for those yellow "enough" flags that would be enough for me to back out of the relationship because of irrational fear. Seeing Jerod's heart for Jesus that Good Friday turned out to be enough to wholeheartedly pursue our developing relationship.

Six months into grief from the tragedy that was forced upon me, Easter 2015 arrived like a dim flicker of resurrected hope. My dad and I had driven to the Verizon Wireless Amphitheater for Passion City's Easter service. It was like no Easter ever before. It was like my own personal Battle of Saratoga, the turning point in the war of my grief. Hope won the war that day.

It was a beautiful day outside, filled with vibrant colors, not to mention the green layer of pollen covering everything. Welcome to spring in Georgia! The sun was shining, and the wind was blowing on my face. Pastor Louie's words of healing pierced my broken and aching heart. The heavy burden I'd been carrying for so long was lifted somewhat; I felt lighter.

Pastor Louie spoke about the various types of death: physical death, spiritual death, and the death of dreams. Physical death is still a big part of this fallen world, but the *power* of death is *gone!* Physical death is *not* the final resting place. Death is a *has been*; it's in the past. Death is done. Death has *died!*

Louie spoke from Luke 24:13–35 about the two men on the road to Emmaus who were disheartened as they discussed all that had happened. *But Jesus* revealed Himself and turned their dashed dreams into a renewed hope. Those two men didn't even recognize Jesus walking along with them on that road of their broken dreams. Louie encouraged me with the reminder that even though I may have put a lot of hope into a dream that has died, the tomb is empty! Jesus walks in and changes the story. And that dream may not come back to life, but a different dream can. A different dream can be born. God's power is not limited, and His story for me is still being written. If I am alive, it is *not* over. There is still hope for God to redeem and restore me. There is still time for the resurrection power to enter my life (Louie Giglio, Pastor of Passion City Church, Paraphrased from a sermon on Easter Sunday in 2015).

Feeling like I was the only one in attendance, I hesitantly stood as Louie asked if anyone had a dream die and needed that kind of hope. That talk was made for me and had been delivered with such impeccable and divine timing. His message had brought the light and hope of Jesus to places in my heart that were so broken and so dark, places I thought had died and would never see the light of resurrection and redemption. Sweet redemption.

What a day that was for me! I didn't expect it to be that life-changing. How could it, right? I didn't have my new husband or my much-anticipated new life; it was supposed to be unthinkably miserable. Instead, in all of God's grace and wonder, He filled my heart with a renewed hope and peace beyond description. God is always good, even when our circumstances are not.

Kevin

Katie and I headed to Sunday worship at Passion City Church being held at Verizon Wireless Amphitheater in North Atlanta. Not only did Katie's mother and I not want her living alone, we also didn't want her being at church alone. Just five months removed from her accident, she was living with frequent tears, nightly nightmares, and all of the implosion that had been her dreams.

On that early spring Sunday, the sun was bright, breezes were stiff, and the temperature was alternately comfortable and cold as we sat waiting for the service to commence. Silently, I wondered what effect the day would have on Katie. I prayed for it to be impactful. We had just come through her canceled wedding date just two weeks earlier, and now were preparing to celebrate a resurrection. My expectation was that this would either remind her in a new way of her loss or hopefully focus her mind on the hope that there would someday be a reunion with her love. After a run back to the truck for a forgotten item, we settled in for worship, which began as usual with several very timely songs about the victory that has come with the resurrection of our Savior.

As Passion City does so well, the anthems reminded us of the hope that day commemorated. The music was unusually good that day, but I remember one song specifically, and it seemed like a direct message from heaven, as well as a loving embrace from our heavenly Father. We came to find that those hugs would become a regular occurrence as wonderful songs washed over our broken hearts. The song title is "Remember."

Never has a song spoken so delicately, yet incredibly powerfully, to the very place that needed it. I'm so grateful for that song; it has become one of my favorites and is on my most-played songs playlist. We could have ended the service right there and it would have been enough, but there was more.

Louie Giglio stood to preach. After welcoming all who had gathered on that special day, he gave his text, which if I recall correctly, was from 1 Corinthians 15. That day turned out to be the first break of daylight in Katie's long, dark night. As he recounted the events of the crucifixion and the burial of Jesus, he built to a crescendo in which the resurrected Christ triumphantly pronounces the death of death (Louie Giglio, Pastor of Passion City Church, Paraphrased from a sermon on Easter Sunday in 2015). It became clear as he elaborated on death's demise, that this message was just for Katie; it had happened again. So many times Louie's messages had seemed to Katie as if no one else was in attendance but her. Through tear-filled eyes, we looked at each other, and without words, smiled as we both were reminded that Jerod was not as we had last seen him. He was now in the presence of the One who had conquered death. By Jesus' death on the cross and His resurrection, Jesus had not only paid for the sins of the world, he had also effectively driven a stake into the heart of death. No stinger left with which to torment the sons of God, the greatest and last battle that each of us faces had been obliterated by our King. Death is dead. Let the bells toll it out!

As we filed out toward the parking lot at the end of the service, the walk seemed lighter and shorter as we shared our thoughts. We both knew many dark days and nights lie ahead, but for a moment, the clouds parted, and we were given the gift of a clear view of our God—the earth-shaking, death-conquering, hope-giving, all-powerful Champion over Satan, hell, and the grave. We knew that day would be one we would look back on and remember. A memorial had been erected on that Easter Day 2015, one of many more that were to come.

Katie

In hindsight, I realize that God had been preparing me in advance to receive Easter and its message of hope. For months prior and through many different venues, God had been speaking these words to me. "You are still here because your story is not over. I have important plans especially for you, and I will help you through every step of the way."

I'd been on the fence about which church to get involved in, knowing without a doubt that I desperately needed a good church home during my walk through this valley. Jerod and I had been involved at West Ridge Church, where he led a boys' Sunday school group and was heavily involved in the children's ministry. I, of course, felt a pull to that church since we had many memories there, but I couldn't take the good without the bad. West Ridge had also been the place of one of my greatest sorrows, the place where we said our final goodbyes to Jerod on this earth.

Before the accident, I'd gone on and off to Passion City Church for a while and felt God's nudging stronger in that direction. After much prayer, I felt God speaking to my heart that He didn't care where I attended, He just wanted me involved with a body of believers somewhere. I felt a deep-seated confidence that He would bless my decision either way. I was also at the point in my life where I was willing to go where God would call me, even if I went alone. I didn't really end up going to church alone very much after the accident though, because my family wanted to make sure I was supported and cared for.

I can say with confidence that if God calls you to it, He will lead you through it. He led me to Passion City and has not failed me once.

On my first Sunday there, while still feeling broken, yet searching for a seat where I might feel comfortable, I heard someone calling my name. One of the mentors God had built into my life from birth was calling my name. Sue Huey had babysat me from my newborn days with help from her daughters, Amber and Dee Dee. Our families had served together in ministry and moved separately to Georgia. We spent many holidays together since neither of our families had relatives nearby. Sue saw me walking by where she and her husband, Clay, were sitting in their usual seats and invited me to sit with them. It became my routine for a while to sit with Clay and Sue. My family joined us as well when they attended with me.

God had laid out every detail of my arrival at Passion City. The series Pastor Louie was in at the time was called, "A Matter of Life and Death." This series addressed many of the major questions people tend to have about death, heaven, and hell as Louie encouraged us to embrace our greatest fears and use them as leverage in God's hands. With this divine perspective shift, we were left with the beauty that in Jesus, even death is life (Louie Giglio, Pastor of Passion City Church, Paraphrased from a sermon in the series "A Matter of Life and Death" in 2014).

It was quite a few months after the accident before I fully embraced perspective shifts and the healing that would come along with them. My first shift was a simple, yet profound, one that came as I was washing my hands in the staff bathroom one day at work. I was looking in the mirror at my teary eyes, thinking about how the Monday following the accident, October 13, was supposed to be the day we met our photographer at Piedmont Park to have our engagement photos taken. We'd already gone shopping for matching fall outfits for the shoot. It was supposed to be perfect.

Initially, my response to that thought was frustration that God didn't grant us those extra four days with Jerod, the time to have our scheduled boat day on Lake Allatoona with his family, followed by our engagement photos that next Monday.

It didn't seem like a big ask, but it didn't take long before I thought, *Wait ... we do have engagement photos, not professional ones, but we do have pictures taken during our engagement.*

One of my favorite photos is of me on Jerod's shoulders at the apple orchard with his dad the weekend before the accident. That photo really portrayed Jerod's personality too, one of the main reasons I love it so much. I was holding onto his face for leverage as he bit into an apple for the picture while wearing his favorite "Breakthrough Blue" sunglasses.

We also had a nice photo taken from a wedding we'd gone to a few months prior, as well as one from my friend's wedding, taken only one day before we got engaged ourselves. That photo from Virginia's wedding has to be my all-time favorite of us; it was taken while we were dancing. You can't see my face, but you don't need to. It's his that speaks so loudly. His eyes were locked on mine, and his face held a sweet enamored smile that I will never forget. To my delight, Jerod had been taking dance classes before he even met me so that when the time came, he would be prepared to dance at his wedding. Jerod was truly one of a kind and certainly *my* kind!

A more profound perspective shift came after seeing a post from Lysa TerKeurst on Facebook. The picture she posted looked like a photo taken from an airplane window. A beautiful sunset shone with brilliant, cheerful colors above a thick layer of clouds covering an obvious dark, gloomy day below. The photo was a timely reminder to shift your perspective above the gray and glum day. Look above the clouds and you'll find the sun is still shining bright even when you can't see it from below (Paraphrased from Facebook by Lysa TerKeurst, December 4, 2014).

That was the first day I remember considering that the storm I was enduring had a different view from above through God's eyes. Maybe there *was* purpose and meaning, not *despite* the storm, but because of it. In the middle of the mess. I knew only God had the power to make good of it all.

The shifts kept rolling in. I'd been writing one of my next blog posts, and God provided an illustration right in front of my eyes during the most bizarre late summer storm. I titled this post, "Good Grief."

Good Grief
by Katie Neufeld
August 5, 2015

One sunny afternoon, I heard an alarming bolt of lightning that lit up the summer sky. It came out of nowhere. It didn't sound far away either. I walked down to the entry, opened the door, and felt another instant confirmation that what I'd just finished writing for this post was from God.

Wow! The sky was painted a beautiful shade of blue with pure white puffs of clouds. The sun was still shining bright, yet this storm was pounding pellets of rain to the ground. The wind was hissing. Leaves blowing. Dark clouds looked far away in the sky. The scene just didn't make sense—but then it did! What a revelation! And I had literally just finished my blog post about it.

Beauty and pain can live together.

It doesn't have to make sense. There's no way it ever could. I became excited as I saw that picture literally painted right in front of my eyes. And just for me in that particular moment.

There's not really an easy way to describe everything that's going on in my life right now. If I were going to put a quick label on it, I'd use something that I recently heard on the radio, more specifically on Dennis Prager's Happiness Hour. In a talk exclusively about living (happily) beyond grief, he zoned in on a critical fact.

The opposite of happiness is not pain—unhappiness is. Therefore, happiness and pain can coexist (If you let them.) (Paraphrased from *The Happiness Hour* by Dennis Prager).

One caller in particular got my attention when he said that in order to be happy, you have to feel the depths of the pain in its entirety. I can wholeheartedly agree with that because happiness, along with most everything else in my life right now, has changed. Actually, it disappeared for a very long time, but it's slowly starting to make its reappearance, just in a totally different way and on a completely different stage. A stage I would've never chosen for myself.

Feeling every bit of the depths of this darkness has created some starkly different, yet totally pure, moments of painful bliss.

This happiness is much simpler than any I had ever experienced before. A type of happiness that shares the front seat with gratitude. Once I discovered for myself that Jesus was the only thing left at my rock bottom, I found that as much as I wanted to run as far away from gratitude as I possibly could, it had a way of finding me anyway. And believe me, I was *not* looking for it. I was hiding from it. I was running away from it—as fast and as far as I possibly could. Because who could ever be thankful for such a devastating tragedy? Who would ever want to?

But I can avoid it no longer. In some of my most painfully beautiful tear-stained moments, I find myself in utter awe and amazement of the way God has been working in my life. When I see just one small piece of the puzzle of God's perfect plan coming together in my life, it fuels my perseverance. Unfortunately, it doesn't answer any of my gnawing questions. It doesn't take away the gut-wrenching pain of loss. It doesn't give me the full picture just yet, but it gives me just enough to piqué my interest and make me want to keep going to see what else is on the horizon.

It fills my tank until the next stop. Even when I've been running on fumes, I've never run out, as much as I thought I would. I've never given up, as much as I've wanted to on too many occasions to count. More importantly, God has never given up on me. As mad as I have been at God, and as much as I've wanted nothing to do with Him some days, He's never left me stranded and on my own. Even in those moments when it feels like He's deserted me, I've found that it was I who walked away.

The most ironic part of this new and slowly emerging happiness is that it's often coupled with painful memories and traumatic flashbacks. I've just learned to accept these painful moments and ride them out like a wave. And what a wild ride it has been! I will often go round and round and end up on the same aggravating dead end, but the beauty of God's undeserved and relentless grace and provision to me while unfolding His plan for my life has given me the courage and persistence to keep walking. Even when fear has a tight grip on my future. Even when anxiety stops me in my tracks. I take just one more step. Just one.

I recently started reading *The Circle Maker* by Mark Batterson. In the beginning of the book, the author talks about the story of the city of Jericho and how God had commanded the Israelites to march around the city once a day for six days and then seven times on the seventh day before the walls would crumble. The author encourages the reader to consider what "Jericho" stands for in his own life (Batterson 2011, 28).

What giant are you marching around and praying over in your life? What problem are you walking around again and again hoping that something will finally change and God in all His power will intervene? A problem. A dream. A miracle. Healing. Whatever that means for you.

As if that chapter in *The Circle Maker* wasn't enough, a friend of mine posted a link the same day to one of Christine Caine's recent posts, which, ironically enough, was about the exact same topic. It was one of those moments where I felt God was lovingly smacking me up side the head with a two-by-four saying, "Hey! Listen! Pay attention to this. It is important."

Christine Caine explained that you have no idea what lap you're on while marching around your own personal Jericho. You may be at the beginning of your battle on day two. You may be on lap five of day seven nearing the end. The frustrating thing is that there's no way to know. But keep walking! Keep going. Keep praying. Keep drawing near to God. You'll hit walls. You'll meet resistance (Caine 2015).

Don't make the wall bigger than God! As easy as it would be, and as much as I sometimes want to, I can't stop! I won't stop. I must keep going. I've come too far to quit now. I must press forward. Just take one more lap. Just one. Because the best is yet to come! And because Jerod would not want me to stop.

I imagine Jesus' followers who were around during His torture, crucifixion, and death felt pretty defeated, to put it mildly. They must have wondered the point of it all. Why should they keep going? They'd given up everything to follow Him, and He'd been put to death.

But unending thanks to God that the story didn't end there! Just like the people of that day, we also don't get to see the big picture on this side of heaven. We, as Christians, know how it ends (and it's good!), but what a tragically beautiful part of God's perfect plan! What unspeakable love He has for us that He would allow His own Son to go through such agony, such undeserved punishment, so that none of us in all of our shortcomings should perish and live apart from Him.

In those darkest of moments during Jesus' death, the plan didn't look so perfect. In the darkest moments of my own life over these last ten months to the day, it seems that God's perfect plan has been shattered into millions of tiny, jagged pieces. But I've come to the conclusion that there must be a reason I didn't die on that dark Thursday in October because I'm still here. God's not done. There have been times during this journey when I haven't been happy about it, but I am alive. And He's still working. What amazement to see such excruciating pain and unexplainable joy coexisting in my life!

"Consider it pure joy, my brothers and sisters, whenever you face trials of many kinds, because you know that the testing of your faith produces perseverance. Let perseverance finish its work so that you may be mature and complete, not lacking anything."

—JAMES 1:2–4

"But we also glory in our sufferings, because we know that suffering produces perseverance; perseverance, character; and character, hope."

—ROMANS 5:3–4

Katie

I started to follow influential Christian leaders like Christine Caine, Lysa TerKeurst, and Ann Voskamp on social media and found that to be healing. In doing that, my days were constantly flooded with timely encouragement and truths about God and His love for me.

One of Christine Caine's e-mails actually became my mantra as I waded through the deep and raging waters of grief. God will get you through what has broken your heart, those wounds you'll never forget (Christine Caine, e-mail to First Things First mailing list, February 14, 2015). That e-mail arrived on the first Valentine's Day after losing Jerod—no coincidence, I believe. I really fell in love with those words because so much of the time I was plagued by the facts that I knew I would never be the same ever again, and I would never just get over my loss like I figured some people expected me to.

This phrase also brings Psalm 23:4 to mind where David says, "Even though I walk *through* the darkest valley, I will fear no evil, for you are with me." And I love that he says "*walk through*," because with Jesus' help, I learned that I'm not going to camp out and pitch a tent in this valley shadowed by death. I'll walk *through* it. No marshmallow-roasting parties in this valley for me! My pastor also helped to remind me through multiple timely talks that I'm not going to die in this valley. Jesus will carry me through when I can't take another step, as He already has and as I know He will continue to do.

Grief plunged me into the deepest and most overwhelming ocean of unexpected loss, into the great unknown. I didn't know how to swim in an ocean this deep and often found myself pummeled by wave after wave of grief, unable to come up for air and fighting against every wave that came my way. Once I learned to let the waves come and go as they may and rest in the hope we have in Jesus, I learned I wasn't alone in my vast ocean of despair.

I was sorrowing, *but not without hope.*

CHAPTER 11

When Words Fail, Music Speaks

Katie

Within one month of the accident, I'd received the newest Chris Tomlin CD, *Love Ran Red*, from three different people, old friends and new. It was quite evident to me that this CD was to be my divine anthem on repeat for the time being. I just love when God is this obvious with me. It was overwhelming how God's gifts to me were so intentional.

My younger brother and I had gone to Passion City one Sunday a few weeks after the accident, finding seats in the back middle section. I like to believe I'm not a habitual eavesdropper, but I couldn't help but overhear the conversation taking place behind me to my left. Ladies in my row and the row behind me were chatting about two nurses who were going back to school. Being a nurse myself, I'm sure that detail was what caught my attention. One of the two nurses they were discussing had the same name as a girl who worked on my unit at work, Meredith. After listening a bit longer, I realized it *was* my friend from work who they were talking about. I debated whether or not to say anything, since I wasn't in the best spirits that day and didn't feel like being happy and social. I eventually decided to follow God's nudging and start a conversation with the lady beside me, the one I thought might be my friend's mother.

She actually turned around from talking to the lady behind us, looked at me, and said, "I hope you didn't get an earful."

"Oh, no problem," I said. "I actually think I know the girl you were talking about. I didn't mean to snoop or anything. I'm a nurse and work with a Meredith."

We then discovered that she was indeed talking about my friend. We continued to go back and forth about a few things with Meredith's job and mine before she asked my name. I told her and she looked at me with compassionate eyes. "Oh, I know about you," she said as she hugged me.

I'd mentioned being out of work for a few weeks due to being in an accident, so I'm sure between knowing those facts and my name, she was able to connect the dots. She introduced me to her husband as the service began. We worshiped together, and after the service she handed me a piece of paper with her name and contact information on it, as well as the Chris Tomlin CD. She told me to reach out to her if I ever needed anything and hugged me once more as we parted ways.

What an angel. God sent her to me that day. He led my steps to those exact seats because He knew I needed some extra encouragement that particular morning. I believe it was no accident or coincidence as there were thousands of seats to choose from in the auditorium, *but God* led us to those two particular seats so His chosen (available and willing) hands and feet could be an inexpressible comfort to me that day.

It was painfully obvious early on that the radio had to be off limits. I realized one day that even my own iTunes library was too much as these songs proceeded to play in this order: "40 Kinds of Sadness,"

"50 Ways to Say Goodbye," and "Misery Business." Even though some of those songs had nothing to do with my circumstances, they were more than enough to put me over the edge. For example, "50 Ways to Say Goodbye" was talking about something completely different, but it made me sad because I didn't even get to say one of them, one of my own ways to say goodbye to the love of my life.

I needed a controlled and safe environment in order to heal. Even the initial instrumentals of certain songs alone could steal away my breath and release an ocean of tears along with the flashbacks that were sure to follow. Initially, the only songs I listened to were those from Chris Tomlin's CD, and *wow*, were they so very healing! As more such songs came to my attention, I added them to my "healing play-list," which we will share in the appendix of this book. I could usually tell from song lyrics which artists had been through suffering; I gravitated toward those.

There were many songs that God provided for me at such divine times. I remember one evening in particular when I was walking to my truck after a long day at work and noticed a heart traced through the dirt on my driver's side window. This time it wasn't a song that brought on the tears, and they weren't even particularly bad tears. These were good ... *good* tears? This was new for me. And how thoughtful someone was to draw that heart! I left it there on my window for as long as I could stand the dirt, which turned out to be quite a few weeks. I just couldn't find it in me to wipe it off as it brought countless smiles to my tear-stained face every time I walked up and saw it again.

I believe it was that same day leaving work as I sat in my truck, buckled up, and turned on a local Christian radio station, hoping and praying I wouldn't regret the decision to forego the safety of my playlist. Jeremy Camp's song "He Knows" was currently playing on the station, the lyrics immediately grabbing the entirety of my attention. It was a timely reminder that He knows. God knows, sees, and cares about my pain.

I researched Jeremy Camp when I got home, only to be reminded that he'd lost his first wife to ovarian cancer just months after they were married and I realized the song was a product of his pain and suffering. I could only hope and pray that God would use me in amazing ways like he used Jeremy.

Music touched places that nothing else could. I remember Shane and Shane's albums, mainly their *Bring Your Nothing* album, being profoundly helpful and challenging during my heavy grief. Some of the most painful songs turned out to be just what my heart needed, the truth I desperately needed to hear and receive. The songs helped fix our eyes on Jesus, letting Him heal us from the inside out.

As I sit here in my living room typing these words, I'm listening to my Pandora piano hymns station, specifically "Take My Life and Let it Be" from *Hymns of Worship Volume 1*. Thanks to my upbringing as a Baptist pastor's daughter, I have a love and hunger for traditional music and hymns, as well as the newer styles. The station I created and listen to as I write provides calming truths as I relive the darkest parts of my life over and over again, which is necessary in writing this book in obedience to what I believe is God's calling on my life at this time. I often find myself in tears over the beauty of heaven's timing when the perfect God-given song begins to play, fitting the topic I'm writing about in that moment. Music is something special and a gift of worship that I pray I never take for granted.

Kevin

Music. So many thoughts flood my mind. Music connects so many of the senses and parts of us: smell, touch, memory, emotions, beliefs. Therein lies both its power, as well as its danger. Years ago, while taking a rare family trip out of state, my parents loaded us in the car to travel to central Kansas for my great-grandmother's funeral. On the trip, my dad wore out the new eight-track tapes he'd just purchased with music by Doug Oldham and also the Gaithers. Some of those songs have become cherished as much for the memories to which they are tied as the songs themselves.

Music has played a huge part in both our pain and our healing. Songs reminded us of truths that would be necessary to make it through our night, however long it might last.

To backtrack for just a minute, in the early days, we wanted Katie close so she wouldn't be alone and also so we could keep close watch on her state of mind. Most of the physical injuries healed in short order, but the emotional and psychological effects were still largely unknown. I repeatedly inquired as to her well-being, and when she disappeared for any length of time, we made a point to check on her. It was one such venture downstairs to which I refer.

It was a couple weeks after the living nightmare commenced that I was walking by Katie's room and couldn't believe what I was hearing. There were a lot of tears in the early days and a lot of reflection. Katie would pore over pictures of Jerod for hours and write in her journal. She and I share a common love—music. Not necessarily the same genre, but we both like to listen to music. As I walked by her bedroom, I heard a familiar song sung by voices I recognized. To make sure I was indeed hearing what I thought I was, I stood quietly out of sight for a few moments and listened to Shane and Shane sing one of their best songs, "Though You Slay Me." In this version, a clip of a sermon by John Piper regarding our suffering in light of eternal glory was edited into the song. It's become one of my favorites.

After the song ended, I entered Katie's room and expressed my amazement at her choice of songs. "Are you a glutton for punishment?"

"No. It speaks to me," she said, calmly. "I need it."

I sat down beside her to hug her but mostly because her response had buckled my knees. Only a couple weeks removed from the accident, she was playing a song based on Job's proclamation after losing everything, being falsely accused by his best friends, and dared by his wife to tempt God to exterminate him. He states that even if God strikes him dead, he will still trust Him, a proclamation I find hard to profess on the best of days, let alone the worst.

Music is powerful and it played a powerful part in our loss and life after it. Songs played a part in ways both expected and unexpected.

Some were too painful to hear while others, though painful, brought peace and healing. Still others encouraged us to fight on even as a handful brought immediate tears.

Katie had begun to build a playlist of both comforting and challenging songs, and we would often compare notes or alert each other to a new song that spoke deeply to our hearts. Sometimes, complete albums became tonic for our souls. Hillary Scott's *Love Remains* was one such album. So many of the songs spoke deeply to our hearts and with perfect timing. It was too much to be a coincidence.

We talk often now about our playlists. The timing of discovering a song and the timing of its play were confirmation of God's active presence in our situation, even when nothing else was visible. Not only that, but I'd find myself rising in the morning with a random tune on my mind, and then I'd realize that God had given me that song for my day. It was His gift to me. As Katie says, "It makes you feel so seen by God." It was as if God selected our playlist, and He did it before we ever needed it. So many artists, songs, and messages birthed before we needed them and delivered by a loving Father at the moment we needed them. God told Israel in Isaiah 65:24 that He would answer before they call. Music was this pre-request answer to prayer for us. It's almost too overwhelming to grasp.

For me, music was still a huge part of my life, and I listened to it often, especially in the car while driving. At church, it was a different story. For the first two months after Jerod's death, when I opened my mouth to sing with the congregation, the floodgates of tears released, making singing impossible. Open mouth … cry; it was reflexive. The songs may or may not have spoken to our situation, but it didn't matter.

I struggled with some of the songs' messages; they seemed to mock me. Where was this God who roars like a lion? What was He doing on October 9, 2014, when the God of angel armies went AWOL? I wondered if I would ever find joy in the songs that once meant so much to me. Listening was all I could do, and although music washed over my parched soul, it still seemed to bring pain to the surface and release it only to be immediately replaced by more. It was like Pitch Lake, one of the Seven Wonders of the World, a place I had visited on the island of Trinidad. No matter how much pitch was removed, it remained full. This was our life with tears.

Music is so powerful because it blasts right past our defenses with the truth or error that it brings. Some have attempted to minimize its power, but look around your car while stopped at a traffic light and observe other drivers listening to their radios. Music overcomes inhibitions, delivers messages beyond barriers, and elicits emotions. During a time of grief when open hands grasp for anything to grab onto, and blind and slipping feet search for anywhere to gain a foothold, good music becomes a piece of solid foundation. God is our Rock, but music provided multiple footholds on our Rock.

If you're reading this and you have input in the choice of songs for a funeral, be careful. Funerals take wonderful songs out of play. "Oceans" by Hillsong is just such a song. In 2014, it was named Song of the Year at the Dove Awards, and as Jerod and Katie's "song," and to honor Jerod's memory and their love, it was chosen for our exit from the funeral.

Once a favorite, "Oceans" has become the best song that none of us wants to ever hear again; it's too painful. It's also become quite cathartic if a good cry is on call. There couldn't have been a more appropriate message for Jerod's loved ones as they were ushered out into waters which swallow up the bereaved. But, to this day, we still find it hard to hear that song.

Just yesterday, Carrie Underwood's song "See You Again" came on at work and ambushed me with emotion. It took a few minutes of reflection to remember why—it was a song from my mother-in-law's funeral. Strangely enough, this experience taught me that the emotions could be tied to the song beyond the memory of the historical significance.

The song "Just Be Held" by Casting Crowns was particularly helpful. Grief can turn a person into that screaming child who beats on the parent in pain, anger, and frustration. In the image of God, the parent holds the child securely, preventing harm and simultaneously absorbing the painful blows and entering into the pain vicariously. Once the fighting has worn the child out, he or she will often melt into the arms of the parents and just be held. This is part of the battle of grief. Inside of us, the battle between trust and control rages. God wants us to come to the end of ourselves and learn to trust. Our fight often delays His comfort.

As we've walked this path since October 9, 2014, there is a growing list of songs that have found a special place in our hearts. Someone was moved to put words to paper about something that had happened in their life, and it became like medicine for our hearts. The timing and similarities of situations amazes me. Some songs seemed as if they were written solely for Katie or for us, songs like "Just Be Held" by Casting Crowns, "Tell Your Heart to Beat Again" by Danny Gokey, and "He Knows" by Jeremy Camp. Both Danny Gokey and Jeremy Camp have written about the early and untimely loss of their spouses. Dan Bremnes has a song, "Where the Light Is," that ministered to Katie's broken heart as well.

As I sat with Katie at Passion City Church, during his Comeback series, Louie Giglio told the backstory to Chris Tomlin's song "I Will Lift My Hands." I recall his exhortation to make a playlist of meaningful and uplifting songs, and that was another confirmation that we were on the right track. The truth resonated with us, and that's what we had been doing—building a playlist. It's a very important part of our journey as it gives voice to our inner groans, exhorts us to not give up, and reminds us that there isn't a test or trial that has come upon us that is totally unique. Others are walking the path in front of us; walk toward the sound of their song.

As a young man, I listened many nights to a soothing deep voice on the radio as I lay in bed. It was a program on the Moody Network hosted by Bill Pierce called *Songs In The Night*. His soothing voice, timely wisdom, and songs of faith were a wonderful companion for a teenage young man trying to find his way to adulthood. In the appendix, you'll find a list of *our* songs in the night.

Before, In, Above, and After the Storm
A Journal Insert from Kevin
July 15, 2017

A friend of mine and I have discussed limits of time and the effects they have on us. Surely, those limits have come into play in our story. We think in a linear timeline; but being outside of time, God is in the future already, and though He doesn't necessarily shield us from all of life's trials, He does prepare us for those events through happenings that seem to be random and disjointed from our present situation.

From her youth on, Katie has had a heart for spiritual things. While she was in high school, there was a group of young people, mostly college age, that occasionally went to an event called 722. It was a gathering led by Louie Giglio and his team at North Point Community Church. She loved to go along, as did a growing number of high schoolers, and it was her introduction to Louie Giglio, whose ministry has been priceless in these past few years of her life.

As the Passion Movement began to grow, eventually 722 went away, but not before one particular event. Coming across a book that had burst onto the scene called *The Shack*, I'd found a critical balance for the God of judgment I'd come to know during my formative years in conservative and overly legalistic Christianity. The love and unity within the Godhead portrayed in the novel, along with the extreme love of God for humans in the face of horrendous evil, had crafted a broader understanding of God's nature. My daughter became interested in the book and loved it, while still struggling with some of the portrayals of God. Why she was interested in such a book that, for her, addressed the problem of evil was a mystery to me but welcome.

We found out that William P. Young, the author of *The Shack*, was coming to 722. She didn't know of anyone else going and insisted (it didn't take much persuasion) that I go with her. We went and heard the story behind the story, which further intrigued me, and ended with us getting to meet the author and getting Katie's copy autographed. All of this was years before her own "Shack experi-ence" was to take place. God, in His providence, had begun to ready the foundation for the extreme weight that was to be laid upon it. The analogy of a bridge with a weight limit sign has been used to describe God's working in our lives to "not allow more on us than we can handle." Instead, we've found God to come in advance of a load far above the structure's ability to endure and to lovingly reinforce the bridge for the coming stress.

About a year before the accident, Katie told me one day about a podcast she'd heard. She'd been listening to the testimony of a lady whose husband had been taken by a bicycle accident on a highway near our home and had been touched by it. Recognizing the story, I shared with her that one of my bosses used to ride with this man. Andrew Pray was the worship leader of a church near us and had been hit by a bus while riding his bike on Highway 41 near Cartersville, Georgia. The testimony was of his wife, Courtney, and of God's pro-vision and her struggle to go on with her young children without her husband.

It touched Katie deeply. But why? Katie was a single young lady in her early twenties, getting established in her career as a nurse and had little besides her faith in common with Courtney. Why was her heart softened and even turned toward this story? Only God knew, but now we also know. Katie eventually met Courtney and shared her testimony with her. Courtney shared some of her insights with Katie, which have blessed her to this day. She's followed Courtney's chronicle and has been infused with hope by her engagement and marriage. Could it be that God, knowing what was coming, made sure that this story made it to the focal point of Katie's heart "for such a time as this?" I believe so with all my heart.

Katie will tell many more stories of God's grace, and you need to hear it from her as well, but there have been numerous instances of God going before her to prepare either the way or her heart so she wouldn't walk the path alone or be destroyed by it. From the family of origin to strategically placed people and events, to timely written and aired songs, God had done what the Bible says in Proverbs 3:5–6 (ESV), "Trust in the Lord with all your heart, and do not lean on your own understanding. In all your ways acknowledge him, and he will make straight your paths."

A song that was written by Scott Krippayne titled "Sometimes He Calms the Storm" expresses what we've experienced. When God chooses not to still the storm, He calms His child instead.

This truth was one to which I had given voice over the years but had mostly accepted by faith. Our family's path in recent years has proven it to be true, and now I stand in full assurance of it. In no way does that mean it's never a struggle, but as we continue to walk this path, we gather more and more evidence of the faithful love of God and His presence in the midst of the storm. He is before the storm, in the storm, above the storm, and after the storm. The only thing that changes is our perception, and we have come to believe that there are seemingly random events in motion now preparing either us or our environment for future things, both good and bad, to come.

"Before they call I will answer; while they are still speaking I will hear."

—ISAIAH 65:24

CHAPTER 12

Heaven's First Responders

Katie

Many people who are enduring or observing suffering often ask the question, "Where is God?" While I still have my questions for Him, I do know that He was very present in our pain. He came to us in a variety of forms: timely messages from my pastor, family and friends who spent time comforting me and listening to me cry and tell the same stories time and time again, strangers who became dear friends, making themselves available and stepping into my pain, taking some of it upon themselves, nature, and music, to name a few.

God went with my mom and me to the Grove (women's worship nights) at my church when I had the opportunity to hear from and meet a widow whose story had profoundly affected me long before my loss wrecked into my life. During the November Grove, speakers talked about gratitude in the unknown, the unexpected, and the mundane. I fought against my desires and human nature and strove to find things to be thankful for in the midst of my devastating loss, because there are always things to be thankful for, even in our darkest valleys. While that endeavor was highly difficult, it was possible. It took a few minutes, but I began to write.

1   Jesus' sacrifice for us on the cross. The story of the cross is something I understand better now, knowing the depths of despair and sorrow I'm now all too familiar with. Thanks to Jesus, even death is now life, and our loved ones no longer have to remain dead in a grave. Because Jesus is alive, so are our loved ones who were believers and have passed from this world to the next! They are more alive now than they've ever been and know Jesus in a way that they never could've known Him here on this earth.

2   The time I had with my sweet Jerod, our beautiful six months and nine days. I'm thankful God sent me this amazing man, literally beyond my wildest dreams, for a life mate of an all-too-short six months, a life mate nonetheless. He restored my hope. He forever changed me for the better.

3   Family, his and mine

4   Friends

5   Your Word

A basic list, but a win in my eyes, because I didn't think I'd be able to come up with anything.

Fast forward to January 2015 when God impressed upon my pastor to preach the "Hope Has a Name" series, specifically the "Hope Sinks" talk. I will *never* forget that Sunday for as long as I live. My heart was bleeding and desperate for hope. Our hope is Jesus. Pastor Louie talked about how Jesus is the cinderblock of hope that doesn't float; He sinks to the bottom of life's pits, however low that may be. Louie proceeded to tell a story about Ryan, a member of the production team at Passion City Church, who two Christmases before was in a car accident with his wife. My radar immediately went off; he had my full attention. They'd been t-boned on his side of the car, yet she was the one who died. It seemed totally backwards. Louie shared how

Ryan had been freed from the angst and the "why did she die and not me?" questions and how he was now happily remarried. That story alone spoke so much hope to me (Louie Giglio, Pastor of Passion City Church, Paraphrased from a sermon in the series "Hope Has a Name" in 2015, Hope Sinks).

Tears had already been flowing by that point in the story. I kept thinking I was done crying, but more tears kept coming with each new detail in the story. I felt like Louie was talking directly to me the entire time, like there was no one else in the room but me. The space seemed like it was getting smaller by the second, accompanied by a dizziness I experienced as I felt the walls were continuing to cave in around me. I sensed God's presence so near as I continued to sob. I'll never know on this side of heaven, but it actually seemed like Jerod was in on this one too, a total out-of-body experience that I hoped and prayed to have so many more of.

Louie invited anyone who needed prayer to stand from his seat. I knew I should have, but just couldn't for some reason. I continued to cry as I remained seated. He then announced that everyone didn't have to rush out, and if you needed prayer that you were welcome to head over to the access space and let someone pray for you. My mom asked if I wanted to and I just floundered. I didn't know what I wanted or needed at that point, and I was *not* one for any extra or special attention.

Thank you, Mom, for getting us there that unforgettable January day. A lady named Kimberly greeted us and led us into the access space where my mom immediately told her why we were there. She just said, "Wow," and her face started to look like she had a story to tell. She began to tell us that she'd lost her son four years prior. My tears had slowed, but they were now surging like an ocean down my face. Even my mom was crying, which was fairly unusual up until my family entered into our season of loss.

Kimberly asked a little about me, my name, the intended wedding date, Jerod's name, and a few other questions. She then asked if we would bend a knee and hold hands to pray. *Unforgettable.* We all sobbed together as she prayed for me and my mom, as well as the rest of my family and Jerod's. She then invited me to the Bible study she led in her home, inspired by her son, called Fully Alive Fridays. Meeting Kimberly and hearing Ryan's story was pivotal for me. I witnessed people further along in grief—those who had not only survived what I'd been enduring but who had also reached the point of thriving. I left Passion that day feeling so seen by such a great God! He is a good Father. He doesn't always give us what we want, but always what we need.

God continued to be ever present in my pain as He chose to use my sweet friend, Allie Shirley, to get me to Passion Conference 2015. It was during my "family group" time late one night at conference when I leaned into God's nudging to share my story publicly for the very first time. Family groups consist of around six to eight people. I tried to avoid dropping my bomb of darkness as I proceeded to evade any of the group questions, but I knew without question that God was leading me down that path of telling some of my testimony.

My heart was racing and my palms were sweaty. I asked God if He wanted me to share and if it would help anyone, and then I followed His lead. I didn't need an audible answer to know it's what He wanted, and I trusted Him. *Wow!* Sharing was *much* harder than I ever expected. I thought the fact that they were all complete strangers would make it easier. *Nope!*

I told them, "Well, I was trying to decide if I wanted to say anything, but I feel like I just need to. So, my fiancé and I were in an accident back in October and ..."

As I trailed off into the story, my voice became shaky, my eyes started leaking, and I got choked up; I could hardly get my words out. Everyone stared at me with wide eyes, their mouths gaping. It felt so good for me to get it out, like a pressure valve released. At that point, it was like word vomit. I answered the previous three questions from the group conversation that I hadn't previously answered in my avoidance. I'd stayed silent as I felt the pressure of having to tell my story building up.

My sharing led to our self-designated group leader, who said he'd usually be quiet and noncontributory, embracing vulnerability and telling his story about losing his fiancé to a breakup. I felt so much lighter. Everyone rallied around me and thanked me personally for sharing. I received some of the biggest and warmest hugs in response to my opening up. Obedience to God isn't always easy, but so worth it and so rewarding, even when you can't see or feel the reward.

Months turned into years as I continued to witness God moving in the middle of my darkest days. To the degree that I stepped out in faith and vulnerability, leaning into the pain and allowing God to use my experiences, He blessed every effort profoundly. One of my favorite times when I was able to physically see God using what little I had to offer was after I started attending a community group at church in the spring of 2015.

One particular night, I didn't feel like sharing my story yet again, because I didn't always want to be known as the girl who lost her fiancé in a tragic car accident. My loss was my entire life at that time, so it was hard to *not* mention my current situation while answering the deep life questions that would often come up while at community group meets. One opportunity after another was laid before me, almost to the point of not even having to grasp for it. That night, the chance to share was almost thrown at me, but I didn't take it because talking would mean crying, and crying is exhausting.

I'd shared multiple times before and had been blessed for it, and hearing my journey had helped others as well, but I just wasn't in the mood that night. *But God* had different plans for me. *But God!* I love *"but God"* stories! But God sent Christine Jarratt to me. As we were wrapping up the night, she saw the rock on my finger and asked when *that* was happening. *Here we go again ...*

At that time, it was too painful to take the ring off, but heartbreaking to leave it on as well. I didn't know what to do. *But God* did!

I answered Christine with the nutshell version of my story. She asked me to repeat it to make sure she'd heard correctly, as it was loud in the room where we were meeting. She expressed her sympathies, then genuinely asked how I was doing. She continually pointed me to Jesus and helped me realize that having my desired husband and family should only be a tool to further *His* kingdom and not mine, reminding me that my dreams were not as important as Jesus and His purposes. That night, I realized what an idol that dream had become in my life.

I told Christine that before the accident, I would've never spent that day before community group the way I did, reading the Bible and listening to podcasts, hungry for Jesus. Now, I have a raw desire for Jesus to a degree I never had before. Christine validated my thoughts as she said that desire is what she wants for people, to know Jesus in that way, but how unfortunate that often people must experience pain or loss to get there.

Once I told her that Jerod was a believer, she told me how Jerod and I were like partners in crime for Jesus, how we worked together here, while his relationship with Christ has now reached its fullness. We're still partners, though—I'm just finishing my job down here on earth. Once I join him in heaven, we'll have a better understanding of that partnership. I just loved this shift in my thinking. Thank you, Christine, for the truth you so boldly told my fragile heart that night, tenderly and with love, but all words I needed to hear. As she was talking, I remember thinking that I would've loved recording the entire conversation, but I'm thankful I journaled about it so I could remember the beautiful details.

Christine asked a few more questions, and I explained how I feel so heavy and weighed down with the tragedy. I still have flashbacks from the accident. She responded that only Jesus could lift those burdens and chains. She hugged me tight and asked if she could pray with me. I, of course, said yes and cried during the entire prayer as she hugged me and held my hands tight. She continued to stay seated and pray over me, even though everyone else was standing to worship with one last song, "Shout Hosanna." *That* was one of those moments ingrained so deeply into my memory that I'll never forget. There was something so heavenly about that moment, prayer with such severe and desperately needed truths being spoken over my life with a voiceover of worship to our King in the background.

Christine finished her prayer, then told me she wanted to connect me with Wendie, a woman who lived clear across the country in California. Wendie had lost a fiancé ten years prior and was now married with two kids. I've never felt a deep soul connection to someone I've never met like I have with Wendie. Texting with her about some of my darkest grief-stricken moments helped me to feel like I wasn't crazy for feeling certain things in grief. She was a best friend, even though we hadn't met—yet. We sent book-sized texts back and forth for quite some time. Her godly support, insight, and encouragement have been invaluable to me.

In the fall of 2017, we were granted a beautiful opportunity to get together for the first time. Since we already knew so many intimate details about each other before actually meeting, it was more like a reunion than a first encounter. The details of our being able to meet in Michigan, neither of our home states at the time, while I was visiting my family were so divine that we knew without question it was God who had orchestrated not only our time together but our entire friendship. Wendie and I have mentioned many times how we have both felt so incredibly blessed by our friendship.

God didn't waste my pain and transparency that night at community group, and He's used every bit of hurt I've turned over to Him. I've since been convicted to live wholeheartedly and undividedly for Jesus with open hands, willing to give back to God any thing or person He's placed in my hands, as well as open hands to receive His good gifts. In the giving and in the receiving, He is good, and we can trust Him with our hearts, knowing that we are safe with Him no matter our circumstances on this earth.

It was in the dark hours early one morning on my way in to work when I realized how clearly God was speaking similar truths to my heart. I was trying everything I knew to reconnect the Bluetooth on my phone to the radio in my truck so I could finish the Passion podcast I'd started the night before. I was so excited because I knew the best part of the podcast was still to come. I tried over and over again to no avail.

I finally called it quits as the radio automatically came on. I turned it until I got to a Christian station, the safest of options during that time of my grief. The *very* first words I heard were from Charles Stanley. He said something like this: "God doesn't just give you something and snatch it away" (Paraphrased from *In Touch* radio broadcast by Dr. Charles Stanley).

Wow! Coincidence? I think not. God nod? It seemed so! Dr. Stanley went on to talk about grace and other similar things, a great message. I didn't realize until later how desperately I needed to hear those words, because that's exactly what it felt like God had done. It felt like He'd given me Jerod just to snatch him back. But God is so much bigger than that with much bigger plans in mind. Nothing about the accident and its aftermath was actually about me. It's about Jesus and the people who have come to know or trust Him more from Jerod's testimony and the godly legacy he left us.

Something similar to that morning in my truck happened later when a dear friend and mentor of mine asked if it was okay to give my information to a friend of hers. That friend has a daughter who experienced something similar and had prayed for me from the beginning, knowing personally some of the pain I was enduring. The mother had called her daughter, Kalyn, to tell her about me. Kalyn had been listening to a podcast, but she paused it to talk with her mom. The first words heard when she returned to the podcast were those taken from 2 Corinthians 1:4, "We serve a God 'who comforts us in all our troubles, so that we can comfort those in any trouble with the comfort we ourselves receive from God.'" She knew in that moment that she needed to reach out to me, being further ahead on a similar path. I immediately got chills when I heard that story from my friend. Wow! God is working even when we don't see Him or think

He is. He's more involved than we will ever know on this earth, doing far more than we could ever hope or imagine.

January 14, 2015

Thank you, Jesus, for loving me so much to be intimately involved in the smallest details of my life. Please work with these ashes that I'm lying in facedown. Please turn them into something beautiful for Your kingdom, as only You can do. I love You!

A large portion of my healing actually came from messages I found that Jerod had already sent me, one of them being an e-mail that we could have never known would become so meaningful. He sent it the day before the accident, October 8, 2014, at 2:43 p.m.

Hey, this sounds fun. I would like to go. What are your thoughts, baby?

I love you forever. ♥

The content was nothing special. He was just asking me about us going to a Braves season-ticket-holder event. It wasn't the question that caught my attention, though; it was his final words in the e-mail. He'd told me that he loved me plenty of times before, but never coupled with the word *forever*. Even initially, it made me smile to read it, but wow, the power it holds now! I believe it was Jesus that day that prompted Jerod to type those words, knowing what a massive comfort they would be to me during the aftermath of his loss.

I love you forever too, Jerod.

I was scouring through his Facebook one day and found one verse reference on his "About Me" page. "Now to him who is able to do immeasurably more than all we ask or imagine, according to his power that is at work within us, to him be glory in the church and

179

in Christ Jesus throughout all generations, for ever and ever! Amen" (Ephesians 3:20-21). Those verses had already been some of my favorites, but now a new light had been shed on them. They were now *our* verses, as we had a front-row view to see the God of immeasurably more doing His work. And the best is still yet to come!

I found another timely Facebook message from Jerod. He told me, "I love you and want the best for you. The most full and filled life, the most joy, the most peace, the most love, the most tranquility, the most happiness, the most security, the most God-honored life possible! *I love you, Katie.* P.S. I've been praying a whole lot."

Even though he isn't here to assist in making my life the most of all of those things that he mentioned, he's now in perfect peace with the God he trusts wholeheartedly to take the best care of me in my days left here on earth. I printed that e-mail and the Facebook message Jerod had sent me. Then I laminated them so I could carry them wherever I went and see the prayers Jerod had prayed over my life, as well as the fact that he will love me forever. What unbelievable comforts they've been!

I've actually discovered so much more about Jerod since I found that message, and every last detail only makes me love him more. He used to text me priceless videos of him talking to me and being silly. I've watched them hundreds of times and experienced just about every emotion in doing so. Not only did he leave me touching messages, but he also left me his wonderful family.

His mother (Carol), his sister (Megan), and I have become something like the three musketeers of sorts, sticking together through thick and thin, but mostly thick, only because that's all we've known in our time together. We've laughed, cried, and acted crazy together. We all desperately needed each other and the support we gave one another, especially during those early and darkest days.

As the closest people in Jerod's life, we knew a level of unrelenting daily pain that few others experienced in the wake of his loss. I'm so eternally grateful for those two women. If only Jerod could see us all together now and the way we cut up and pick at each other—jokingly, of course. Jerod always made comments about how he wanted the top ladies in his life to hang out and be close. He could've never known, though, that he wouldn't be physically present as those relationships blossomed.

Katie – Jesus in the Unexpected

As I've said, I work as a pediatric nurse and was terrified to start working again due to fear of what I might see that would remind me of what I'd lost. But Jesus, of course, met me here too. I still wore my engagement ring at the time, and it wasn't long before this sweet family asked me about it. That was actually the first time I shared my story with a patient's family, and Jesus blessed me immensely through the sting of sharing. I could see it in their eyes; they felt some of my pain. They took some of it upon themselves. Somehow, it made me feel lighter.

The patient's father was a youth pastor at a local church, and the sharing of my story ended in that precious family circling around me and simultaneously praying the most heartfelt prayers over me. That experience was pivotal for me, reminding me yet again that Jesus really was walking in the valley of my grief with me, hand in hand, carrying me when I just couldn't take another step. I also learned that Jesus will use every bit of my willingness to share my story to bring glory to Him! But He doesn't stop there. Because He *is* God, He takes it one step further. He makes a way for my willingness to share to come right back around and bless me too! Nothing is wasted. For His glory and my good.

Meeting that family was like God saying, "See? Just wait. I see you. I hear you. I know you. I know where you are. I know you're hurting, and I love you. Beauty is coming."

The patient's grandmother had a peaceful, heavenly-sounding voice as she spoke encouragement over me, telling me how God loves me so much and He knows my pain. He's been there, and I can trust Him. She talked about how diamonds go through a tough process of becoming beautiful, how they're put under fire and stress. Then after they're made, you still have to polish and refine them. Encouragement kept flowing out of that room. The grandfather said to me later that day how he could tell from my countenance when I walked into their room that I was different. That I loved Jesus. That I was anointed. What a special day and an unexpected venue for such healing to take place. God truly is walking every step of this journey alongside me.

Some of my earliest encouragement came in the form of a card from a stranger, Laura, who had heard of my story through a close mutual friend, Dee Dee, who had asked for prayer for my family and me after the accident happened. Laura asked for my information and sent me one of the most wonderful cards with timely grief tips. She told me that even though I felt so alone, I was not. She'd lost a fiancé many years prior and was reaching out to make herself available for any support, being very familiar with what I was sure to be experiencing during those initial days of grief. These were some of her tips:

1 Be prepared, the next two months are going to hurt, and it will be hard for even the most well-meaning people to understand. If you need to, allow yourself to skip happy holiday celebrations. People who love you will understand.

2 It is okay to grieve for as long as you need to, and do not let anyone convince you otherwise.

3 You *will* laugh again, and when you do, try not to feel guilty about it.

4 You are not weak if you cry—even if it seems like you start for no reason.

5 Although the pain will ease as years go by, you will always have a sensitive spot in your heart.

6 Survivor's guilt is real. Do not let it eat you alive.

7 As much as it hurts right now, do take care of yourself.

8 Above all else, listen to your heart, not to other people. When you are able to move forward with other relationships, you will know.

Profound advice from someone who would become a dear friend, one who would sit across from me at Panera for hours on end listening to me blab about whatever hurt my heart was feeling that day. Tears were always a part of our time together, especially because I knew I could be transparent with her about what I was feeling, knowing that she just knew. She'd been there.

Some of the most memorable words Laura told me were as follows: "I remember bringing myself to the point of constantly repeating to myself that God authorized an early homecoming that I did not. It was so hard to submit to the fact that God is God and I am not. I never wanted to play God, but I sure as heck wanted my fiancé back, just like you want Jerod back. I do believe with everything in my heart that God has a plan for your life as well as mine, and even though it feels like He has abandoned us in a dark chasm at times, I am confident that there is something more, and maybe we will catch a glimpse of it on this side of heaven. If there is anything at all I can do for you, let me know. It is so hard, and you are not alone."

That's how it went for months. God kept sending person after person to me through so many different venues to help me along to the next step and to remind me that I was on His radar. Complete strangers continued to send me cards (some sent multiple timely cards), and some people met with me to share their stories of redemption, which instilled so much hope in my heart that my life would not always be so hard and look so dark.

I also received a Happy Heart Box from a dear friend, Dee Dee, that first holiday season. The thoughtful gift lifted my spirits and brought a smile to my face and to my heart. The box was filled with pretty, girly, and inspiring things, like a bracelet, scarf, and cards with inspirational words on them, etc. I didn't know what giving back to others would look like on the other side of my grief, but I knew after receiving that special box that I wanted to do something. I didn't want to go through hardship for nothing. I wanted to do something with the encouragement I received from others, like Pastor Louie had explained once. He likened it to a sponge. We soak up the vitality and encouragement from our community and from others to the point where we are overflowing with all of it. We then need to take that fullness and encouragement we've absorbed and wring it out on others until we're dry again, just to soak up more goodness.

I made a dear friend, Kristen, at a retreat in Ellijay, Georgia. I *didn't* want to go and almost bailed, despite the two-hour rainy drive to get there and the hundred dollars I'd already spent to attend the weekend retreat. I was lost in heavy rainfall on dark, scary, tree-covered gravel roads. But if my time with my new "frenemy," grief, has taught me anything, it is to persist for things that matter. I had no idea the healing, peace, and hope that the weekend would bring, but I committed myself to finding the place. The very place I'd switched my entire weekend of work, including Friday, to be there. Not to mention, I was missing my nephew's second birthday to be present. The retreat where initially there was no room for me—but accommodations were made.

I truly felt like a new woman when I returned home after that weekend. But, at first, I absolutely couldn't wait to leave and get back to the comfort of my bed and technology, since we were in the mountains with no signal. As it turned out, I was the *last* person to leave.

Kristen had asked about my ring at one of our meals that weekend, not knowing the weight of what was coming with my answer, and with that explanation came the ever-faithful companion, tears. We ended up spending most of our waking time together that weekend, complete strangers who turned into dear friends. Kristen had endured many major hardships in her own life and had a perspective on things that changed the way I grieved in the best way.

Her creative mind comes up with the most perfect and beautiful analogies for every situation, something that speaks so well to me, being a visual learner. She talked to me about "future tripping" and how worrying about things that hadn't happened—or may never happen—could drain me of strength needed for today, making me trip where I was at in that moment. I'm honestly still working on being completely present in the day I'm in and not worrying about what lies ahead or the things we can't control.

Kristen told me a few other grief analogies that will forever stick with me. She said, "Grief is like throwing a journal into the creek. That is the tragedy. But to move forward, you have to start peeling away the pages one by one. It's a long and tedious process. Meticulous. But if you don't do this, the pages dry up and get all smudged, becoming an impossible task to do later. As painful and annoying as this process of peeling the pages of your story apart can be, it's necessary. And in this process of grief, you are naturally in a very exposed position. You don't have to stay that way, though. You don't have to expose your underbelly. Start politely saying no to things. You don't have to talk about it or go to that painful place if you don't feel up to it or don't have the energy to do so."

Kristen's analogies weren't always easy to absorb. I didn't want to hear some of them, but they were still necessary, nonetheless. "All of the emotions of grief, pain, and tragedy in life are like bricks, each one a heavy burden. Anger. Bitterness. Anxiety. Loneliness. Depression. Guilt. Regret. You can either carry this heavy bag of bricks around *or* you can use them to build a foundation."

Kristen's words and friendship challenged me and helped me realize that even though my story may not be beautiful right now, it will be one day. She encouraged me to keep going because I have to stick around to see the beauty that God will create from my story and my pain. My life will be beautiful again in time. It may always be messy because—let's be real—life is messy, but it will be a beautiful mess.

It was even the analogies for daily living that were so comical and helpful. Kristen once told me, "Being a depressed and glass-half-empty person is like picking up poop after your dog, putting it in bags, and stapling it to yourself. The more bags you add, the heavier and stinkier you get. You get used to them though, living in it all. Other people, however, don't like being around you because you stink so badly."

We made it a point as we were both nearing the first-year anniversaries of our losses to try to celebrate the lives of Jerod and Kristen's father while still paying our tearful respects to them. It truly is a precious gift that God has given me, all of the dear friendships that have emerged and blossomed out of the ashes of my loss—additional family and new friends who I love and will cherish for the rest of my life here on earth.

Not only people, cards, meals, or the like, it was also unexpected baskets of encouragement and church signs! God used anything and everything in all of His grand creativity to walk me through this valley.

My great-aunt Joan and her church sent me a thoughtful "promise basket" in the mail. It was full of everyday and household items with applicable Bible verses attached to each item.

- **Comb:** "Indeed, the very hairs of your head are all numbered. Don't be afraid; you are worth more than many sparrows" (Luke 12:7).

- **Pillowcase:** "When you lie down, you will not be afraid; when you lie down, your sleep will be sweet" (Proverbs 3:24).

- **Kleenex Pack:** "He will wipe every tear from their eyes. There will be no more death or mourning or crying or pain, for the old order of things has passed away" (Revelation 21:4).

- **Heart Cookie Cutter:** "Because of the Lord's great love we are not consumed, for his compassions never fail. They are new every morning; great is your faithfulness" (Lamentations 3:22-23).

- **Dollar Bill:** "And my God will meet all your needs according to the riches of his glory in Christ Jesus" (Philippians 4:19).

- **Flower Mug:** "And to know the love of Christ that surpasses knowledge, that you may be filled with all the fullness of God" (Ephesians 3:19 ESV).

- **Candle:** "The Lord is my light and my salvation; whom shall I fear? The Lord is the stronghold of my life; of whom shall I be afraid?" (Psalms 27:1 ESV)

A blog I'd written called "Woman, You Are Highly Favored" touches on the story about the church sign. Read on to find that blog post.

Woman, You Are Highly Favored
by Katie Neufeld
May 31, 2015

My engagement ring is the most beautiful ring I have ever seen. Of course I'm partial, but I just love it. We picked it out together, and Jerod knew it was the one that I without question loved the most. Now there are days when I get so angry about the current circumstances of my life that I can hardly stand to wear the ring because of the emotional pain it causes me. So, I start to reconsider if I want to continue wearing the ring all the time.

Despite my grief, I've decided that it's not time to take it off yet. My ring has surprisingly been a tool through which God has been bringing healing to my hurting and broken heart. Oh, the irony that one of the very things that so often surfaces the deepest aches, pains, and brokenness could also make way for my healing. This, my friends, is without a doubt the hand of God in my life. I love when I'm able to see so clearly His work in my life ... to know He is still there ... to know that I am not forgotten ... to know that He is doing something with these broken pieces ... to know ... or have a growing hope that my story is not yet over.

Some of the venues God has used to bring healing have been totally unexpected too. I would actually deem the various places He has used as some of the most unlikely. I'm not sure why I make these assumptions though, because one thing I've learned about God through all of this is to expect the unexpected, unlikely, and seemingly impossible.

He permeates the unexpected, the unlikely, and *the impossible. He can use them all ... We just have to give them to Him.*

I recently had to part with my rings so that two loose diamonds could be fixed. One diamond had already fallen out of my ring a while back, so that made it slightly easier to part with them for a few days. I felt like I left my child with a stranger. I also felt naked and lonely without them. The guy who helped me must have sensed all of that, because as I walked out of the store, he told me, "We'll take good care of them."

The weekend started out depressing with having to leave my rings behind and only got worse as I drove home Friday night. I started seeing boats and jet skis heading up to the lake for the holiday weekend, one that was so amazing and unforgettable for me last year. The pain was suffocating; it felt like a stubborn elephant sitting on my chest.

Once I got home, I spent another lonely Friday evening staring at the wall, going in and out of sleep, until I was finally tired enough to go to bed. Saturday morning proved to be a much-welcomed guest—it was like the fresh crisp air after a good rainstorm. A stranger (I think) paid for my breakfast in the Chick-Fil-A drive thru. That person will never know how much that meant to me and how impeccable the timing. Somehow, that individual's generosity made me feel incredibly loved, like God had placed me there in that particular moment to receive a sweet gift.

Woman, you are highly favored.

Those words became the theme of my morning. And it wasn't hard to come to that conclusion when God smacked me in the face with those exact words posted on a church sign I drove by on my way home. "Woman, you are highly favored." Chills shot through my entire body. Our heavenly Father must know that He has to be very obvious with His loving gestures or I will completely miss them as they slip into the heavy fog of my grief.

That morning, everything was obvious.

Woman, you are highly favored. So much so that this meal is on Me. So much so that I want you to know that this is all from Me, so here is a very clear message for you. Look at this church sign. Woman, you are highly favored. And while I am at it, have this cloud that I made just for you. It is shaped like a heart with an arrow going through it. Because I love you. Because I care so deeply about you. Because you are mine.

Woman, you are highly favored.

Katie

I didn't really consider the significance of that one particular church sign until much later in my grief, but there it so faithfully stood along the main path I traversed time and time again from my parents' house to the closest nearby town. There it stood in silence, preaching many desperately needed truths and love to me, always delivered right on time.

Just a few months after that initial sighting, I drove by again and saw the sign had been changed to, "If you are going back to school, God is too." Its messages were nothing fancy or over the top, but they were always just a little nudge from God to my aching heart. And here He was reminding me again, *Hey! I'm still here with you. No matter where you go. How deep or wide you go. I'm along for every bump, turn, crash, and stall in the road.*

And no matter how long the road, He kept gently nudging me to just keep going. Take one more step. Keep going because as followers of Jesus, no matter what happens, we still win! Because in light of our earthly perspective, the best is still yet to come!

Keep going because unbeknownst to you in that moment, God is weaving threads into a beautiful tapestry. It's difficult to tell in the moment how God is using or directing you, but know that He is.

Kevin

Initially, there was another group of caregivers that were the hands and feet of Jesus to us. Our focus was on caring for Katie, and as is often the case, caregivers put their own needs in the background to handle the triage of the moment. We did as well. We took time off work, interrupted our schedules, missed our own church family to be with Katie, and altered our lives in many ways.

One of the reasons we made it through grief's early days is that we had others who cared for us. Initially, extended family rushed at great expense to be at our side. Meals were brought in to us for several weeks. Members of our church rallied around us in prayer and offered a listening ear when we gathered with our Bible study group. Random phone calls or messages asked what we needed. Others to whom we had ministered during times of their great pain and loss rallied to our aid in a knowing way and yet with limited words.

Many struggle for what to say, but those with unwanted experience in grief and loss know there is very little that can be said. One dear friend who had lost a sister and her sister's son (her nephew) in an accident came alongside us in support. That kind of sacrificial act means so much more to us today because we know the pain and heartache that it brings back just to show up. Even as we have written about our story, the pain is dredged back to the surface and the pain of loss is emotionally draining. Katie has even been tormented by the recurrence of nightmares some nights. Loss hurts ... caring hurts as well.

Members of a family who had been through their own loss just several years prior to ours became a lifeline to us. They were the first family to join our small flock in West Georgia after our arrival to lead that church. Our kids had grown up together, and without family in the area, they'd become our family in many ways, especially during holidays we spent at home. Their sixteen-year-old son was one of the most delightful children we knew, and though he was not one for a lot of words, his smile was infectious. Their son, who was a specimen of fitness and committed to a life someday in the military, went unconscious while playing basketball with friends at his house. After several days of living at the hospital as all efforts were made to save his life, he went to heaven. We stood with this family, though I was no longer their pastor during that time, and tried to be of some encouragement.

Russell and Lisa and their family had moved to a different community, and we were no longer at the church where we met, so we had limited contact ... until Katie's accident. Once again, we found ourselves crying and grieving together, but this time our roles were reversed. Because of their experience, they were present with such words of comfort and encouragement, and they remained present for us as we navigated the dark valley.

I recall several bits of wisdom they shared with us that prepared us for where we were going. "You are numb right now; you don't know it yet, but you will. You think the pain can't get any worse, but it will. We still hurt from our loss, but *know* there are good days still ahead of you, though there will be times you won't believe it." Truer words have never been spoken.

A little word here about such a statement. Those who have not been through loss tend to try to stop tears and speak soft, encouraging words. Only someone who has been through loss would be so bold as to tell us that it gets worse, *a lot worse*, before it gets better. That was invaluable to us, especially when followed by the assurance that there will also be better days ahead. Their experience gave them that wisdom, and we needed it spoken into our lives. Pain and loss gives credentials, but there is a cost in personal pain to be that involved. And the opportunity to be that for others is the driving force behind our writing.

In twenty-eight years of vocational ministry, I'd seen some tragic losses. Though many of them as followers of Jesus had risen up, even beside the casket to boldly proclaim God's faithfulness and wisdom, I'd also seen these public professions followed by private meltdowns. Having never gone through the type of loss we now faced, we didn't fully understand, but we've learned to give room for grief. No two situations or people are the same, and we all mourn differently. For example, I put a memorial sticker on my car for Jerod, something I'd thought of as a little too sentimental previously, but now use as occasion to pray for a car's occupants. So many carry private pain that no one around will ever know.

Emerging from the valley of grief, we wonder just how those without Jesus make it. If this world is nothing but random pain followed by death, especially untimely death, what is the point? Thankfully, faith was interwoven in our foundation like rebar in concrete construction. But even concrete can have chunks knocked loose by accidents and trauma. Believers aren't spared from the pain of this life, but we have meaning and hope in our pain.

Even this book was birthed from our desire to live out our faith publicly and honestly. We didn't want to portray the stoicism that is often carried as a façade to be a testimony to the watching world. Jerod's death hurts … still. It stinks … still. It doesn't make sense … still. But thanks to Jesus and His children, we've navigated the dark night and have emerged with stronger faith, stronger hope, and stronger purpose.

CHAPTER 13

Your Breakthrough is Coming

Following is the story of a life impacted by Jerod and the events of his home-going.

Breakthrough: My Testimony
by DeAnna Welsh

I've told short versions of this story a few times on Facebook and Instagram, but I've always felt they didn't quite encompass the magnitude of change that occurred within me and in my life at the time. So here I can go more in depth, and I truly hope these words "pay it forward" and someone is changed from it like I was. I used to be afraid to "go tell it on the mountain," but now I'm bursting at the seams, and I hope to never contain myself. This is my testimony.

I had become a pro at going through the motions. During the week, I submerged myself in motherhood and work. My two boys were top priority as always, and little did they know they provided a much-needed distraction from the chaos I folded neatly and tucked away in the back of my mind. I'd left their father after nearly six years of marriage and was stunned that my life had taken the turn it did. In rare, quiet moments I would get overwhelmed with the reality that I was a divorced mother with two little guys who depended on me. I was wrought with thoughts of failure and plagued with guilt that this was the best I could do for them. I'd always promised myself that I would never divorce. That no matter what, I'd find a way to make it work, and I would endure whatever pain and loneliness it took to avoid putting my two precious boys through divorce.

But suddenly there I was. Despite many attempts at saving our marriage, I realized there was something missing between us, and sadly, we never figured it out. I moved my sweet boys out of the home they knew and had failed at the one thing I'd promised not to. The guilt was heavy, and yet every time I looked into their big, blue eyes I felt their unconditional love. I didn't deserve it.

For a long time, I tried to make it up to them. I became obsessed with being as present as possible when I was with them. I wanted to soak up every second, remember every funny thing they said, keep them close, and was anxiously aware that my time with them as children would one day be over. That wasn't necessarily a bad thing, but on the weekends they spent with their father, I found myself completely lost. When they weren't there to distract me from all the pain, guilt, and fear held in my mind, I began to look for other distractions.

During my darkest days, I found myself in places I'd be ashamed for my parents to find me, much less my children. When the boys were away, I used alcohol to numb the painful reality that I was a thirty-something divorcee. The scarlet letter "D" burned a hole in my heart each time someone asked about my marital status or asked me or the boys, "Where is your husband/father?"

Judgmental comments were overheard many times, and often I felt like an inadequate woman whose status only reflected the fact that I was "used goods" with a lot of "baggage." Those labels seemed to overshadow the mother I was to my children and the hard work I put in every day to support us on my own. To make myself feel better, I entertained relationships that were superficial, and after having my heart broken a few times, I came to the conclusion that feeling nothing had to be better than feeling anything at all.

I'm not one to feel sorry for myself, so I began strategically numbing myself to all emotion. I carefully built an impenetrable wall around my heart. I distanced myself from friends and family. When someone mentioned God, I'd dismiss the thought that He had nothing better to do than to deal with my mistakes. I'd made my bed in life and accepted things the way they were. I truly believed love didn't exist outside of movies and books. I wasn't happy for my friends and family who proclaimed love for someone; I pitied them for believing in something they'd eventually find out to be a lie. During those days, my world was very dark and quiet when my children weren't around. Saddest of all, I was perfectly okay with it. I'd convinced myself I could do life alone with no help from God, family, or friends. Without them, it was easier to deny emotion, and that had become the only life I was comfortable living.

Little did I know that while I had let go of God and love, He still had a very firm grip on me.

One day my step-mother suggested a Tae Kwon Do class for the boys and their cousin. She signed them up for a month to try it out, and they ended up really enjoying it. So, every week I'd take them to class, and the change I witnessed in them was enough to pull me ever so slightly out of the darkness I'd been in for so long.

I hadn't realized until they began to develop a relationship with their instructor just how hungry they were for a male leader in their lives. Their little-boy hearts grew bigger, and they stood taller with each class. Mr. Hicks provided the discipline and confidence they'd yearned for that I simply could not provide on my own, and I saw them blossom under his guidance for many weeks. Throughout that time, I became amazed. They inspired me, and slowly I felt warmth flow back into my stone-cold heart each time I saw Mr. Hicks show kindness and love to his students.

There was a familiarity in his eyes. At first I didn't recognize what it was. It had been so long since I'd opened myself up to see Jesus that

I could hardly make out His light shining through those kind eyes as he taught my boys. I remember sitting in that metal chair as my boys kicked and shouted, tears burning my eyes as I held them back, realizing that the same light shining from Mr. Hicks was buried deep somewhere inside me too. The thought scared me, and I was afraid to chip away at the wall I'd so carefully built the last few years.

I've always been a huge fan of music; it's been relevant my whole life, and often it's been a song that either brought me solace during a difficult time or sometimes ignited something within that brought forth clarity and perspective. During the late days of September and early days of October 2014, it seemed the song "Oceans" by Hillsong United was always playing when I turned on the radio or even when I was in a store or some other place where music would be playing in the background.

After noticing this a few times, I began to listen to the lyrics. I wasn't quite sure I could relate to the Holy Spirit giving me the kind of trust needed to go wherever God would lead me. It was a beautiful song, and I couldn't help but feel the tug in my soul each time I heard it, though I couldn't explain why.

One evening as I was preparing dinner for the boys, I received an e-mail that said Mr. Hicks had been in a terrible car accident and class had been canceled. I silently prayed he'd be okay and went about the rest of my evening, though in the back of my mind, I wondered if things were actually going to be okay.

On Friday, October 10, 2014, I received an e-mail that confirmed what all of us—parents and students—had feared. As I sat my phone down in shock after reading that e-mail, "Oceans" began to play on the Pandora station I'd been listening to. I fell to my knees on my kitchen floor. It was clear to me in that moment that God was trying to tell me something. I still didn't know what, and I didn't understand if it had anything to do with Mr. Hicks. All I knew is that I needed to start listening, and the wall had to come down.

On Tuesday, October 14, 2014, my boys and I walked into the doors of West Ridge Church for the first time. I'd been in church off and on my whole life, but it had been a long time since I'd felt the presence of God. As I sat down in my seat, it was undeniable that He was there with me. Mr. Hicks was lying peacefully before us. His family and friends told story after story, making it apparent that Jerod Hicks didn't need a eulogy; his life was his eulogy. He left this world a much better place than when he first got here. He was obedient, he was fearless, and above all, he allowed Christ to shine through him so others could be saved.

As the service came to an end and they began to move Mr. Hicks's casket out of the room, I heard the familiar beginning of the song that had become the theme to those last several days. The hair on my arms stood up, and tears flowed freely from my eyes. I surrendered to it all. The wall came crashing down, and I sat in that chair in the arms of my two sons weeping in the midst of a love so intense it overcame the years of numbness and brought me out of the dark. I was home. My Father wrapped His arms around me, and it became clear in that moment, He'd been leading me there for some time. He'd never let go. He'd never given up. And for the first time in years, I felt worthy of love, and I believed in it.

My life has not been the same since.

"Breakthrough" is the name of Mr. Hicks's Tae Kwon Do school, and I don't know what exactly he had in mind when he came up with that, but that place was the catalyst for the biggest breakthrough in my life and the life of my boys. My boys and I knew him as the instructor of that school for six months. In just a short time, his obedience to God and love for people impacted our lives in ways I could have never imagined.

I've been attending West Ridge Church ever since that day in October 2014. Soon after that day, I realized what those lyrics meant to me: My trust in Him has no borders. In the last few years, I've faced situations that have required huge leaps of faith and enormous amounts of trust. Through it all, I've kept my eyes on Him, and He has constantly reminded me Who I belong to. He presented love to me not long after that breakthrough, and my feet wandered into territory where I'd once decided to never tread again.

God brought Bradley, a man who would later become my husband, into my life and taught me how to love like Jesus through some of the toughest tests of love and faith I have ever experienced. I'm no longer content with being alone, and I have an understanding of marriage that I've never had before. My husband and I are members together at West Ridge and have fire in our hearts for Christ. Each day, I find myself bursting with love and joy. Instead of walking in darkness, I strive to shine the same light that saved me. If you'd told me a few years ago life would look like this, I wouldn't have believed you.

I used to think those passionate hand-raisers in church were strange; now I know where their passion comes from. His love, the relentless pursuit of our hearts, and the infallible grace He gives amazes me every day. This must be how David felt when he wrote Psalm 103:2, 4. "Praise the Lord, my soul ... who redeems your life from the pit and crowns you with love and compassion."

I hope this post somehow conveys His love—that glorious and unfailing love He has for us all—and how critical it is for us to fill ourselves up with it so we can give it away.

Katie

While DeAnna's testimony speaks for itself, I'm amazed as I consider how our worst day was the moment that God used to dramatically change her life's trajectory. Don't discount the way God may still be using you even when you feel you're at your lowest with nothing left to give. When you're running on empty. Trust that the God who holds all the moments won't let one of them go to waste.

It Came to Pass
A Journal Insert from Kevin
March 5, 2016

It is not until now, March 2016, that I felt like I could write the words for this post; some things just take time. You won't be able to see clearly until you look back in retrospect, but knowing what is going on—what to expect—will help as you go through the seasons of grief. In August of 1978, my journey took me to Bible College in northwest Indiana. During my years there, we went through several very hard winters, including the blizzard of 1979. During one winter, the temperatures dropped below zero for a month straight. I remember because I worked outside! I was the weekend replacement at the full-service islands of the truck stop where I worked. Temperatures approached zero during the week, only to plunge at the end of the week to twenty to thirty degrees below zero. One question remained. Would it ever get warm again?

Like experiencing a never-ending winter, it's normal to think while grieving that the current pain will last forever or that the light is gone forever out of your world. The situation seems so permanent (some parts are) and so debilitating that hope can be lost. What I'm sharing is for those who find themselves in that frame of mind.

There are definitely seasons of grief, and others have written about them and broken them down. My purpose is not to come up with a list, because we find that there are variations from one to another. The anger stage was not one that was really part of my experience. It surprised me that there never were really any feelings, good or bad, toward the driver of the vehicle whose choices that day ended Jerod's life, shattered Katie's dreams, and ripped out the heart of a family and a business. Actually, I have more anger as I write about it now than I felt at most any time since, so maybe my anger stage is yet to come.

The point is that things *will* change but never as fast as we wish they would. Looking back, we've gone through periods of shock, denial, survival, and healing. As I've taken time to reminisce, it's much clearer now than ever. Distance and time have given us a clearer perspective. The following is what I've observed in Katie's world.

Initially, we surrounded her to help her just stand on her own feet. She took extended time off work. Her job as a nurse had many emotional triggers that she needed to be shielded from initially. What we could not provide was empathy. We loved her, but she was walking a road we'd never walked, and we were little help navigating it. God, in His grace, provided contacts who did what we could not. Oftentimes in pain people ask, "Where is God?" We didn't have to wonder. He came to my daughter in the form of others who had experienced similar losses.

Katie made contact with a couple of ladies who had lost fiancés tragically. One made herself available to Katie for talks over a shared meal on multiple occasions. Several times, they must have talked for four to five hours. Another who continues to bless Katie is a dear friend she has yet to meet. This friend lost her high school sweetheart, a marine, to the war on terror as he gave his life on foreign soil. She and her husband have provided valuable wisdom as our daughter has navigated her dark valley, but especially during the early days of shock. During that season, many others gathered around us, providing meals, prayer, support, and encouragement. Family from Michigan and Colorado, friends from church, and friends of Jerod spoke words of comfort and compassion.

There was also a season of excruciating pain; that lasted for months for Katie. As much as it helped to walk with those who had similar experiences, a certain amount of loneliness is still experienced by the griever. No two losses are alike. Let me say it one more time for emphasis: *No two losses are alike.* Let it sink in. Part of the grief process is very personal, and no one else can do it for you. I feared that part the most. We could surround Katie with multiple layers of support, but we couldn't put the fight in her to survive. Would she retreat into a dark cave never to return, or would she emerge victorious? Going into the cave is not a choice, but coming out is.

To our great relief, she has come roaring out. She has the heart of a lion. As a result of this lonely season, made more lonely by the type of loss she experienced, she's discovered strength that has amazed everyone around her. This strength has come from the Father she grew to know better while in the cave. Over the years, she'd come to *own* her faith in God, but in the last year and a half she has come to *know* the God of her faith.

It seems there was also a season of rest. Limit the variables. Just breathe. During that time, we tried to do things that kept Katie, and even us, outside of the cave. It felt like we were trying to distract, but it was important to have some things to look forward to. Katie and I went skiing in Colorado, and we also went to Las Vegas on a trip I'd won at work. Evenings at home were spent as a family just sitting together in casual conversation.

There was a distinct change as she moved into the season of healing. For the first year, all of our attention was directed to the past that hurt, the dream that had been lost, and the next step. Having stabilized, we then began to raise our heads and dare to look further down the road. For Katie, that began with a two-day retreat. She called me on her way home to inform me that she'd just had her "weekend at the shack," referring to the bestselling book by William P. Young. She bubbled over as she told me about her experiences. As it turned out, who she met while there was more important than the weekend itself.

It was a very unlikely friendship with a new friend who was God's agent in turning Katie's head. Kristen's role in Katie's story was quickly clear. Spring was coming. This friend was so different from Katie in age, temperament, life situation, and many other ways. She had her own story of survival, but she helped bring out the fighting spirit needed for Katie to thrive.

Katie's church also became very important during that season. Her pastor, Louie Giglio, had many words that seemed to be just for her. Timely messages connected with her, and she began to look for opportunities to serve. She started attending classes at Orange Theory Fitness and also signed up for a 10k and half marathon on back-to-back days. Ready to have her own place, she's put a contract on a house and is well on her way to building her new life. She's even begun to date, something she never envisioned having to do again.

Recently, in our Bible study group at church, prayer was asked for a particular individual who had made a series of bad choices with disastrous results. This dear couple was saying how it was more than they could handle to keep attempting to rescue this person. I took the opportunity to share with the class what we had learned from walking through this period with our daughter.

No single person is sufficient to be all that another needs.

My wife and I have given ourselves to our daughter, but there are others that God has brought into her life, many others, who have each had a part in her healing. We each do what we can do, but none of us is enough on our own. We have limitations, and we need to learn to accept them.

Here is what we have learned about seasons of grief:

1   There are seasons of grief. Things will change. Keep on struggling. Don't give up.

2   There will be different people sent into your life during each season. Some will come and go, others will come and stay, and some will leave. Don't expect any one person to be your "everything," except God.

3   Learn to recognize God's hand and His grace in those He brings into and takes out of your life.

4   Accept your seasons. Yours may differ from others you know. Enjoy both the similarities and the differences. Variety is the beauty of life.

5   You could be the key to someone else's season change. Be alert.

CHAPTER 14

I Don't

Katie

I knew the next time I stood face-to-face with death would be too soon. Except this time, it wasn't my mortality that was at stake. We knew my fourteen-year-old dachshund, Roxie, was entering the beginning of the end as her health continued to decline throughout the summer of 2016.

That girl helped me blow out the candles at my sweet sixteen and had been my faithful furry friend through my darkest of nights, sensing my pain as she would cuddle up next to me. The vet believed she was suffering from congestive heart failure, which in turn made it difficult for her to breathe. She would find a corner and position her head as she struggled to take a full breath. Seizures were not uncommon for her either during those final days. She'd been on and off medication to alleviate the health problems in her older age, but the problems persisted. It was truly heartbreaking to experience. I'm thankful, though, that I wasn't present for any of the seizures. I don't want to remember her like that.

I was on the phone with my mom as I drove home from work on September 1, 2016. Her tone changed when she knew I was home. I immediately knew she had something to tell me and it wasn't good. She'd already told the news to my roommate at the time, Paige, who was ready to meet me with open arms and a big hug when I walked in the door. (I had since moved to Woodstock into my first house.) My mom had taken Roxie to the vet that day and had decided it was time.

Roxie was in such bad health by that time. My mom had talked to me beforehand to ask my wishes of how involved I wanted to be in that final decision of Roxie's life. I'm not sure if it was denial that I exhibited, but I wanted no part of any more death. I wanted no part, nor could I handle any part. It was not even two years removed from the accident that turned my life upside-down, and I was far from ready to deal with more death on a personal level.

The tears immediately began to fall after my mom told me the news. She had to put Roxie down. When I finally walked inside, Paige was available to listen to anything that I wanted to talk about.

I grieved heavily for two days.

Paige was a godsend! To backtrack, in 2016, my counselor had given me the wise advice of not planning and finalizing a trip to Europe at the same time as buying my first house, especially since I was still unable to handle even minimal stresses well, due to the grief I was still enduring. I didn't listen. And, well, I'm just plain stubborn. I paid for it, though, in my heightened level of stress and anxiety. My dad and I had a blast in Europe, and soon after I got back, I was moved into my new house! It had a pool too. My blog post, "For His Glory and My Good," best tells the story of my meeting Paige.

For His Glory and My Good
by Katie Neufeld
August 12, 2016

I don't have any really profound things to say this time around ... scratch that. God has shown Himself faithful again, and I can't wait to share! I actually had most of this post already typed out when it all came together late one afternoon. I got off work early that day and had planned to go to the top of Kennesaw Mountain to intentionally spend some alone time with Jesus. No distractions. A breathtaking view. After sitting in traffic for an hour to get home, I decided I would find somewhere closer to home. Long story short—that didn't end up happening either. I was bummed since my grand idea of getting away from bills and responsibilities around the house (including the bedside table I've been meaning to get out of my truck for days and assemble) in order to fill my soul crashed and burned. *I thought.*

It was while I was sitting on my living room floor, finally getting around to assembling this table, that it all became clear. (I'm taking a break from assembling to type this—gotta get it out while it's fresh on my mind!)

You don't have to go anywhere grand to experience Jesus.

He met me on my living room floor on a partly cloudy Tuesday afternoon. You see, I'm not an expert with tools and assembling things. I'm always sure I *can* do it, but that's what dads are for, right? So, why bother? But seriously, what on earth is a cam lock and how do these things even work?

Pausing on cam lock story for now.

I actually want to share a little bit of what God has been doing in my life first. I'm overflowing with gratitude and joy as I've seen Him move and lead me further into His divine purpose for my life. I also am completely in awe of the way He's been answering my prayers and using my pain for His ultimate glory and for my good. I've felt things lately that I've never experienced before.

It was late one lonely night at the new house I'd just bought. I'd been dealing with frustration after frustration with this new house and was coming to the end of my rope with it all. Putting another "For Sale" sign in my front yard seemed like the best idea of all. I was still going to Passion City Church, where I plan on staying for a very long time, but had considered trying out the big church that's just down the road from my house, First Baptist Church of Woodstock.

I'd heard about this church and seen it all the time on my way home, but never got around to trying it.

Late on that lonely night, my dad was trying to help out in any suitable way he could find. He searched the church's webpage to see what they had to offer for someone in my life stage and with my life experience. Past the college years. A young professional. Not into the games of those in their younger twenties.

My dad stumbled upon the Young Singles page. He planned on sending a message to the Young Singles leader, Kelly, to see what it was all about, but of course made sure that it was okay with me first. I probably wouldn't have ever taken that step, but I'm so thankful he did! He was doing what any good father would; He was looking out for me, making sure it was a mature group of young people and not just a glorified youth group. He knew I didn't need any extra drama or stress in my life as I had plenty of anxiety related to my house and pool, not to mention the grief and healing I was still working through.

So he sent the message asking Kelly what the group was all about, letting her know where I was at, and making sure it would be a good fit for me. Much to our surprise, he heard back from her that same night. She told him it was totally a God thing that she was still in the office to see and respond to his message so quickly.

Then the ball really got rolling. I didn't even ask God specifically for this group of friends, but I could see the writing on the wall. I knew what was coming, and I liked it! Kelly called me a few times just to chat, and she also invited me to some upcoming singles events. Just to be clear, I did *not* like the idea of being in a singles group. The word *single* can sometimes be such a nuisance. Frankly, it can be a downer with the way everything has played out in my own life.

The leader thought it would be better for me to ease into the group knowing a few people in advance, so she gave my number to one of the girls in the group. Jamie started texting me, and we set up a date and time to meet for lunch.

The night before we met, push came to shove. Experiencing a difficult, emotional evening alone at my house, I contacted my realtor to see what the financial damage would be if I moved closer to home. Needless to say, I went into the lunch the next day wondering what the point was to meet new people from FBCW if I wasn't even going to continue living in the area.

I spent that night crying out, asking God why I'd gone through what I had, why He didn't stop me from buying the house, and just why this and why that. In hindsight, some of my cries of desperation made sense, while others I'll just conveniently forget about. It just kept on coming. I continued crying for most of the night, which ultimately led me to this prayer: I told God I either needed Him to send me a roommate or I was going to move out. I hadn't sensed His direction prior to that night regarding whether I should stay or go, so I just figured it didn't matter. I was wrong. But God!

I met Jamie the next day, and at the last minute, I found out her friend, Paige, was meeting us for lunch as well (a last-minute change of plans for Paige too). I was excited to meet a second potential new friend who also attended FBCW. The three of us had a great lunch and connected well, I thought. I remember Paige saying that she was moving up to Woodstock and had a potential roommate already lined up. It was later that same week when I felt strongly that I needed to just let Paige know that if her rooming situation didn't work out that I'd been looking for a roommate.

Little did I know that day at lunch that Paige's other rooming situation would later fall through and I'd just met my future roommate. A complete stranger, but God's hand was on the whole situation and I knew I could trust Him. And because I trust Him, I trust that He sent Paige my way so that I would stay here at this house.

I'm still not quite sure why He wants me here or what He's up to, but I know He's moving and working it all out in ways that only He can. I've been completely blown away to see even small glimpses of what He's up to in my life, and it's good! Ever since Paige has moved in, I've felt more at ease in so many ways. Who knew just getting a roommate would help me get back to my normal eight hours of restful sleep instead of waking up every thirty minutes to an hour leaving me exhausted before ten a.m. every day. It takes a huge load off me financially, and I've just felt way better overall. Thank You, Jesus! You are faithful. To be transparent, the answer to my many prayers for a roommate made me wish that God always answered prayers so quickly.

In my entire life, I've never been as sure as I am at this moment that I'm exactly where God wants me to be, smack dab in the middle of His will for my life. It is mind-blowing to think how much things can change from moment to moment and how only a couple weeks ago I was so desperate to get back to a place of comfort and move closer to my parents' house. God just kept showing me that I'm right where He wants me. Thank You, Jesus! Your ways are so much higher than mine. I am thankful, and I praise You!

The coincidence to me, but not to God, is that His direction in all of this is happening while I'm in the middle of a small group Bible study on the book *Restless* by Jennie Allen. It's all about finding your purpose, and it's very eye-opening and inspiring. In studying this book, I've seen more clearly the ways in which God is shaping my life. I knew my purpose would be related to the accident and the strength I've found in God, and I *thought* it would be with my blog and love of writing. That may still be true, but it has taken an unexpected turn. In the last week alone, two different women have asked me to speak and share my story at their churches this fall.

First thoughts: *Awesome!* Yes. Sign me up ... Wait. What am I actually signing up for again? I've prayed for many months for God to use my story and pain for His eternal story and all for His glory, so these opportunities are just His answers to my prayers. I feel a bit like Moses now though.

I'm no public speaker, God! I can't. I am going to stutter. I'll forget what I'm talking about mid-sentence. I'll pass out. I'll get up there and cry my eyes out. I can't.

Well, like my earthly daddy always said, "Can't never did anything." But really, me? No. I can't. *But God* can. With His divine strength and unparalleled power, I'll push through my terror of public speaking. With His comfort and peace, I'll share whatever He places on my heart for these groups of women and teen girls. And we can know with confidence that whatever comes out of my mouth will truly be from God, because my stepping on any stage will be a miracle. I truly am so excited to be used by God in this way. It is just so unbelievable looking back at this rollercoaster of a journey I've been on. What impossible lows and super high spiritual highs. What redemption. Hope. Perseverance. Because of Him. Thank You, Jesus, for facing your undeserved torture and death so that we can live with the hope that because You conquered death, so can we. I am in awe.

Back to the cam bolts.

I had no idea what this piece even was coming into this project. But God knew. I'm no public speaker, but God is! He's the ultimate Teacher. I have *no* idea what I'm doing, but God does, and He's leading me into greater things than ever before. I can't do this, but He can! I have no idea how all these little bolts, screws, cam locks, and rails go together, but He sees the end result of all of this work and effort going into this bedside table. He also sees the big picture of all of the effort and work I've put into moving forward in my grief and healing.

He has this beautifully grand picture of how it will all turn out here on earth and into eternity, but all I can see right now are these weird cam bolts and awkward hinges that I have no clue how to even fit together. I have to trust, though, that God has gone before me to place each and every nut, bolt, and screw of my life exactly where they should go to bring about the most glory for Him and the most good for me.

Life is so full of these moments where nothing makes sense. Why does putting this bolt here and that screw there make any sense? The H1 cam bolt is sticking out funny from the drawer front, P14! How could that ever work? Maybe that cam bolt is supposed to stick out funny so it meets the cam lock in just the right way so it locks into place. That's so similar to how we're placed directly in the path of exactly where God wants each of us so that we can meet the right people and connect in deep God ways that would've never happened otherwise, moving us forward into God's perfect plan.

One thing I've learned and now also believe without a doubt is that we were never supposed to build anything great without an instruction manual—the Bible. Just like the instructions tell me *exactly* where to place each screw, hinge, and bolt, the Bible gives us clear instructions on how to live to our greatest potential and impact eternity in the biggest way possible in the time we are given here. Let's make it count! But unlike instruction manuals and part kits, the Bible never leaves any parts out and never leads you down the wrong path.

One last thought. *Our God is a God of beautiful exchanges.* He's taken my ashes and made beauty. He's taken my sorrow and given me His joy. He's taken my pain and is using it for His glory. And He's taken this night and turned disappointment of missing the mountaintop Jesus experience into complete fulfillment assembling my bedside table on my living room floor, and He was here all along ...

I love you, Jesus.

"Who is like you, Lord God Almighty? You, Lord, are mighty, and your faithfulness surrounds you. You rule over the surging sea; when its waves mount up, you still them."

—PSALM 89:8–9

"Jesus looked at them and said, 'With man this is impossible, but not with God; all things are possible with God.'"

—MARK 10:27

"Truly I tell you, if you have faith as small as a mustard seed, you can say to this mountain, 'Move from here to there,' and it will move. Nothing will be impossible for you."

—MATTHEW 17:20

Katie

Paige had also been in school at the time studying to be a counselor. *God was just showing off now!* My own personal counselor! Paige made it clear that this would most certainly be a conflict of interest and unacceptable professionally. I knew that but was still so thankful to have such a wise new friend for a roommate. We'd really been enjoying getting to know each other and were a great fit for living together.

After two days of grieving heavily over losing the dog I'd spent so many of my transitional years with, I was ready for a break emotionally. Labor Day weekend was approaching, and I had a pool in my backyard. Two plus two, right? Carol, Megan—Jerod's mom and sister—and I planned a girls' day that coming Saturday at my house. Grilling out and a pool party sounded like a great idea, and it truly was!

Saturday arrived, and it was a beautiful sunny day. We all chipped in, each of us bringing various items to create an incredibly delicious and filling post-swim dinner. The day was going perfectly and could not have been better. We swam. We laughed. We ate. We relaxed. We were planning to wind down and watch a movie as we were finishing up dinner when my phone rang. My mom was on the other end of the line telling me that my three-year-old nephew Mason was being rushed to the top children's hospital in Atlanta because some of his blood counts were in the same range as those with childhood cancer.

Say what?

I could hardly believe what my ears were hearing. Mason had been sick on and off for months and was scheduled to have his adenoids removed soon. Since he'd had fevers for a week and a half already, his doctor decided to run some basic labs on him, and the results were shocking and really just unbelievable.

Being an experienced nurse, though, I wasn't bothered by hearing this because I knew collected blood clotted from time to time, creating skewed results. In the hospital, we'd have the test redrawn just to see normal results follow shortly behind. I told my mom this kind of thing happens all the time. He'd be okay. I hadn't directly talked with the medical professional that gave them the news, but I wasn't worried. My mom told me that my brother and sister-in-law, Cori, wanted me to meet Mason at the hospital, since I'm the only medical professional in the immediate family and because they were currently out of town for a good friend's wedding in Washington, DC.

Please Wake Me Up!
A Journal Insert from Kevin
September 10, 2016

Life has been a blur the last two weeks. Heck, it's been a very different world for the last five years. Vickie and I were talking about that right before we got hit from behind on our way home from seeing Mason at the hospital. As I checked the Facebook page for Mason, I saw the update: "Chemo, Day 4." Why is chemo part of an update on my grandson? What happened? Wake me up! Pinch me. Hit me in the face! Do whatever it takes to get me out of this nightmare.

The last five years are filed under the heading "Loss." My wife lost her father and rock to cancer in just a few short months, followed three months later by the loss of my job and semi-voluntary loss of my career and identity as a vocational pastor. Then we lost her mother after a slow decline over several years. Things were looking up—grandkids, last child in college, job going well, daughter engaged to a wonderful man who had become like a son to us. Oh, yeah, we lost him too. It's a miracle we have our daughter after the accident, but her life is forever changed, and we spent the last two years trying to accompany her through her nightmare.

I don't think I am a pessimist, but I recall thinking not very long ago, *what if we're not out of our season of pain?* Not sure why my mind went that way, but it was a harbinger of the last two weeks.

My wife has headed up the 9/11 lunch for first responders for a few years now, and she works very hard on it. This year, she had less help than ever before and was trying to do far more than one person should. Part of what she provides is bags filled with candy made by her sister in Michigan. My wife was to make a day-and-a-half trip on standby to help make and bring back the candy. She asked me one night if I'd make the trip, since she knows I enjoy travel and she had too much to do. On August 31, I boarded a flight to Detroit and worked remotely for a few days while hanging out with my brother-in-law and catching up with family I hadn't seen since my mother-in-law's funeral.

In the meantime, I had to cancel an appointment for Roxie, our old dachshund, because of her failing health. On Thursday morning, Vickie informed me that the dog wasn't doing well and she was taking her to the vet. We were then faced with whether or not to put her down. The decision was easy, but the ramifications were not. Roxie was Katie's dog, and our daughter had experienced enough death to last her a long time. By the end of the day, Roxie was gone, and we grieved the loss of our good friend. My brother-in-law, Herb, and I went to a baseball game in Utica on Friday night, and I kept an eye on flights, intending to catch one back to Atlanta on Sunday. Then I got what we have come to know too well as "the call." Eventually, everyone gets one. I thought we'd already hit our quota.

My son, Taylor, and his wife, Cori, were in Washington, DC, for a wedding, and her parents had kept the kids. After some recent illness, Mason had been in and out of the doctor's office. On Friday he went back and they drew some blood. Around five p.m. on Saturday of Labor Day weekend, they received a call telling them to take Mason directly to the hospital where a team was waiting for him.

Taylor and Cori got the call while sitting in the audience during the ceremony. I was next in line to take that same call, and everyone began the mad dash from DC, Detroit, Carroll County, Woodstock, and Paulding County to the children's hospital in Atlanta. Before catching the last plane out after ten p.m., Mason's parents received the doctor's report that their middle son probably had leukemia.

The cascade of bad news began. It was confirmed as leukemia. We hoped for the lesser type, ALL, but the diagnosis was AML, the hardest kind to conquer, and soon Mason was headed to a hospital where they specialize in treating that type of cancer. We've spent the last week going back and forth to see him, trying to figure out how the family will juggle all that has to be handled—jobs and work schedules, making sure that the other children are cared for, providing personal items needed at the hospital—and oh, the 9/11 show must still go on.

The 9/11 lunch went well, and we made our way back to the hospital Friday afternoon where everyone was getting farmed out for the weekend. Taylor and Cori were going to spend a night at home with the other two kids and out-of-town family. We waited to walk out with Taylor and Cori and head home. We were dealing with the Friday-evening rush hour, the sunshine slowdown, and traffic stopping suddenly. I braked in time—the car behind me, not so much. I heard screeching tires and looked, trying to find out where they were, then quickly found out.

Really? After one of the toughest blows of our lives, Jerod's death and Katie's still-ongoing recovery, Roxie is gone, our most tenderhearted grandchild is in a fight for his life, and we get creamed in rush-hour traffic. There's not even enough time to recoil from the recoil anymore.

Katie

I hesitantly started packing a bag of snacks and things to take with me, unsure of how long we would be at the hospital with Mason. Carol and Megan supported my decision one hundred percent and graciously helped clean up dinner and the pool floats. It was a bummer for sure to stop the fun we were having just to go to another hospital, but I knew I needed to go. The "what ifs" only grew larger and scarier in my mind as I sped to the hospital to meet my family. *What if* it wasn't a mistake? *What if* the labs were completely accurate? *What if* another valley was on our horizon? *What if* Mason died? More death. I remember distinctly what song was on the radio when those thoughts flooded my mind and caused me to worry heavily— "Just Breathe" by Jonny Diaz.

214

My mom and I later talked and realized we were both listening to the same radio station on the drive in, both given the timely gift of that song. *Breathe, Katie. Just breathe.* I started breathing hope. God got us through losing Jerod; He would get us through whatever was on the horizon for Mason. He was telling us—*just breathe.*

We sat in the emergency room for hours. Waiting. I hate waiting! Not doing anything was difficult to handle. My mom and I decided to walk up to the unit where I work and get comfortable up there for a bit. That was the best thing we could've done. My coworkers were wonderful, offering comfort and prayers as we continued our vigil. Finally, we received some answers, and the doctor confirmed our greatest fears. *Leukemia.*

Mason was admitted to the first floor, where kids with cancer were admitted, until his team of doctors knew enough information about what type he had to make a treatment plan. Necessary action took him away from the hospital where I work. In reality, that was a small disappointment, but after the massive blow that took all of our breath away, any more felt unbearable.

We were all shocked, sick to our stomachs, and at a loss for words. That first night in the hospital will forever be burned in my memory. The doctors waited—even though it was after midnight—until Taylor and Cori arrived so they could all talk face-to-face. My blog post, "Come On, Sunday," describes well the details of the early days of Mason's diagnosis.

Come On, Sunday
by Katie Neufeld
October 2, 2016

As I sit here in my bed, finishing out my birthday, watching *Homeward Bound* and eating a delicious cinnamon roll from Ikea, heated for just the right amount of time, mind you, I can't make these tears stop rolling down my cheeks. For the past week or so, two words in particular have been stuck in my mind. Simple words, yet profound.

I don't.

I believe those words will forever be burned into my memory. It's a different form of torture than I'm used to, being a fly on the wall to hear my precious three-year-old nephew cover his mouth and cry "I don't" while being poked and prodded and coerced to take loads of medicine he's never had to take before in his short life. It broke and will continue to break Aunt KK's heart watching you endure all of these new and unwanted—yet necessary—medical tasks, like a true champ, I might add. Shoot, you're handling it way better than I am.

As a matter of fact, kids seem to handle a lot of things better than adults. There have been many instances in the last two weeks as I've spent time in the hospital with Mason that I've wondered why I spend all this time trying to improve my adulting skills when I should really be focusing on becoming more childlike.

It became more clear last night as the tears were flowing, with the help of a few cherished friends, I might add. There are days when Mason doesn't even know he's sick, but Mason does know that he has two parents who adore him and who won't leave his side. He knows that he's not alone. He knows that he's getting gifts pretty much anytime anyone walks in his door, even from the nurses! He asks now every time you walk in if you have anything for him!

He doesn't worry about how hard the road is and will be, partly because he just doesn't know, as a child, what a typical leukemia course is like (we have no clue either), but also because his parents and family don't overwhelm him with the scary details of what is to come. Even if he did know the details of what and how many things he would have to do that aren't fun, I just have this feeling that he would forget it all the second someone else brought him some Spiderman or Paw Patrol toy.

What a perfect picture of what our heavenly Father is to us! Just like Mason's relationship with his earthly mommy and daddy, our heavenly Father doesn't leave us to fight our battles alone. Deuteronomy 31:8 says, "The Lord himself goes before you and will be with you; He will never leave you nor forsake you. Do not be afraid; do not be discouraged." We are never alone.

Our Father loves us.

"And I pray that you, being rooted and established in love, may have power, together with all the Lord's holy people, to grasp how wide and long and high and deep is the love of Christ, and to know this love that surpasses knowledge—that you may be filled to the measure of all the fullness of God" (Ephesians 3:17–19).

Our heavenly Father also knows how to give us good gifts. Matthew 7:11 says, "If you, then, though you are evil, know how to give good gifts to your children, how much more will your Father in heaven give good gifts to those who ask him!"

Our Father wants to take our burdens and fight for us. From reading Exodus 14:14, we learn that, "The Lord will fight for you; you need only to be still." We just have to learn to let Him, a grueling lesson I'm still learning myself. How exhausting these long earthly battles can be when we take it all upon ourselves and by ourselves. May we all be a little more childlike in the days ahead. More faith and less worry.

But I just can't stop thinking about Mason's two-word mantra with his new medicines. Oh, how those two words resonate so loudly in my own life right now.

I don't.

I *just* don't, okay?

I'm beyond over it! I don't want to have to keep fighting. I'm so sick of these battles. *Fighting* for my sanity. *Fighting* for positivity. *Fighting* for my faith. *Fighting* for hope. *Fighting* for my future. I don't want to be a professional griever. I don't want to always be sad and crying. I don't want to deal with the major anxiety with which I now suffer. I just want to return these cards I've been dealt and start over. Where's my royal flush?

I didn't want to lose my Roxie (the dog that had been through it all with me) two days before getting Mason's leukemia diagnosis. I surely *didn't* want Mason's leukemia diagnosis. I didn't want to lose Jerod, but I didn't really have a choice in the matter. I did, however, have a choice in how I responded. I chose to be the victor and not the victim. I chose not only to survive, but also to thrive! Now to figure out how to bring that winning attitude into the battles going on right now.

While those are a few of the "I don'ts" that I think about often, I can't write off the "I do's" that *I do* have. Even though I'm not particularly a fan of the words "I do" at the moment, I *do* have a supportive and loving family. The same could be said of Jerod's wonderful family and my amazing work family. I *do* have the encouragement and support of some really wonderful friends who have spent time with me and continued to point me to Jesus in the middle of these relentless storms. I *do* have the hope that because of Jesus, I have nothing to fear. Nothing this world throws my way can ever change what I have in Jesus. A hope beyond the shadow of any death, even my own. An anchor to hold me fast through any and every storm.

I just finished the book *Through the Eyes of a Lion* and loved it! So much of what Levi Lusko wrote resonated with me in every way. But the last words in the book—wow! He totally nailed it!

Saturday eventually has to end.

That's where I feel I am and have been for the last two years. Stuck on the longest and most torturous Saturday of my life, referring to the day between Jesus' death and His resurrection. *Saturday*. I've been in a holding pattern, waiting for this or that for years now. And Levi is right. Whether my Sunday comes on this earth or when I enter heaven and meet Jesus (and tackle Jerod), Sunday is coming. There's never a Saturday that isn't followed by a Sunday. There's never a winter that isn't followed by spring. There's never a night that isn't followed by morning. Thank You, Jesus, for being all we could ever need. Now come on, Sunday!

"He called a little child to him, and placed the child among them. And he said: 'Truly I tell you, unless you change and become like little children, you will never enter the kingdom of heaven. Therefore, whoever takes the lowly position of this child is the greatest in the kingdom of heaven. And whoever welcomes one such child in my name welcomes me.'"

—MATTHEW 18:2–5

"There is surely a future hope for you, and your hope will not be cut off."

—PROVERBS 23:18

Kevin

I've never been one to see either God or Satan behind every rock, tree, or bush. Our limited view behind the curtain of events as exemplified in the story of Job leaves me reluctant to assign credit or blame to events, and yet I believe God is with us and with us always. Sometimes it's so evident that it sends chills down the spine and raises goosebumps on the arms.

One of the memories that stands out so much to me was the following story as told by Mason's parents. Upon receiving the news of Mason's very serious condition and the need to rush home immediately, they left the wedding ceremony and made a dash to the airport. It was Saturday evening of Labor Day weekend, and flights, they discovered, were scarce. The planes were also full. I'm not sure how one sits and waits when their child is hundreds of miles away with a potential diagnosis of cancer. It is beyond imagination what it would be like to wait all night for the next day's departure. I prayed they would find a flight, and my prayer was answered. The last flight out at seven p.m. had two seats left, and Taylor and Cori had them.

Now the wait began. Seated nearby, a dear lady observed the distress that was written all over their countenances and the tears that flowed freely. Being impressed to get involved, she came over, introduced herself, and identified herself as a pastor and asked if there was anything she could pray with them about. After cluing her in on the news they'd just received, she bowed her head and prayed earnestly for them, for Mason, and for the situation. She then sat and waited with them to board the plane.

Once boarding began, she said goodbye, and after a few words of encouragement, entered the plane. What a gift she had been to them and how seen and loved by our Father they felt. The situation hadn't changed, but God had shown Himself present in the midst of their nightmare. Eventually, their names were called and they boarded. Walking back through the plane, they came to their two empty seats to find … you guessed it. Next to them for the flight back to Atlanta was their angel, the lady who had seen them, listened to God's promptings, and had comforted and prayed for them.

There can be no doubt in my mind that God's hand was in that chain of events and had been as early as whenever the flight schedules and seat assignments were made. God reached down into time and had a divine appointment planned for a dear lady He trusted to listen and obey. Through God's providence, three people had planned their trip, but God directed their steps.

"We can make our plans, but the Lord determines our steps."

—Proverbs 16:9 NLT

There were to be plenty of times in the months that followed that I'd wonder if God was present, but on that evening, there can be no doubt. And that evening became a monument to which we would cling for hope in the coming days.

Katie

After what I'd already endured, I thought for sure this diagnosis would be a death sentence for Mason. I'd fought for and found hope in my own loss, but that battle was far from similar to this one. My loss happened so quickly, I didn't have much time to pray for a miracle, but this, *this* was much different. I felt this would be a battle of ups and downs while we just waited for the other shoe to drop. It was all bad news for a long time. Leukemia.

Then we found out he had the worse type with the lower chances of remission. While we knew God was bigger than all of that, it was still hard to come to terms with the reality of the whole situation. Within seventy-two hours, Mason had already received his first dose of chemo, as well as his central line placement and his first bone marrow aspiration. This was the way the medical team was able to assess how much of his blood was comprised of cancer cells.

It was still hard to believe the reality of Mason having to fight such a horrible disease. I remember thinking, *wait! Stop! What is even happening right now? We're talking about* my *nephew?* Within the first round of chemo, we also learned that Mason had a gene, FLT3, which makes the cancer more aggressive and more difficult to treat. It all sounded the same to me. *Death.*

Mason's condition had changed, but God's position had not. He was and is still on His throne with limitless power and ability to change any and every situation we will ever face.

I'd been reading Priscilla Shirer's book, *Life Interrupted*, which is all about how your latest disruption may often be your most persuasive testimony (Shirer 2011, 36). The part of the book that really shipwrecked my heart and encouraged me on many occasions acknowledges that what you're dealing with may very well be the most painful and intimidating thing you've ever faced. But sometimes the Lord puts you in difficult circumstances, in between the Red Sea and Pharaoh's armies, so that His power and sufficiency is on display for all to see. And for some, God's mighty work in your life may be the greatest story they will ever read (Shirer 2011, 43).

Others call these tough times being stuck between a rock and a hard place. Either description is spot on. That's exactly where I feel like God has placed my family and me, between a rock and a hard place. We were stuck with Mason in between cancer and death. But as Priscilla says, it is in the middle of this hard and sometimes impossible-seeming place that God's power is on display and where God ultimately gets the most glory. This was especially true for us, because the only way Mason would survive leukemia would be a miracle, and one that would put God and His mighty power on display. I've learned that this specific placement, living between two impossibly hard things, turns out to be a front-row seat to see God in all of His mighty power move mountains and fight our battles right before our eyes! It's a painful gift to walk this road. A terrible privilege.

I'd witnessed God move mountains and perform miracles in my life before, but I still had the most difficult time carrying over the hope I'd found before into this new and daunting battle. It was so different. This new fight certainly brought into the light my fear of losing more people in my life.

Jerod's mom encouraged me on many occasions with the words, "God still does miracles." While I highly doubted that He would perform this miracle for *us*, her words repeatedly went through my mind and reminded me that we did have hope. Even if what we deem as the worst happened here on earth, I remembered time and time again the ways that God had taken care of my family and me through the valley that we'd already walked through and thought we were escaping.

Mason's future remained bleak for a long time. Many tears were shed, some of the most unforgettable moments, tear-stained. I remember the day that a mentor of mine came over to my parents' house. Few words of encouragement were spoken, but what meant and stood out the most to me was that my mom, my mentor, and I all shared tears and hugs together over the journey. It hurt and we all acknowledged that. In my experience, shared tears have always meant more than words ever could.

It took a lot of time, prayer, and Mason's bone marrow transplant in February of 2017, but we started learning to survive in the dark while hoping for the light. Good things started happening, though. His counts improved with each check after the transplant. It was 11:38 on the morning of March 22, 2017, as I was putting household things into my storage unit preparing for another move, one that was closer to my parents' house, when I received a text message from my brother, Taylor, Mason's dad. After a long and grueling six months, Mason had now been pronounced *cancer free! Hallelujah!*

I cried the happiest of tears in my truck as I read that text message. It was one of those moments when I felt heaven about as near as I imagine that it can get on earth. It felt like crowds and masses of people were cheering and rejoicing along with us, just another one of those out-of-body experiences that will forever stick with me. And if Mason's miraculous healing wasn't enough, there was more. That day, March 22, had been the day that Jerod and I were to be married in 2015. How kind is God to give such a sweet gift on that impossibly hard day, scarred by the death of my fiancé and the death of my dreams. Only God. Thank You, Jesus!

CHAPTER 15

An Assortment of Our Favorites

Kevin

One of the most helpful habits we developed after our loss was the practice of journaling. It may not be beneficial for everyone, but it became an avenue for us to release emotion and process our pain. It also laid down markers, some to revisit and others to never lay eyes on again. Following are a few of our entries that we thought might be helpful.

Katie

Emotionally, I felt incredibly scarred by those last few years. Scars are a sign of strength, though—His strength. Below is a blog I wrote, "Scars Tell a Story."

Scars Tell a Story
by Katie Neufeld
January 13, 2016

Scars tell stories — and who doesn't love a good scar story? We've all heard stories that start with those three famous words, "Hey, ya'll, watchiss!"

Well, I've been thinking a lot about wounds lately, physical and emotional. Quickly after an initial physical injury, the body is already automatically at its natural work sending the necessary cells and other healing properties to the site of injury in order to begin its healing. Specifically when a bone is broken, sometimes before true healing takes place, it must be rebroken and set into place in order to promote the highest level of functioning after healing is complete. And if that wasn't painful enough, just wait for the physical therapy to begin! Therapy always focuses on the weakest places. In enduring the struggle of physical therapy, one is choosing to embrace the pain of healing and recovery in order to get back to the highest level of functioning possible. All with a good physical therapist. Still, healing is excruciatingly painful.

The same is true of healing emotional wounds. Again, there's a choice. In all of the anger and bitterness, one can ignore the injury altogether and never live up to his full potential, or he can choose to dig deep into the most painful of places in order to bring what's dark to light. *His* light. To expose the lies of the enemy that have crept in. To expose the hurt and disappointment for what it really is. To focus one's energy instead on God's promises and His truths, even when He seems absent or uncaring. It's only in directly facing the pain that true and complete healing can begin.

I've heard stories of people coming out of physical therapy *stronger* than they were before the injury even took place. Weakness becomes strength, but not without grueling amounts of time and effort and not without divine intervention. It's possible for one to come out stronger on the other side, but he must choose to set aside all of the things that don't better him, all of the negativity. When any wound is placed in the Great Physician's more-than-capable hands, the hurt that could have destroyed one's life can turn into his greatest strength, one that could potentially save the lives of others. One that could help others in the middle of their darkest nights. One that is better and more useful if shared, when one is ready, of course.

I'm seeing all of these things happening in the middle of my own story. I've been able to use what once was crippling as a strength, a secret weapon. Like the choice of enduring physical therapy, my healing was very much a choice that I had to make. A process that I had to endure and embrace. One that fully exposed my vulnerability. One that got harder in the breaking before it got better in the healing.

I'm not so naïve to think that my struggle and healing are over, for I know that healing is a rather lengthy process, but so far, I've come through the struggle a stronger woman. One who is still afraid, but doesn't let fear stop her. One who will try most anything at least once, even if it means going alone. One who burns with purpose and intentionality. One who embraces a challenge because I can usually say that I've been through far worse and done much harder things. And how empowering this is! (Hopefully, this will be enough to get me through my first—and maybe last—half marathon that I signed up for next month.)

Scars tell a story. A story of victory, strength, and courage in the face of adversity. The story of someone who never gave up. Scars mean that what tried to hurt you didn't defeat you. Because what was meant to harm and completely destroy you, God turned around for good, using it to save the lives of others. Thank You, Jesus, for redeeming my pain and exchanging my weakness for Your strength and for renewing me day after day. All glory to You, Jesus. I trust You.

"That is why, for Christ's sake, I delight in weaknesses, in insults, in hardships, in persecutions, in difficulties. For when I am weak, then I am strong."

—2 CORINTHIANS 12:10

"You intended to harm me, but God intended it for good to accomplish what is now being done, the saving of many lives."

—GENESIS 50:20

A John 6 Moment
by Kevin Neufeld
February 25, 2018

Jesus' earthly ministry came in like a flash, but perhaps there was nothing that propelled it any more than the endorsement of the camel-skin-wearing, locust-eating evangelist who told the crowds which he had drawn that there was someone else they should follow. So begins the gospel of John. It started at a wedding in Cana where Jesus turned water to wine and was followed by a series of miracles and healings. All of these factors converged to swell the crowds that followed Him.

In John 6, we find Him starting to do more than just miracles; He begins to talk like a madman, in the opinion of many, as He calls Himself the bread from heaven. The message gets a little stranger as He explains that unless they eat His flesh and drink His blood, they cannot have eternal life. The growing discomfort with the way His teaching was turning resulted in what John 6:66 (ESV) tells us: "After this many of his disciples turned back and no longer walked with him."

Two thousand years later, I believe this scenario has been and continues to be replayed at least once, and even repeatedly, in the hearts and lives of those who call themselves followers of Christ. It happened to John the Baptist as he sat in jail contemplating how his seemingly promising career as the forerunner of the Messiah had been derailed. In Luke 7:19 (ESV), he sent two of his disciples to ask Jesus, "Are you the one who is to come, or shall we look for another?" John must have wondered if he'd bet on the wrong messiah or if he'd wasted his efforts. For others, it was simply the hard teachings of

228

Jesus, while still others stumbled because their reality didn't match expectations.

Whatever the reason, we all will face at least one John 6 moment when circumstances scream *run!* It's usually more complicated than that, but at the very heart of the issue is whether or not we'll bow to the Lord or if we'll choose to be our own lord and demand He submit to our wishes. In such times, it would make sense to run from God, and many do. But there's also a choice to run to Him in spite of circumstances. Katie's accident was such an event for her.

Katie had followed Jesus with increasing intensity over the years. She made a profession of faith at a very early age and had never shown any evidence of falling away. As a teenager, her interest increased, and she continued to follow with a very devoted heart. In college, nursing school and a job took much of her time, but she attempted to stay faithful to church and her walk with Christ. At some point, she read Eric & Leslie Ludy's book, *When God Writes Your Love Story*. That became her dream and her desire. Upon graduation, still being single, she committed her story to God.

While a number of her peers were getting engaged and married, she remained single and unattached ... until Jerod swept her off her feet. As her parents, we didn't have an icon in mind, but if we had, it would have looked something like Jerod. He was passionate about his faith, a strong witness, a successful businessman, a learner to his very heart—and one who was not afraid to say he didn't know and set out to learn. He was a young man who had placed himself under the tutelage of a number of godly men. We couldn't have been more thrilled for Katie. Jerod fit with the family so well that our grandkids were already calling him "Uncle Jewod," and he embedded himself in my heart and became like another son to me. God's plan was wonderful, and we were enjoying it; it really was good to let God write your love story. He treated Katie so well as both a gentleman and also a provider. There was no doubt in my mind that he would give her a good life. I only hoped his love of fast cars and boats did not get him in trouble. Little did I expect that the speed which took him home would not be his own.

The accident was as if someone had hijacked the manuscript and begun to write a different story.

When two young people who have committed themselves to pursuing God and His kingdom find each other and set out to do it together, it's a red-letter day! After Katie read *When God Writes Your Love Story*, she set out to let God write her own, and we loved the way He was writing it—*until now*. Watching your daughter keep a high standard for her life mate, finding him, losing him, and listening to her wail in sorrow is more than this dad's heart can stand. I wrestle with the Author of her love story and life over the script. It stinks! But I'd rather limp for the rest of my life than not wrestle.

I've walked with God too long to believe that He makes mistakes. I don't always understand, but He's trustworthy. So, while my understanding is screaming that He messed up the script for her and Jerod's lives, my faith struggles to accept that the story isn't finished. And I wish I could peek a few chapters ahead and see in advance how this turns out, because I cannot see how a finer man for my daughter could exist than the one He just let slip out of her hands.

There have been multiple times when I've faced a disappointment and wondered why God let it happen, but my most decisive John 6 moment happened just a couple years later as our grandson was diagnosed with a very tough form of leukemia. My wife and I had both studied at a Christian college for ministry and set out early on, in spite of minimal resources, to pursue ministry. She has served over twenty-five years in Christian education, and I'd served in various aspects of pastoral ministry for twenty-eight years. In 2011, after the economy crashed and my position at a new church plant was cut, I sought secular employment where I continue to this day. That didn't end my ministry; it just ended it vocationally.

We'd tried to do the right things, had taken some uncomfortable stands, and had gained many friends and lost others through ministry. We carry with us today some scars that will always remind us of battles we faced. In some cases, it's more like a limp, but following Christ has sometimes cost us in ways we wish we could change. Even now as our peers begin to retire, we face the prospect of working on for a good while. One day, it all weighed down on me as we faced the uncertainty of life for our three-year-old grandson fighting cancer and the chaos it had injected into our family's life, and I cried out to God. "All that we have done for You, and this is what we get in return?"

It no sooner left my lips than I was convicted that God had blessed me far beyond what I deserved. As I wrestled with Him over days and weeks, I came to the point where I literally had to give my grandson to God and admit that he didn't belong to me. If God chose to let us keep him, I would praise and follow Him; if He chose to take Mason to heaven, I would do no differently.

It may not be so dramatic for everyone, but each of us faces some John 6 moments where we have to decide who will sit on the throne of our lives. It may be hard Bible truths, life's tragedies, shattered expectations, broken relationships, poverty, illness, or a host of issues. But, in the end, as Job found out, it is God who gets to ask the questions. In John 6:67, Jesus asked the twelve if they wanted to go away as well. Peter quickly answered for them and said that He was their last and best option.

I'm so thankful that He promised, in Isaiah 42:3, that He would not break a bruised reed or quench a smoking wick. It may be a pitched battle within to make the right decision. It is not easy in many instances. Even as Peter made his confession, Jesus replied that out of the twelve, one would be a devil. Personally, sometimes it's maddening that Jesus doesn't join me in my pity party, but He calls me to be strong in His strength, and when we come to the end of ours, we find that His strength is boundless.

So fight on, brother or sister, and run *to* Him ... even when it seems to make more sense to run *from* Him. What is your John 6 moment?

He's Mine!
A Journal Insert from Kevin
September 28, 2016

I've really wrestled with Mason's illness, especially after all that we have been through in the last two years with Katie and last five years in general. I've come to call it my season of loss.

On Sunday, during our class at church, the following question came up. What is the root of our struggles? It was a good question, and I asked myself, *What is at the root of my own struggle?* You shouldn't ask questions you don't want answered. It came to me in one word—*ownership*. I want to control my world. I'm told by my culture that I need to control my finances, my career, my relationships, my health, my weight, etc. I don't do well in the passenger seat of life, but the movie *Bruce Almighty* emphasized that each of us is woefully unequipped to handle the driver's seat as well.

As a pastor, I didn't push baby dedications, though we did them from time to time. I imagine the story of Samuel in the Bible birthed that tradition, but what's caused us to carry on that practice? The cynic in me fears that, at worst, it's a chance to get *my* baby up in front of the congregation for all to fawn over, but for many, it's merely the way we used to do it. Right now, I think of it in terms of Mary, the mother of Jesus, more than Hannah, the mother of Samuel. The Bible tells us that Mary kept many things in her heart and pondered them. She gave birth to a Son who was born to die a cruel death. Did it hurt any less due to her understanding, or did it hurt more because of that knowledge? If we knew that giving our children to God meant He'd take them from us, would we still dedicate them to Him?

The answer became clear to me as I looked at a picture of Mason and several questions came to mind, perhaps from the Holy Spirit.

Who is this?

My grandson.

Why?

He carries my genes.

Where did they come from?

I can see where this was going.

And who chose his hair color, beautiful eyes, and his genetic makeup?

You know.

And what can you do about his current condition?

Very little. So, this human I call mine is not really mine?

Right. And if I made him, do I not care for him?

I would think so, but this is an odd way to show it.

Will you trust Me with this?

What are my options?

Trust yourself ... or Me.

Wow! May I be dismissed?

I've often thought when officiating weddings that I should shout "for *worse*, for *poorer*, in *sickness*, and in *poverty*." Perhaps we should take time to stress the gravity of dedicating a child to God. Ask Abraham.

I give up, Papa. He's Yours ... but please, let us keep him here. Please?

Joy and Sorrow
by Kevin Neufeld
February 2018

The lessons we've learned from the events of the past years are numerous. Much of what we've told others over the years has echoed in our ears as we've faced tragedy as part of the cast instead of mere observers. Some truths have been reinforced, while others are new and fresh. It's difficult to know whether these truths are new or just seem that way, but we find ourselves talking and understanding differently, and a deepening of understanding has also resulted. Such is it with the topic of joy and sorrow.

What is the relationship of joy to sorrow? On October 8, 2014, all was right in our world. I was happily and gainfully employed, enjoying the grandkids and our growing family, happy in our church, and preparing for our daughter's wedding. Life was good. Occasionally, inventory was taken in my mind of how blessed we were. On October 9, everything changed.

Our existence went instantly from one of joy to sorrow, from laughter to tears, from relative ease to excruciating pain. Parts of those first few days bring tears to my eyes just by their mere recollection. If pre-loss life was ninety-five percent joy and five percent sorrow, surely post-loss levels were at least 180 degrees opposite, though I would have struggled to find the five percent joy. And that is how I'd looked at joy and sorrow before the accident. To increase joy, one must reduce sorrow, or at least deny or overlook it.

Joy and sorrow can coexist.

One thing that has become increasingly clear in the post-loss world is that joy and sorrow can coexist. The absence of sorrow may be happiness, but it's not joy. The removal of as much sorrow as possible in no way guarantees joy; often it seems to grow the feelings of entitlement. In one of the saddest admissions of my years of ministry was the day I said to myself that the church ought to take care of their pastor—me—in such a way that I could give myself without distraction to the needs of the flock.

The Holy Spirit immediately reminded me that the Author and Finisher of our faith had nowhere to lay His head, no home, no reserves, and no concern for it. He instructed us in history's greatest sermon that we are to seek first His kingdom, and He would take care of us. Ease and comfort rarely cause spiritual growth, and the lack of sorrow does not guarantee joy.

Great joy and great sorrow can coexist.

The loss of our future son-in-law brought us sorrow beyond what we could have ever imagined or measured. Beyond one hundred percent. One of our early discoveries was the myriad of ways that there are to cry. There are quiet tears, wailing, screaming, sobbing, sniffling, and dry crying when tear duct reservoirs have been emptied. There is also angry pounding, questioning tears, tears of pain, and inner tears. I could go on, but that's not my point. The point is that our sorrow was beyond description or measure. Early on, only our faith could suggest that it would ever be any different.

With the passage of time, we found that, though the sorrow receded very little, there was a new companion that joined it—joy. We found ourselves spending a lot of evenings just hanging out at home together in conversation and simple pleasures. As we shared memories and stories, we'd laugh and simply enjoy each other's presence. As we lived with our loss, we also grew to realize the blessings accompanying the loss. We lost a son-in-law, but we did *not* lose a daughter. Looking at the pictures of Katie's wrecked car, we were struck with how few injuries she had and gratefulness for the grace we'd been granted. (I've never posted pictures out of respect for Jerod and his family, but the vehicle was almost unrecognizable.) There was no reason that we should still have our daughter. This created a great tension of mixed emotions.

We also found joy in other things. Our Bible study group at church prayed for, listened to, and encouraged us. Friends and family surrounded us. Distant friends reconnected with us. New friendships were discovered. We met the first responders who attended to Katie and Jerod and were touched by their care for our loved ones. As that happened, our sorrow may have decreased slightly, but our joy grew much more than our sorrow receded. We discovered that great sorrow and great joy can coexist.

Great joy and great sorrow increases the potential capacity for the other.

As we unravel our ball of tangled thoughts, we discover also that growing joy increases the capacity for great sorrow, and growing sorrow can increase one's potential for joy. With family members who are in law enforcement, we live with the constant awareness of the fragility of life. As family members have been added, we've rejoiced, but our potential for loss grows along with it. The more one has, the more one has to lose. The more one loses, the greater capacity one has to find accompanying gains. Our capacity for comfort has increased along with our enjoyment of each other. Every day with Katie is one beyond what we could have had.

Therefore, the very accomplishment of survival, which we know as aging, increases one's potential for both joy and sorrow. It's our choice whether we experience joy; life will take care of the sorrow. It's the nature of a fallen world. Ultimately, as a Christian, I believe that joy comes from God, and it's the fruit of His presence in our lives.

> *"But the fruit of the Spirit is love, joy, peace, patience, kindness, goodness, faithfulness, gentleness, self-control; against such things there is no law."*

—GALATIANS 5:22–23 ESV

Psalm 4:6–7 (ESV) says, "There are many who say, 'Who will show us some good? Lift up the light of your face upon us, O Lord!' You have put more joy in my heart than they have when their grain and wine abound." Scripture wisely affirms that joy is not the sum of good fortune but rather of trust in God. This brings one last truth along this line of thought.

Increasing joy is the best way to overcome increasing sorrow.

With time, life will increase sorrow. An elderly man once confided that growing old was not all it was "cracked up to be," but that with long life comes increased funerals. In his words, "You just watch your friends die. Eventually, you have more there than here, and you would rather just be with them." The elderly mother of a preacher friend once bemoaned the fact that she thought she would have been with Jesus by now.

To keep from being overcome with sorrow, one must purposely pursue joy. Our world is a killjoy with its twenty-four-hour worldwide news cycle. If it bleeds, it leads. In an article recently passed around the office, the author gave suggestions for positivity: turn off talk radio. Simply put, without effort, sorrow will overwhelm joy. As we employ the Philippians 4:8 filter and screen the thoughts allowed to enter our minds, we will find our joy increasing and outweighing our sorrow.

While joy and sorrow can coexist, it's not like being happy and sad at the same time. We find that we can really have joy in our hearts and tears in our eyes. And these tears are not tears of joy. It's one of the most confusing of emotional quandaries to experience. Here are some examples:

1 I have joy beyond description that Katie survived her accident. Looking at the vehicle afterwards reminded us that we could have easily lost our only daughter. But before our hearts can bubble over, we realize we lost Jerod, our son-in-law, and the family that Katie would have had. That's heartbreaking.

2 "Oceans" was their favorite song, and the family chose to have it played as the funeral procession exited the service. The words of that song have such profound meaning, especially for our circumstances, yet we cannot endure hearing it because of the tragic memories it evokes. Many times we've been ambushed as it came on the radio. Usually we turn it off, but occasionally I'll lean into the pain and let the words minister to my heart. It's a moment of joy that such a song exists and that God is using it, while at the same time, it's a moment of great sorrow in its baggage for us.

3 Our grandsons were over this evening; they are truly our pride and joy. As we watch our son's family grow and grow up, we have joy for him and his wife as they watch their family take shape. At the same time, there's sorrow over the fact that my daughter should be experiencing this right now. She rejoices with them as Aunt KK, but I often wonder about the pain it must bring to be reminded of what she has lost, or at least has been delayed from having.

You get the idea. Joy is not subject to our environment or circumstances. It comes from knowing that even with the shattered pieces of what we call our lives, there is a Creator and Redeemer who is working all things together for good. It comes from counting your blessings, and it comes even in the middle of pain. As the Bible reminds us, we sorrow but not as those who have no hope. Hope is what makes sorrow bearable, and for us our hope is centered in our Savior. Hope is why sorrow and joy can coexist, and hope has a name—Jesus. He who conquered sin and death awaits us and assures us that though Jerod is not here, he's not gone. Though Katie's and our dreams have been crushed and altered, there is reason to keep going. Hope is an anchor for our souls.

So, if you see us with tears in our eyes and smiles on our faces, we may just be having a "good cry," as we have learned to call it.

Filing a Complaint Against God
A Journal Insert from Kevin
October 3, 2016

For the last couple years, we've been working our way through some dark days and darker nights. We've walked through Jerod's death and Katie's loss and thought we only had to recover from that and get back to a normal life eventually. Without any warning, we've been thrust into a new valley with the diagnosis of leukemia for our three-year-old grandson. Not only is it leukemia, it's the harder type to treat, and he has a genetic anomaly that places him in the toughest five percent of those who have AML.

I've confided in close friends that I've wrestled with God over this one. When is enough, *enough?* We're tired. We're weary. We're struggling to make it through our days, and we're missing a lot of sleep during our nights. The entire family has been pushed to our limits, and I've expressed my disdain for our situation to God. Then this happened.

Sunday was pumpkin carving day. It's a bit early, but Mason will be back in the hospital the last half of the month. Such is the cancer life; live today—there may not be a tomorrow. Our youngest son, Caleb, came home for the weekend to visit family, but he's also our pumpkin carver. He did one for us, and then he sat Mason on his lap and they carved one for him. Caleb had to leave to go back to school, so I was elected to carve one with our oldest grandson, Brady. His was to be a "scary ghost pumpkin," as he called it.

It wasn't a terribly difficult one to do since I'd seen Caleb do several previously. I secured the template and marked the pumpkin for carving. As Brady looked on, I began to carve out the largest piece that would need to be removed. It would reveal the outline of the ghost, and all that would be left were the eyes and mouth, which I'd already marked. Once the large piece was removed, he could see the ghost shape and was happy until he concluded that I was finished.

After several attempts at explaining to him that I wasn't done, he began to cry and ran into the other room to "tell on me" to Grandma. I'm not sure why he didn't hear or understand, but he was sure that his pumpkin was ruined. Heartbroken, he'd run to where he thought he'd find a sympathetic ear, but having heard our conversation, Grandma spoke sweetly to him. "Grandpa is still working on your pumpkin. He's not done yet. When he's done, your pumpkin will be fine. You need to trust Grandpa." After several attempts, she at least stopped his crying and bought me some time.

I called him into the room to reveal the eyes and mouth cut out and the carving complete. His demeanor changed suddenly and drastically as he danced with delight. "I love my pumpkin, my scary ghost pumpkin! Thank you, Grandpa! Thank you, thank you, thank you." As I looked at him, I saw me, and I think I saw a smile breaking on my heavenly Father's face.

He is me. I think I'm all grown up and mature, but I'm just a more complicated version of my grandson. I find myself complaining because I don't like the way things look right now, and I assume that the present is the final product. But God is still at work. I may be able to see the outline, but pieces of the puzzle are missing. There may be enough missing that the outline is nothing like what the end product will be. I need to trust the Father. He just used my grandson to remind me of an important truth that I thought I already knew but needed to hear again, just as Brady needed to hear from Grandma what I had tried to tell him.

CHAPTER 16

Three Dances on Hold

Katie

I wish I could tell you I have some stereotypical happily-ever-after ending to my story, but that just isn't my reality, the stereotypical part anyway. My life is happy, but it goes much deeper than that. The beauty is that I am still in process. My story is still being written. The beauty is in the process, not the destination. I'm still here, and I haven't given up.

The last few years have been beyond unbearable at times. If someone had warned me ahead of time about the darkness that was coming before God had fully prepared me—if in fact it is possible for one to be at all prepared for life's tragic events—I without a doubt would not be writing this book of hope and healing that the Lord so graciously provided. How merciful is God that He doesn't overwhelm our feeble human minds and that He spares us the knowledge of what lies ahead in each of our futures. Some of us may be desperate to know what's ahead so we can plan and prepare, because who doesn't love to make a good plan? God promises to be with us through it all, though. He meets us wherever we are, not where we want to be or where we thought we'd be, and He fights for us!

"The Lord will fight for you; you need only to be still."

—EXODUS 14:14

"In their hearts humans plan their course, but the Lord establishes their steps."

—PROVERBS 16:9

My plans haven't always lined up with God's plan, maybe not even half of the time if we're being real here. In my mind's eye, I was to be happily married by now, living in this beautiful Pinterest-inspired home with two kids and maybe one on the way, living the dream. While I'm not living the dream I'd nurtured in my heart for I can't even count how many years now, I'm still living a dream—a different and greater dream that God has birthed in me.

No, my anxiety is not gone. No, I'm not married. No, I don't even have any prospects on the line. No, I don't have any human children. Yes, I still grieve Jerod's loss. The world will always be less without him. Yes, I still struggle with the fear of a good day. Because that's what Jerod and I were having, a good week rather, right before everything fell apart right in front of my eyes and there was absolutely nothing I could do about it.

I still fight a major battle after I experience those beautifully imperfect, almost heavenly days. It's that little voice whispering in my ear. *When are the chips going to start falling? When will the other shoe drop? Who's going to die this time?* I start to brace myself emotionally. Those thoughts quickly evolve into fears that will sneak into my mind and run rampant unless I immediately take those destructive thoughts captive, recognizing they are *not* of God, and replace them with the truths I *know* about who God is and the promises He has made. Taking every thought captive isn't an easy or a one-time-fix-all task, but it's a critical skill to learn and put into daily practice that will serve you well when those thoughts start to creep in that you *know* are not of God. Anything that is not wholesome, not helpful, not pure, not true.

> *"The world is unprincipled. It's dog-eat-dog out there! The world doesn't fight fair. But we don't live or fight our battles that way—never have and never will. The tools of our trade aren't for marketing or manipulation, but they are for demolishing that entire massively corrupt culture. We use our powerful God-tools for smashing warped philosophies, tearing down barriers erected against the truth of God, fitting every loose thought and emotion and impulse into the structure of life shaped by Christ. Our tools are ready at hand for clearing the ground of every obstruction and building lives of obedience into maturity."*
>
> —2 Corinthians 10:3–6 MSG

While there are still things I've consistently prayed for that have not culminated into anything according to the human eye, God has been doing so much in my heart! He's been changing me from the inside out. For a while, I prayed that God would either grant me these desires that I believe He planted in my heart so long ago, change them, or take them away completely. These desires had become too much for my broken heart to still dream about.

After the unapproved burial of my dreams, the surrounding soil of grief in my life became fertile ground for growth. God tilled the soil with timely songs, messages, and people's influences on me. The healing waters of my tears saturated the parched ground, but to our eyes nothing was happening, just like the cocoon from the outside. The light crept in through the cracks of my broken heart, and over time—a lot of time—beauty returned. And with the beauty came the perspective shifts. With those thought changes, suffering became a gift, the gift that no one asks for, but also one that produces changes and forges friendships that few want to return.

Of course, I'd still want to return to a day when Jerod was here with me, but I'd never want to give back the passionate fire God birthed in my heart to help others going through deep suffering. While I didn't always like the changes in me, I'd never want to return the new set of eyes I've been given, because with them, I see the broken. I also see the beauty. I see and feel God moving in new and powerful ways. I feel more alive than ever. I *really* notice the vibrant hues of the sky now, birds soaring high, and the wind blowing softly on my face, surrounding me like a tender embrace.

The highs are higher and the lows aren't as bad after having endured worse. There was a day when I never thought I'd hear myself laugh again, but now I find myself laughing all the time, deep hearty laughs. Laughs so deep that I end up having to take my inhaler! The Bible speaks louder than ever. It actually draws out so much emotion now that verses frequently bring me to tears, and usually not sad ones, happy and thankful tears!

I'm actually in the middle of reading through the entire Bible for the first time, unbelievably so, as a pastor's kid. My mentor and I are going back and forth daily with readings, talking about what God is speaking to each of us about that day, until we're completely finished. And then we'll start again. It really is amazing how each time you read a passage from the Bible, it can show you something new or in a different light. That's just the beauty of one of the ways that Jesus moves in our hearts.

While I absolutely hated receiving this "gift of suffering," I've hesitantly, yet wholeheartedly, grown thankful for it. My relationship with Christ is as strong as it has ever been after going through the refining fire of suffering. I've never been as thankful for the cross and our victory through Jesus' death and resurrection as I am now. It's so real to me now, like a special connection I have with the God of the universe, my co-sufferer who suffered *for* me so that death would not be the end of the road. Death no longer has the final word.

Suffering pointed me heavenward and loosened my grip on this world as I remembered that this broken world is not my home. I longed for more and began to realize that my suffering was producing something good and that God wasn't wasting any of it. The deeper my suffering went, the deeper my surrender grew as sorrow stripped me of my comforts, helping me realize that I already had all I ever needed in Jesus. When I reached my rock bottom, I found that Jesus *was* the Rock at the bottom, that sure and steady Rock that I could hold on to, the Rock that I realized was already holding on to me. And in those darkest and lowest moments, when He was all I felt I had left, I realized like no time ever before that He was all I'd ever needed.

Pain and suffering opened doors that otherwise would have remained closed, as my grief and Jerod's legacy have inspired me to do things I never imagined I would or even could do. There was a guilt associated with starting to truly live again, like I shouldn't be happy because Jerod wasn't here, but I pushed through and made the conscious decision to be happy anyway. Even if it hurt. Even if it took all I had. I wanted to live again and felt I owed it to Jerod and his massive absence to live again, live fully for two now, and it was up to me to do just that.

I have since run a 10K and half marathon in one weekend at the most magical place on earth. I'm not a huge runner either, mind you. I started a blog, which is when I truly realized my love for writing. I realized that God didn't bring people to comfort and help me just for the encouragement to stop with me and to be for me alone. I've feared going and doing things alone but have gone and done them anyway. I signed up to serve as a Doorholder (volunteer) at my church, even though I knew only a few other Doorholders before committing to a team.

I've embraced opportunities to share my Jesus story of healing with women and teens. I felt terrified, anxious, and unqualified to give those talks but did them anyway, regardless of the possible out-come. Even if I passed out on stage. Even if I started crying violently and couldn't stop. *Even if.* I preached to myself: God is bigger than all of my *even ifs*, my *what ifs*, and my *fears*.

Public speaking has always been a major fear of mine, even back to my senior year of high school. It was then that I accidentally refuted my own point in debate class, thanks to my anxiety of public speaking! I was also fine not trying quite as hard as I could have with my studies to avoid having to give any speeches at graduation. I was quite close to having to give the Salutatorian speech. Funny story about that is the very stage I was avoiding in giving that speech is the stage God led me right back to in sharing my story with the women of First Baptist Church. God is so worthy of our trust. He brought me through those talks and used my pain and story to help others, beautifully and perfectly answering a prayer I'd prayed for months. I just wanted Him to use me. I would tell Him, "I am willing. I am available. And I want to be a part of Your eternal story!" He was that day, is now, and will forever be faithful.

I am now unashamed to talk to anyone about my story and what Jesus has done! Before the accident, I was never that person who would openly bring up Jesus in random conversation. Now He is the center of it all!

There really is so much power in pain! It's like a secret weapon. When distressing things came up, I could usually say that I had done harder things. And I just want to tell you today that you can do *way* harder things than you ever thought or imagined you could do. With Jesus' help, we can scale any wall and take down any giant. He's already done the work and defeated all enemies, including the last and the worst, death. And while we're at it, I just want to say how much I've grown to dislike the phrase, "God won't give you more than you can handle." I believe in this fallen world, there will be many things that will happen to you that will be far too much for you to deal with on your own. I believe God allows those things to happen so we learn to rely solely on Him for our every need, our every breath.

Paul knew about having too much to endure as he talks about in 2 Corinthians.

> "We do not want you to be uninformed, brothers and sisters, about the troubles we experienced in the province of Asia. We were under great pressure, far beyond our ability to endure, so that we despaired of life itself. Indeed, we felt we had received the sentence of death. But this happened that we might not rely on ourselves but on God, who raises the dead. He has delivered us from such a deadly peril, and he will deliver us again. On him we have set our hope that he will continue to deliver us."
>
> —2 Corinthians 1:8–10

The key, I learned, is to put God between us and our circumstances instead of letting our circumstances come between us and God. Look at God, not the seemingly immovable mountain of trouble or despair looming like a giant in front of you.

Suffering has this way of liberating us from the petty concerns and worries of everyday life. It clears the clutter and idols and helps us realize that Jesus really is all we need. I now appreciate the little things, laugh louder, love harder. Honestly, I love the new me! I feel like before, the Bible was in black and white, but now it's in HD color! Verses come alive and jump off the page, and things just make so much more sense now than they ever have.

After traveling on the highway of grief for some time, I find that I'm actively looking for opportunities to pull off and help people who are broken down, overwhelmed by their own entrance onto the highway. I remember all of the people God sent to my family and me, and I've been praying to be one of those people for someone else. When I feel compelled to step out, I pray I always obey and follow God's lead, even when it's scary and uncomfortable, as suffering usually is.

In hearing and responding to God's nudges, it was in the summer and into the fall of 2017 when I felt God whisper to my heart, "It's time." Pastor Louie had been going through the *People of the Fine Print* series in July of 2017 when he zoomed in on some of the lesser-known, yet essential and impactful characters of the Bible. The week he spoke about Dorcas, a woman who made clothes for the widows and the poor, was the day I knew I was receiving a clear direction from God regarding what He wanted me to do next.

We all have a story of grace to share with the world. What can you do well? How can you use what you can do well to look for the last and least of these? How can you bring dignity just by doing what you do well (Louie Giglio, Pastor of Passion City Church, Paraphrased from a sermon in the series "People of the Fine Print" in 2017)?

I've always loved writing and have had many people tell me that I should write a book about my story and what God has done in my life over the last few years. I just never felt the time was right. It was one of those big mountains of a task that I thought was a really good idea, but for someone else and not me. It was something I would idealize, but not something I pictured myself hunkering down and actually doing anywhere in my near future.

After hearing about Dorcas, I just knew it was time. The tipping point of inspiration that led to the beginnings of this book also happened to occur during a week that I'd spent out of work, sick, and lying on my couch resting. God had my full attention. If *I* didn't write this book, then who would? Someone else for sure. But *I* wanted to be used!

I'd prayed for months on end for God to use me, my story, and my pain, not letting any of it go to waste. I knew God called me to help hurting people, but I had no experience writing anything more than my blogs and Facebook posts. Thanks to the encouragement of many, my dad and I finally sat down and discussed what it would take to start this massive project.

We had *no* idea what we were doing or how we were going to do it. We didn't have to, though. God provided and led us so beautifully, quite literally from step to step through the entire process, using many dear friends of ours who were willing to step into the process with us. Now here you are, reading about the fruit and beauty God created with our pain. It brings me to tears to read back through and see from a different perspective the overwhelming faithfulness of God as He gently led us through the pain and healing and subsequently through the writing process. Goodness, He is *so* good.

As I have sensed this strong calling on my life, I have also experienced supernatural peace about my singleness like never before! God has filled my lonely places with abundance and purpose—just another way I knew He was nudging me to put my story on paper in order to share with the hurting world that is now so very evident around me.

For weeks that turned into months, I continued to feel so strongly in my heart that God was telling me to put into print the journey that He's had my family and me on for these last years. I thought, *Well, here we go!* God had brought us through much harder and more painful things; I knew I could trust Him with this too. I also knew dragging these painful and traumatic memories back to the surface in order to write this book would cause some expected distress, so I wasn't surprised when the gory and frightening nightmares of people dying started revisiting me. *But God* has been fanning the flame in my soul and encouraging me to just keep going. Keep telling the story. Keep typing the words. Keep creating the peaceful environment of writing space. Keep listening to My voice. And don't stop.

As I've continued writing, I've considered that I may have remained single for such a time as this. If I were married or had children, I doubt that I would've been able to make completing this book a priority. I'm certain writing could easily have taken a back seat to the new and exciting (and scary) first days of dating someone new.

I've prayed and am trusting God to bring my life's partner in His perfect timing. He sees the big picture and all of the exciting things He has planned for me outside of the wonderful world of dating (Ha!). So, I have to keep trusting that if God wanted me with someone right now, then I would in fact be with him right this very second. And that brings me peace, remembering and preaching to myself that God in His limitless power is completely *able* in an instant to bring these dreams of mine to reality. And I will rest in that.

Honestly, I've struggled quite a bit as I've prayed about what God wanted me to share in this final chapter of the book, primarily because my story doesn't have that Hollywood, happily-ever-after ending right now, that clinching grand finale. A few Sundays after I started praying for guidance, I was worshiping at church to the new Phil Wickham song, "Living Hope," and God revealed what I'd been searching and praying fervently for. The ending. And it was as clear as day! One of the lines from the end of the first verse ...

The work is finished, the end is written ...

There—my answer. My ending is already written! I'm still alive; therefore, it's *not* over. Even if my life here on earth were done, my life in Christ would only just be starting. 1 Corinthians 2:9 says, "'What no eye has seen, what no ear has heard, and what no human mind has conceived'–the things God has prepared for those who love him."

Even if I did have that husband I've been praying and longing for these past years, it still wouldn't be the end. And even if we shared a godly union of hearts, that should still never come before Jesus and the work He has for us here on earth. What the world has to give will never satisfy. And while things here on earth can be good, they should never be our end goal. Jesus is our goal. Intimacy with Him and co-laboring to advance His kingdom is the goal.

On earth, we're living in the in-between, the time between receiving the promises God has made to us and the second coming of Christ when He will come back for His bride, His followers. While this is the ultimate wait for believers, we're all waiting for something every day. Waiting for the barista to prepare your third caffeinated drink before ten a.m. Waiting for the end of the workday. Waiting to hear if you got the job or not. Waiting for that big promotion. Waiting in traffic. And in Atlanta, let's be real—there is *always* traffic. Waiting to meet that special someone. Waiting on a much-needed vacation from everyday life. Waiting for a phone call. Waiting for test results. Waiting for healing. Waiting for a breakthrough. Waiting for happy days to return. Waiting for the world to change. Waiting is a universal thing that everyone is familiar with in some way or another.

Even if God Doesn't
by Katie Neufeld
December 13, 2015

I've been reading a lot about Advent recently, including Louie Giglio's book, *Waiting Here for You: an Advent Journey of Hope*. The common thread among all the advent material seems to be waiting, patience, and longing, with a bit of unrest thrown in there as well. But let me start with this.

I hate waiting.

Whether it's waiting in line, waiting on dinner to finish cooking, or waiting on bigger things like healing or for a breakthrough, I hate waiting. To take it back a bit further, imagine the four *hundred* years of deafening silence that came and went between the prophecies of Malachi and the birth of Christ. How's that for a wait? And I don't even like waiting in traffic! That is many generations of waiting for God to come through on a long-anticipated promise. How many of us would've given up on the wait after, say, even ten years? How does one keep his faith alive during an extended wait like that? How do one's hopes not become dashed?

Then suddenly one night, God came through on His promise, just like He said He would. God's timing is certainly not mine. But He's never late; He's always on time ... His time. His perfect record of faithfulness strengthens my faith in the silence, in the waiting. Even when it feels like nothing is happening, the waiting is not wasted. God is working while we wait. Even when I don't believe these very words I'm typing, I must repeat them to myself over and over because filling my heart and mind with these truths is what fuels my trust and keeps me closely connected with Jesus during the wait.

Sometimes, I'm not even sure what I'm waiting on, but I know there is something. Continued healing, of course. Maybe a glimpse of what my purpose is through all of the pain of this chapter in my life. That would certainly be nice. I guess I'm just not sure what happens when this dark season of my life fades and another begins.

The future can definitely be scary, but lately, as I've seen God's hand directly at work in my life and in the lives of others, I get a little excited for the possibilities! This is a new thing for me anyway. When looking into the future, all I used to see was darkness and all kinds of miserable-looking things. Now, I'm seeing God directly using my story in a variety of very cool and breathtaking ways!

I've found myself praying for Him to just put me in His story, wherever that may be. Quite an unnerving prayer, but sincere nonetheless. I pray for God to use my experiences for His glory as an anchor of hope and redemption for others. Even though my story doesn't have the cliché happy ending right now, there is still joy, although different from any I'd ever experienced in the past. A more pure form of joy.

There is still life, reborn and renewed. There is still hope in Jesus to come through. There is contentment in knowing that God knows exactly where I am, is with and for me and has always been, and has a plan to use this chapter of my life for profound good beyond what I could hope for or imagine. There is a strength not my own.

I am a survivor. I am a fighter. I am an overcomer.

I have come to the conclusion that while I may not have all that I *want*, I have all that I *need*. Emotional pain is still very much a part of most of my days, whether it is a minute, an hour, or even longer, but He has also given me something new. He has filled my cup, and I am overflowing Jesus and His promises. He has given me a new wholeness in Him that I have never experienced before. Honestly, it is a wholeness that I never thought possible after such tragedy, and even just in general. And while I've never felt more broken than in this chapter of my life, I've also never felt more alive. I cannot say that I will ever be thankful *for* the accident and its devastating aftermath, but I'm finding ways to be thankful *in* these circumstances. I quite like the changes it has made in me through the fire and the fight.

Yet, I feel conflicted. I go round and round asking God, "But can't I have what I need *and* what I want? Other people get both. Why can't I?"

I go round and round on that train of thought until I get tired and discouraged enough to just rest. Rest knowing that *even if God doesn't give me what I want, I already have all that I need. In Him.* I will rest knowing that the God who has carried me this far will lead me until I am home. He's held my heart long before day one when it shattered in too many pieces to even begin to look at. But that's when He said, *Don't look at all of that. Look at Me.* I will rest knowing that even if things don't finish as I desire here on earth, I can know that all will be right one day. It will all end well one day, just maybe not here. But maybe so. Who knows? We'll have to wait a bit longer and see ...

"If we are thrown into the blazing furnace, the God whom we serve is able to save us. He will rescue us from your power, Your Majesty. But even if he doesn't, we want to make it clear to you, Your Majesty, that we will never serve your gods or worship the gold statue you have set up."

—DANIEL 3:17–18 NLT

"Rejoice always, pray continually, give thanks in all circumstances; for this is God's will for you in Christ Jesus."

—1 THESSALONIANS 5:16–18

"Be joyful in hope, patient in affliction, faithful in prayer."

—ROMANS 12:12

Katie

Lately, I've been considering this question: What does it look like to wait well? While I feel like I'm constantly learning something new about waiting well, I know that *waiting does not give you a pass from doing.* Waiting can easily be mistaken as a passive activity, but waiting *well* is an active thing you do. Waiting well looks a lot like being useful for God's kingdom. Psalm 37:3 describes a great way to actively wait well. "Trust in the Lord and do good; dwell in the land and enjoy safe pasture."

If we are trusting in the Lord and focusing on Him during the wait, our eyes will inevitably be less on ourselves and our anxieties and more on the needs of others. When we turn our eyes away from ourselves, we remember, or maybe notice for the first time, that there is a world full of need and hurting people all around us every day, desperately waiting for us to give of our time, lend a helping hand, and do good. Opportunities to serve others are hundreds of miles away, but they're also in our cities, in our neighborhoods, and in our homes. Opportunities helping people with yard work they can't do themselves. Walking dogs. Watching children for widows. Loving strangers, as well as our neighbors.

In our modern world of technology, opportunities to help others while we wait are available without even having to leave the house! How's that for a pajama Monday for those of you with Mondays off work? A friend just shared on Facebook about an app called *Be My Eyes* that was designed to help blind people with minor daily tasks they cannot do themselves. The service is provided through live video feed with a volunteer who quite possibly might live across the world. Checking expiration dates. Adjusting air conditioning. Checking clothes for stains.

Just last week, I was thrilled to be able to be eyes for someone and evaluate a piece of mail to decipher whether it was a bill or not. Seeing even the basic needs of others is a good reminder of how blessed we are and of how much we have, despite how we feel. In the hustle and bustle of living in this world full of brokenness and suffering, it's easy to forget how much we have when we're zoned in on our pain. I know I have way more than I actively recognize on a daily basis.

For starters, all of my five basic senses are intact. I can see the beautifully painted canvas in the sky every day. I can hear the birds chirping me a chipper good morning. I can smell sweet honeysuckles blooming and my dog when she needs a bath. I can feel the warmth of towels and sheets just coming out of the dryer on a cold day. And I can taste a delicious meal when I actually cook one. I usually have food to cook, and when I don't, I can get in my truck and drive two minutes down the road and get some, thanks to my full-time employment. I'm blessed beyond measure.

I love what Jon Bloom, who writes for *Desiring God*, expressed about waiting. We're all waiting on God for something and that thing is often at the center of our focus. Eventually, we may realize that helping others and doing good in the wait brought about our most significant bounty (Jon Bloom, e-mail to Desiring God mailing list, June 12, 2018).

Psalm 37:4 dives in a little deeper when it says, "Take delight in the Lord, and he will give you the desires of your heart." While this verse was consistently bringing pain and questions for me early in my loss, I see it now with new eyes. A few years ago, I kept wondering why my life felt like the backwards version of this verse. I thought I *was* delighting in the Lord, yet He let the desire of my heart die, and I had to watch. With fresh eyes and new perspective, I learned that I was looking at this verse backwards. God should've been the desire of my heart, not Jerod.

Jon Bloom explained that we can *know* God will grant us our heart's deepest longings when God *is* what we long for. When this shift takes place and God is at the center of our affection and desire, our focus shifts. We are no longer waiting for a what, but rather a Who. "O Lord, we wait for you; your name and remembrance are the desire of our soul" (Isaiah 26:8 ESV) (Jon Bloom, e-mail to Desiring God mailing list, June 12, 2018).

Waiting well looks like being in the Word and in prayer daily about where and how God wants to use you. It looks like trusting God with the process, the in-between that we are living in here on earth, with the things we may never understand on this side of heaven. It looks like finding contentment and joy in the messy middle of your story, despite circumstances that may have broken your heart. Joy may look different from the happy picture you have in mind. I've found that joy and sadness often live together and tend to bring out the vibrant colors of the other. Because I've known deep sadness, I find great joy in little things. Because I've known deep joy and love, I experience profound sadness when that love changes or is lost.

"Even in laughter the heart may ache, and the end of joy may be grief."

—PROVERBS 14:13 ESV

"Sorrow is better than laughter, for by sadness of face the heart is made glad."

—ECCLESIASTES 7:3 ESV

While joy may seem hidden or lost forever when you're in the middle of life's darkest moments, it will eventually return. Time does not heal wounds, though—God does. And when He does, joy will surely look different than it ever has. There was a particular joy I found in shifting my thoughts to an eternal perspective. In doing that, I was reminded that no matter what happens here on earth, whatever bad news, diagnosis, or death, the best is *still* yet to come.

Fellow traveler, I want to encourage you in the wait that even when God seems remote or distant, He has not forgotten about you. He is *with* you every step of the way and He is *for* you! He created you on purpose and for a purpose. I pray He grants you overwhelming peace and dare I say, joy, for the road you are traveling and for whatever may lie ahead.

Kevin

A few years back, I was impressed to start giving each of my children a personal letter for Christmas. Of course there was the usual array of gifts, but they fell short of conveying to them everything I wanted to give. It's not clear what motivated my decision because the first letters were written in 2011, before the losses we've experienced in recent years. Yet, I can't help but wonder ... Had God planted the desire in my heart for the season that was coming? Looking back, He seems to have done that repeatedly, so it wouldn't surprise me if that was the case.

Here is what I wrote in the Christmas 2015 letter to Katie:

Dear Katie,

Another year. So fast, yet so long. And what a year it has been ... for all of us. It is still a detour from what we thought would be our path. In fact, the rest of our lives will have a bit of a detour scent to them. It is a broken road.

But, in the midst of this broken-roaded detour, I find myself drawn ever closer to my fellow passengers. Doing this past year with you has been bitter and sweet, but it has been good. You have healed, grown, matured, and amazed me so much. While there are still ups and downs, you are trending up. You are finding a way to love and remember Jerod and still look forward to your chapter two.

I must admit that there are still times I want to slam my dash and scream. Those are the moments when I think of what could have been. Then I watch you stand up as a bridesmaid for a friend or celebrate the birth of a new niece and wonder just how much it must hurt. Honestly, I don't want to go to another wedding till I dance with you at yours. No disrespect or ill will to those who get to enjoy it; it's just your turn now. It has been your turn for some time, but time has chosen to stand still while you process and change gears. It is not lost on me how you must still hurt silently.

Then I watch you reach out to others. You have become such a beautiful person, not perfect and not always good company, but you have a depth of beauty unmatched among those who have not known such pain. I have been blessed to be your dad, and I can tell you that if we were picking daughters and I had my choice of any girl in the world, I would choose you.

Who knows what 2016 holds for you? Who would dare to guess? But this I know: God is working *in* you and *through* you for *His* glory and *our* good. I believe there will be a day when we will have a better perspective on life now. It is my prayer that there will be wedding bells and a chapter two. Regardless, I know you have at least three dances left: one with me, one with Papa, and one that has been put on hold … with Jerod. I can't wait to be present for all three.

Merry Christmas, my dear.

Love,
Dad

This year marked the first anniversary of Jerod's death, along with its many firsts for Katie. You can pick up the raw emotions from the letter, but it was also the time when the early rays of hope were coming on the horizon. It was also the first time that I became aware of how important those letters were, as Katie informed me that she not only kept them, but she read them again from time to time. There was no way for me to know just how meaningful the last paragraph would be to her as she clung to the hope of the "three dances."

To be sure that the reader understands, let me explain. The three dances are all still future and still in the hope column. First, I have hope that there will be a father and bride's dance. Not knowing when, but knowing that it's still her desire, and she is much more ready now

THREE DANCES ON HOLD

than in 2015, I still pray for that day and am sure that I will need a pocket full of tissues. Second, she *will* have a dance with the Father she has come to know, love, and trust with her pain and loss. "Papa," the name for God that we have both come to love, is preparing a place for us with Him and a marriage supper for us. Not only do I plan to be there, it is my hope that you will be there as well.

As you have read, loss hurts even for those who believe in Jesus Christ. We grieve just like all who suffer loss, but we do it differently; we do it in hope. Our hope is not wishful thinking. It's based on a cruel cross and an empty tomb. If the cross in all of its horror does not take place, we are still in need of a sacrifice for sin. If the tomb is not empty, our hope is blind and ill-placed. Paul said in 1 Corinthians 15:19 (ESV), "If in Christ we have hope in this life only, we are of all people most to be pitied." Because Jesus has conquered death, His promise to us that we can expect our own resurrection is not only possible, but true. It is our desire that if you have not secured this hope that you will accept this gift from the God who is pursuing you. His love for you brought Him to this earth to live and offer the perfect sacrifice to end all sacrifices for sin. It also causes Him to pursue you even now.

The third dance is the other one I'm very sure about. In Hiram, Georgia, there is a cemetery where you can find a marker for Jerod Hicks, but he's not there. He's with the God he loved and served, and he's awaiting the arrival of his earthly love. He's joined the great cloud of witnesses spoken of in Hebrews 12:1–2. "Therefore, since we are surrounded by such a great cloud of witnesses, let us throw off everything that hinders and the sin that so easily entangles. And let us run with perseverance the race marked out for us, fixing our eyes on Jesus, the pioneer and perfecter of faith."

No doubt he would be proud to watch Katie continue to run her race, though his is finished. As family and friends often do at the end of a race, I'm sure he will be waiting for her to break the tape at the end of hers. And I can't help but wonder if this will not be a dance of three as Jerod, Katie, and Papa celebrate the long-expected reunion.

Epilogue –
Tips for the Grieving and Tips for Those Caring for the Grieving

This book is finished, but our story isn't. It would've been much easier if Katie had already met and married someone and started a family, but we've been led to write now ... even while the story is unfinished. But aren't all of our stories unfinished right now? Writing as we have done without resolution and a feel-good ending in some ways gives greater credibility to what we have written. Our desire is that others will take encouragement and find that their dreams have also been planted instead of buried. Beyond just telling our story, we hope that you have picked up nuggets of truth along the way that will bless you on your journey.

We wanted to end the book with a place where griever and comforter alike can go for a summary of what we've discovered in our journey. We hope these will nourish your soul and become batons of truth that can be handed off to others who will be blessed as well. We're not saying that all of these will help in every situation. Grief is very individual, even when many circumstances are quite similar. Our hope is that you'll find your path widened or leveled by a handful of these observations.

TIPS FOR THE GRIEVING

1   God promises to be with you in each and every situation but often He shows up through people. Don't discount that possibility.

2   Be honest with others about where you are emotionally and what you need from them. They won't know unless you tell them.

3   Open your phone first to Scripture, not social media. You will notice a difference in your day. Let God's words and promises fill your heart and define you rather than the ups and downs of social media.

4   Replace your worry about the days ahead with worship to the God who holds each of those days.

5   You are not a victim of your circumstances. God ultimately rules over your circumstances. He loves you and you can trust Him.

6   Fill your days with songs of worship and praise to God. You may not like it or agree with the lyrics right away, but sing the words until you believe them.

7   Grief is not always forward motion. It is not linear, but rather all over the place. Keep pressing on. Keep taking baby steps.

8   It's okay to be angry. God doesn't tell us not to be angry. He just tells us not to sin in our anger.

9   Ride your emotions out like a wave instead of resisting or forcing. In order to survive, it is important to swim *with* the rip current until it settles enough to swim back to shore. Swimming against the current of grief is exhausting.

10   You are not going crazy. As much as it may feel like you are. You may never have been through anything of this magnitude before. Be gracious with yourself. It is okay to not be okay.

11 Catch some rays. Splash in puddles. Dance in the rain like no one's watching. Let yourself be refreshed in God's creation.

12 Crying does not equal weakness. And you're not crazy if you start crying for seemingly no reason at all.

13 There is no timeline to grief no matter what anyone tells you. Grief is different for everyone.

14 Be gracious with your comforters. Pain can create awkward moments and no one responds perfectly. Your comforters are just as unsure of how to best comfort you as you are. Overlook any insensitive comments and move along knowing they most likely meant well.

15 Consider counseling. Life is hard. Don't be afraid to get help!

16 Watch out for triggers or things that push your "reset button." Once you know what these things are (a song, a smell, a place, etc.), it's okay to avoid them. Know that some are unavoidable (holidays and special dates) and may feel like an emotional pounding that sets you back to square one. Try not to shove those feelings. Feel them and then let them pass.

17 It's okay to be happy. Just because you're feeling happy one day doesn't reduce the love or grief you feel for who you've lost. Sorrow will return soon enough.

18 It's okay to tell people "no" with no offered explanation.

19 Give yourself permission to have good and bad days. Guilt may creep up when a good day comes along. Understand it's okay to have them again.

20 Exercise if you can. You'll be thankful for the rush of endorphins.

21 It's okay to skip happy holiday celebrations. Those who love you will understand. Know that holidays and anniversaries will be painful. Sometimes distraction will help and other times leaning into the pain will be what is best. Be open to either of these options.

22 Try not to look ahead with worry and concern to things that are months in advance. Take each day one step at a time, even one minute at a time if you feel the need. Often, you may dread those big days so much that by the time the day actually arrives, it's not near as painful as the days and weeks prior.

23 Music stitches songs and words into the very fabric of our lives. Choose wisely. Also, don't miss the providence of God in giving songs to musicians well in advance of your need for the very time and nature of your pain. Our faith has been bolstered by knowing we're not alone and by repeatedly meeting the God who sees.

24 Ask the tough questions. Thomas Jefferson said, "Question with boldness even the existence of a God; because, if there be one, he must more approve of the homage of reason, than that of blindfolded fear." Truth can stand the test of examination, but in the end, when we get to the end of our power to reason, we must trust something ... or someone. We have found God worthy of that trust.

25 Let the fact that others have survived suffering and loss give you hope. We're grateful that others blazed a trail before us. We hope to develop it further to aid those who follow. Suffering is a terrible thing to waste.

26 Connect with someone who entered this road of suffering before you. Their friendship and advice will be invaluable and will help to validate many of your feelings.

27 Consider writing letters to your loved one. This can be especially helpful if your loss was sudden or traumatic, leaving much unsaid in the wake of their loss.

28 If and when you're ready, use what could be an impossibly hard day to do something fun or something that you and your loved one had wanted to do. It may still be sad, but it can be meaningful. Use it as a way to remember and honor them.

29 Find someone else who needs help and reach out, focusing on them for a time. Not only will it help you to focus on something other than yourself and your loss, but it will also provide meaning and most likely a positive experience for both of you.

30 It's okay if you feel angry at your loved one. Feel the anger even if it doesn't make sense and then let it pass.

31 Although the pain will ease as years go by, you'll always have a sensitive spot in your heart.

32 Survivor's guilt is real. Don't let it eat you alive.

33 As much as it hurts right now, do take care of yourself.

34 Grief sometimes seems a bit like wandering in the wilderness like Israel. You keep going in circles and seeing the same things over and over. You *will* come out of the wilderness, but you'll see the same things repeatedly before you do.

Tips for Those Caring for the Grieving

1   Say their name. Talking about the loved one who has died may bring tears. The grieving will thank you for the opportunity to shed them. The grieving like when people remember their loved one. If it seems awkward, imagine how awkward it is for such a large part of someone's world to be instantly gone with no one wanting to speak their name. They may be gone but don't let them be forgotten.

2   Instead of saying, "Let me know if you need anything," just pick something and do it. Those enduring heavy grief usually can't join enough coherent thoughts to know what they need. Instead, just pick something and do it. Make a meal. Bring dinner. Be a listening ear. Watch their kids for a few hours. Buy them flowers. Get them a massage or something relaxing. Just be there.

3   Be careful with clichés. When you tell a griever they're so strong, it may make them feel more misunderstood and unseen. The griever is most likely feeling about as weak and numb as ever and may be doing only what is absolutely necessary. You may not see them behind closed doors.

4   Keep a keen eye on those enduring suffering and don't be afraid to directly ask them if they're considering self-harm. They may not tell you otherwise. One can get depressed in the midst of deep suffering.

5   Just because someone looks cheerful on the outside doesn't mean they aren't feeling pain on the inside. They may be waiting to release the floodgates until they're in a safe place. Only ask how they are doing if you plan to stick around and find out.

6   Don't try to stop the tears. Tears are healing. They're a way for the hurting to release some of the heaviness and pressure. More than likely, tears are more uncomfortable for you as the comforter or friend than for the hurting. Give them the gift of shared tears. They won't forget it.

7   Don't hesitate to get counseling for you too. You may be so focused on helping your friend or family member that you don't consider how the loss affected you. Don't be afraid to seek wise counsel from a pastor or counselor.

8   No one person or family is adequate on their own to handle grief and loss. Trying to do it all would've been a disaster. God sent various comforters into our lives at different times and for specific reasons. Each has brought his own value and unique gifts to the story; some have only made a cameo appearance and others have joined for the duration. None of this could have been predicted, but it's the healing part of looking at the story in the rearview mirror of life.

9   Try to be ready and willing to listen to whatever the griever has to say even if it's the same story for the 100th time.

10 Be prepared to step in it a time or two. Be prepared to apologize as well.

11 Give them an invitation to share what hurts and what helps. They will appreciate the offer.

12 Understand that no two losses are the same no matter how much they look alike. Don't compare losses. This only brings additional and unnecessary pain to the grieving.

13 Less is more. Less words. Less advice. More hugs and more listening.

14 Don't try to force laughter but don't avoid it either.

15 Make it a point to check in with the grieving after all the crowds have died down in three months, six months, nine months, etc. This is often when the numbness and shock has lessened, allowing for more intense pain.

16   "How are you?" can be a complicated question for the grieving. I found it was often used as a greeting, and my answer was usually too long to tell someone in passing. Consider just saying "Hello" and hugging them when there isn't time to listen to the complete answer. When you ask how a grieving person is doing, be prepared that the answer may be all over the place. No moment, hour, or day was all good or bad.

17   Remember the significant days and reach out. A card. A call. A message. Your thought will mean so much to the grieving on their difficult day.

18   Don't give up on them. Even if they tell you no to multiple invitations to go out, keep asking.

NOTES

Batterson, Mark. *The Circle Maker: Praying Circles Around Your Biggest Dreams and Greatest Fears.* Detroit: Gale Cengage Learning, 2011.

Caine, Christine. *Possessing the Promise.* April 12, 2015. www.youtube.com/watch?v=-m03voQ2K9Q.

Lachrymatory.com. "Tear Bottle History, 2003-2008." www.lachrymatory.com/History.htm (accessed June 11, 2018).

Shirer, Priscilla. *Life Interrupted: Navigating the Unexpected.* Nashville: B&H Publishing Group, 2011.

Tchividjian, Tullian. *Glorious Ruin: How Suffering Sets You Free.* Colorado Springs: David C Cook, 2012.

Young, William P. *The Shack.* Newbury Park: Windblown Media, 2007.

OUR HEALING PLAYLIST

1   Broken Hallelujah by The Afters
2   Draw Me Nearer by Meredith Andrews
3   Worth It All by Meredith Andrews
4   You're Not Alone by Meredith Andrews
5   Death Where Is Your Sting by Cory Asbury
6   Garments by Cory Asbury
7   Water and Dust by Cory Asbury
8   You Won't Let Go by Cory Asbury
9   You Were There by Avalon
10 Fall by The Belonging Co
11 At Your Feet by Dan Bremnes
12 Beautiful by Dan Bremnes
13 Born Again by Dan Bremnes
14 Faith Is by Dan Bremnes
15 He Knows by Dan Bremnes
16 Heart On Fire by Dan Bremnes
17 I Am Sure by Dan Bremnes
18 In His Hands by Dan Bremnes
19 Over by Dan Bremnes
20 Where the Light Is by Dan Bremnes
21 Wide Open by Dan Bremnes
22 No One Like Our God by Lincoln Brewster
23 Greater Things by Mack Brock
24 Into Dust by Mack Brock
25 He Knows by Jeremy Camp
26 My Desire by Jeremy Camp

ABOUT THE AUTHORS

 Katie Neufeld is daughter to Kevin and Vickie Neufeld. Katie graduated with a Bachelor's degree in Nursing from North Georgia College and State University and now works as a pediatric nurse in Atlanta. She enjoys traveling, hiking, and adventures with her fluffiest companion, Dusty Rose Doodle.

Kevin Neufeld is the son of a pastor and was a pastor himself for twenty-eight years. He now works in banking and is involved in ministry nonvocationally. Kevin and his wife, Vickie, have three children and three grandchildren and live in the Atlanta area. He enjoys nature, reading, minor league baseball games, and is an avid Denver Broncos fan.

Thank you for taking time to step into our journey with us. We would love to connect with you!

Connect with us through e-mail at: *Plantedhopebook@gmail.com*

We are also on Instagram at @plantedhope and on Facebook under the Katie Neufeld author page.

Our heart in sharing our journey of hardship and healing has always been to bring hope to others. Help us do this by sharing about the book on social media using the hashtag #plantedhopebook.

Called to Hope,
Katie and Kevin